Ethical issues in social work

It has always been recognised that the practice of social work raises ethical questions and dilemmas. Recently, however, traditional ways of addressing ethical issues in social work have come to seem inadequate, as a result of developments both in philosophy and in social work theory and practice. This collection of thought-provoking essays explores the ethics of social work practice in the light of these changes.

Ethical Issues in Social Work provides up-to-date critical analyses of the ethical implications of new legislation in community care and criminal justice, and of trends in social work thought and policy, such as managerialism, user empowerment, feminism and anti-oppressive practice.

This book provides important and stimulating reading for social work students and their teachers, and for all practitioners and managers who are concerned about the ethical dimensions of their work.

Richard Hugman is Senior Lecturer in Social Work at Lancaster University and was previously a social work practitioner. **David Smith**, a former probation officer, is Professor of Social Work at Lancaster University. They are joint editors of *The British Journal of Social Work*.

Professional Ethics

General editors: Andrew Belsey,
Centre for Applied Ethics, University of Wales College of Cardiff
and Ruth Chadwick,
Centre for Professional Ethics, University of Central Lancashire

Professionalism is a subject of interest to academics, the general public and would-be professional groups. Traditional ideas of professions and professional conduct have been challenged by recent social, political and technological changes. One result has been the development for almost every profession of an ethical code of conduct which attempts to formalise its values and standards. These codes of conduct raise a number of questions about the status of a 'profession' and the consequent moral implications for behaviour.

This series seeks to examine these questions both critically and constructively. Individual volumes will consider issues relevant to particular professions, including nursing, genetic counselling, journalism, business, the food industry and law. Other volumes will address issues relevant to all professional groups such as the function and value of a code of ethics and the demands of confidentiality.

Also available in this series:

Ethical Issues in Journalism and the Media
edited by Andrew Belsey and Ruth Chadwick

Genetic Counselling
edited by Angus Clarke

Ethical Issues in Nursing
edited by Geoffrey Hunt

The Ground of Professional Ethics
Daryl Koehn

Ethical issues in social work

Edited by Richard Hugman and David Smith

London and New York

First published 1995
by Routledge
2 Park Square, Milton Park, Abingdon, Oxon, OX14 4RN

Simultaneously published in the USA and Canada
by Routledge
270 Madison Ave, New York NY 10016

Transferred to Digital Printing 2006

Typeset in Times by J&L Composition Ltd, Filey, North Yorkshire

British Library Cataloguing in Publication Data
A catalogue record for this book is available from the British Library

Library of Congress Cataloguing in Publication Data
A catalogue record for this book has been requested

ISBN   0–415–10109–3
        0–415–10110–7 (pbk)

Contents

Series editors' foreword

Applied Ethics is now acknowledged as a field of study in its own right. Much of its recent development has resulted from rethinking traditional medical ethics in the light of new moral problems arising out of advances in medical science and technology. Applied philosophers, ethicists and lawyers have devoted considerable energy to exploring the dilemmas emerging from modern health care practices and their effects on the practitioner–patient relationship.

But the point can be generalised. Even in health care, ethical dilemmas are not confined to medical practitioners but also arise in the practice of, for example, nursing. Beyond health care, other groups such as social workers, addressed in this volume, are beginning to think critically about the kind of service they offer and about the nature of the relationship between provider and recipient.

One visible sign of these developments has been the proliferation of codes of ethics, or of professional conduct. The drafting of such a code provides an opportunity for professionals to examine the nature and goals of their work, and offers information to others about what can be expected from them. If a code has a disciplinary function, it may even offer protection to members of the public.

But is the existence of such a code itself a criterion of a profession? What exactly is a profession? Can a group acquire professional status, and if so, how? Does the label 'professional' have implications, from a moral point of view, for acceptable behaviour, and if so how far do they extend?

This series, edited from the Centre for Applied Ethics in Cardiff and the Centre for Professional Ethics in Preston, seeks to examine these questions both critically and constructively. Individual volumes will address issues relevant to all professional groups, such as the nature of a profession, the function and value of codes of ethics, and the demands of confidentiality. Other volumes will examine issues relevant to particular professions, including those which have hitherto received little attention, such as journalism, social work and genetic counselling.

Andrew Belsey
Ruth Chadwick

Notes on contributors

Julie Browne is a Ph.D. student at Lancaster University.

Ann Davis is Senior Lecturer in Social Work at the University of Birmingham.

Kathryn Ellis is a Lecturer in Social Care at the University of Luton.

Richard Hugman is Senior Lecturer in Social Work at Lancaster University.

Charles Husband is Professor of Social Analysis at the University of Bradford.

Geraldine Macdonald is Reader in Applied Social Services at Royal Holloway College, University of London.

Kenneth Macdonald is University Lecturer in Applied Social Sciences and a Fellow of Nuffield College, Oxford.

Mike Nellis is a Lecturer in Probation Studies at the University of Birmingham.

Naina Patel is a Development Officer at the Central Council for Education and Training in Social Work, Northern Region.

Steven Shardlow is a Lecturer in Social Work Studies at the University of Sheffield.

David Smith is Professor of Social Work at Lancaster University.

Maurice Vanstone is a Lecturer in Applied Social Studies, University College Swansea and a Senior Probation Officer, Mid-Glamorgan Probation Service.

Sue Wise is Senior Lecturer in Social Work, Lancaster University.

Chapter 1

Ethical issues in social work: an overview

Richard Hugman and David Smith

INTRODUCTION

Ethical issues are at the heart of a discipline such as social work. Social work is concerned with the care of people who have a variety of needs, with family relationships, with social responses to offending and with needs arising from structural causes (such as poverty). These are each, in different ways, moral concerns, embedded in the *mores* of society, and so are laden with social values (Timms 1983; Horne 1987). Herein lies the crux of the problem, because value-statements, being views about what is desirable in society, are highly contentious. They say 'what *ought* to be the case' (Shardlow 1989: 3), and so open up the potential for disagreement between individuals on grounds of belief and perception (for example, of politics, culture or religion). Not only does this mean that an activity such as social work will always reflect values, because it is required to intervene in important aspects of everyday life, but that it will often be disputed because the goals of social work may not necessarily be equally acceptable to every member of society. To this extent, ethics and values are inherently 'political', so any exploration of their implications must be concerned also with the contested nature of social work activity.

The choice for social workers, therefore, is not whether their work has an ethical dimension, but whether or not ethical questions are addressed explicitly and how they are to be explored (England 1986). The various chapters of this book engage in just such a task through the examination of a range of contemporary social work issues, each of which poses specific challenges to social work practice and policy. At the same time, it is recognised that the treatment of social work as a unitary phenomenon in such matters as questions of ethics is likely to be mistaken (Timms 1983: 2). Within, as well as outside, the profession there are different perspectives, and the discussions of the different contributors to this volume reflect a range of approaches and positions to the topics under examination.

ETHICS: THE MEANS–ENDS RELATIONSHIP

Ethical propositions are statements of value related to action. In the instance of social work with which we are concerned here, ethics concern the way in which that occupation is practised, organised, managed and planned. Value-statements may draw on abstract or ideal notions but at the same time they necessarily carry with them implications for the way in which individuals act and the relationship between people as members of social groups. For example, if we accept as an ethical principle that social workers should demonstrate a 'respect for persons' (Butrym 1976) then we must also be able to say something about the context in which action demonstrating respect occurs and by what criteria we may decide that respect has been demonstrated. To do otherwise is to be 'hesitant and clumsy' in our analysis, or even to lack analysis altogether (Timms 1983: 28). Timms goes further, and argues that ethical principles are not fixed directions in the manner of an instruction manual but are the basis for making choices in situations where a range of actions is possible (*ibid.*: 31–2). Similarly, Horne (1987) and Shardlow (1989) have been critical of writers on ethics and values in social work who have not grounded their understanding within a grasp of the concrete historical demands facing social workers day by day.

We shall return below to the specific example of 'respect for persons'. At this point what we are emphasising is the extent to which questions of ethics and values have been dealt with as discrete issues in the social work literature, rather than as facets of a wider concern with the tasks social workers have to accomplish, the methods by which they work, the organisation and management of their services, and the way in which all of these things are judged. As statements of value, ethical principles provide an important yardstick by which particular actions can be evaluated. Moreover, they represent a measure through which the relationship between means and ends should be made clearer.

To illustrate the connection between means and ends Jordan (1990: vii–xiv) sketches out a fable in which the Director of Social

Services in a mythical department is challenged by service users to justify the way in which the outcomes of services fail to reflect formal principles and objectives. The charge is that the immediate meanings of phrases such as 'value each client as an individual', 'promote human potential' or 'assessment of need' (*ibid.*: viii) are contradicted by the experience of receiving services. This, Jordan appears to be suggesting, is because social work methods, theories and systems often serve to aggregate people by type of need or problem and to deny services users' own perceptions of their lives, thus communicating other, unstated objectives such as 'controlling costs', 'limiting criminal behaviour' or 'rationing scarce resources'. This may be as a consequence of decisions taken elsewhere – for example, in Parliament – but if this is the case then the inherent values (as ideal objectives) are dominated by particular economic considerations or concepts of justice, such as retribution or deterrence, which are remote from social work practice. In such circumstances questions of ethics will concern the principles governing the allocation of resources or access to power in decision making (*ibid.*: 144).

Jordan is indicating that ethical issues cannot be divorced from the standpoint of the actors involved. To the extent that this involves access to resources and decision making we are talking about social power. Social workers, along with other 'caring' professions, exercise considerable power (Hugman 1991), and so this must be addressed in any discussion of ethical issues in social work.

THE 'CLASSIC' WRITING: DECONTEXTUALISATION

Those writers who can be seen as forming the 'classic' phase in the formulation of social work values had a common interest in elucidating codifiable sets of principles. Probably the most influential of these was the 'seven principles of case-work' outlined by Biestek (1961). These principles are:

1 unconditional acceptance of the client as a person;
2 a non-judgemental approach to clients;
3 the individualisation of the client;
4 the purposeful expression of emotion;
5 controlled emotional involvement;
6 confidentiality;
7 self-determination for clients.

Similarly, Butrym (1976: 47) outlined three principles or 'propositions', namely:

1 a respect for individual persons;
2 a belief in the social nature of each person as a unique creature depending on other persons for fulfilment of her or his uniqueness;
3 a belief in the human capacity for change, growth and betterment.

For Butrym these propositions underpin Biestek's principles listed above (1976: 48–55). They are statements of value or belief which provide the rationale for the more action-oriented ethical principles which Biestek had described.

Halmos (1978) similarly relates his understanding of the guiding ethics of social work (and other counselling professions) to questions of 'ethics' and 'morality'. However, Halmos's work highlights a problem which has continued to be a source of confusion – namely, the extent to which a concern with 'ethics' can be separated from what he calls 'moralising' (Halmos 1978: 182–6). 'Moralising' is defined here as the making of judgements about the moral worth of other people or their actions as the basis for the provision of a social work service and so is regarded as antithetical to the establishment of an ethical code for a profession. In this context the rejection of moralising in favour of a concern with ethics is equivalent to Biestek's (1961) assertion of non-judgementalism.

A more recent example of the apparent failure to grasp this distinction is evident in the *Report of the Panel of Inquiry into the Circumstances Surrounding the Death of Jasmine Beckford*, in which the social workers concerned claimed that their non-intervention was guided by the principle of non-judgementalism because they did not form a negative view about the consequences of the father's parenting (Blom-Cooper 1985: 293–4). A different understanding of what 'non-judgementalism' means might have suggested that it was the approach taken in the assessment and not the parenting practices in themselves which should have been subject to evaluation against an ethical principle of this kind. The parenting itself had to be judged, irrespective of any moral view of the parent(s), because social workers are obliged to consider the safety and well-being of children (see, for example, Wise 1988).

The first code of ethics for social work in the UK developed by the British Association of Social Workers (BASW 1975) represents an attempt to spell out the implications for practice of general ethical propositions of the kind listed above. This requires a recognition that social workers are not free agents, but employees of various agencies, and they may have several points of reference as a consequence (the client, colleagues, other professions, the employing agency and the general public) (BASW 1975).

However, Horne (1987: 4) argues that because the BASW code starts from an idealist set of abstractions, it, like the contemporary statements by the qualifying council (CCETSW 1976), fails to provide adequate guidance for social workers in the resolution of day-to-day conflicts of interest and the discharge of their responsibilities. The conclusion drawn is that implications of ethical principles must not only be spelt out but also must be located in the legal, organisational and political contexts in which social work is inevitably practised. The underlying charge is that the lists of principles on which the early BASW and CCETSW documents were based are decontextualised and therefore idealised in their portrayal of social work.

THE 'CRITICAL' WRITING: POLITICISATION

A similar criticism is made by the body of writing which can be grouped loosely together as 'radical social work'. However, although these writers share with others the view that social work ethics must be grasped from the perspective of what actually happens in practice, the underlying theory on which this position is based is that of Marxist (or sometimes neo-Marxist) materialism. For example, Bailey and Brake (1975), Galper (1975), Corrigan and Leonard (1978), and Simpkin (1979) all argue that the framing of ethical questions as well as the answers at which one arrives are derived from the class positions of those involved. In other words, values are inseparable from the material relations of society.

For Simpkin the roots of orthodox social work values are to be found in Kantian philosophy, especially that element which posits the humanity of each individual person as an end as well as a means in our actions (Simpkin 1979: 97–100). This requires the recognition of each actual person as an instance of the 'general human individual' and so establishes ethics as impersonal principles, divorced from any recognition of the specific characteristics of any one person. In this way, the Kantian approach leads to an apparent removal of ethical issues from the subjective world of social relations to the level of abstraction. It is this, Simpkin concludes, which results in notions such as 'respect for persons' being taken out of the social context in which social work is practised. The 'individualisation' of the client which follows therefore serves, at best, to disguise the social origin of problems with which people are faced (such as poor housing, unemployment and low income). At worst it results in a covert blaming of victims (which is not made explicit, because that would be judgemental).

It may be argued that the 'individualisation' which Biestek (1961) claimed as central to social work ethics was important in that it emphasised the status of the client as a unique person, with the rights and claims which that entails. However, the radical social work position is critical also of this argument as taking the individual out of context. What the materialist framework of radical social work points to is, rather, the location of human individuality in various groups formed by divisions within society, of which the most usual instance was class. In these terms ethics must be built not on the assumption of a general humanity, but a humanity that is divided within current social structures. It is impossible to speak or act in this sense without recognising that every person is a member of a specific social class and other objective groupings.

The critics of radical social work frequently focus on the detail of 'radical practice', arguing that it is barely distinguishable from 'orthodox practice' (summarised, for example, by Langan and Lee 1989). At the level of values, Timms (1983: 104) identifies a central theme in radical social work writing of 'the truly human', which, he points out, itself makes an assumption about general humanity. Timms may be mistaken when he goes on to say that a Marxist definition of 'truly human' does not exist (Marx, after all, was engaged in part in a critical 'philosophical anthropology'; see, for example, McLellan 1970). However, he is accurate in his conclusion that what we are presented with is a set of claims which compete with 'orthodox' values and which themselves make philosophical assumptions which require elucidation. Moreover, many Marxisms and neo-Marxisms have developed, so it may be inaccurate to speak of one single position.

THE CONTEMPORARY SITUATION

The radical social work critique, while it may sometimes be seen as remaining oppositional (Langan and Lee 1989), has also had a marked impact on 'conventional' social work values. This can be seen most clearly in the extent to which structural explanations of the problems faced by social work clients are now incorporated in practice and teaching which would make no explicit claims to being 'radical'. Nowhere is this more evident than in the terms of the *Diploma in Social Work* (DipSW) set out by CCETSW (1991). Although still founded on primarily liberal principles involving the recognition of competing value positions, social workers are now expected to develop an awareness of structural oppression, understand and counteract stigma and discrimination of both individual and institutional kinds, and promote policies and practices which are non-discriminatory and anti-oppressive (CCETSW 1991: 16). As such, these terms attempt to contextualise ethical principles in the manner called for by critics of earlier CCETSW documents (see above). At the same time, as Husband argues in a later chapter in this book, they may fail to recognise other dimensions, such as that of culture, in which different concepts of the individual are normative.

To what extent, then, has the definition of core ethical principles in social work shifted between Biestek (1961) and CCETSW (1991)? Although the CCETSW document does not provide a list in quite the same way as Biestek, it is possible to identify key points which can be compared between the classic formulation of thirty years ago and the current position. In Table 1 Biestek's seven principles are listed alongside implications embedded in Paper 30 (CCETSW 1991: 15–16).

The shift in the ethical implications for social work illustrated in this comparison can be summarised as one from notions which are abstract and wide-ranging to those which are more specific in scope. This can be seen in point 2, where the move from non-judgementalism to anti-discrimination focuses on the areas in which social workers might introduce moral judgement, based on their own social position and experience, in relation to class, race, gender, sexuality and disability. Similarly, the general principle of confidentiality has become a more specific injunction to respect privacy and to maintain confidentiality within the limits of law, policy and procedure.

Not only does this development show something of the influence of radical critiques on social work, but there may also be a degree of convergence. As Pearson (1989) acknowledges, there are limits to what social workers realistically may be expected to achieve, because they are grounded in powerful and concrete social institutions. Therefore, a focus on issues of discrimination and work which

Table 1 Comparison of ethical positions 1961–1991

Biestek (1961)	CCETSW (1991)
1. Acceptance	1. Respect for clients' dignity and strengths
2. Non-judgementalism	2. Non-discrimination and anti-oppression
3. Individualisation of the client	3. Commitment to the value of individuals
4. Purposeful expression of emotion	4. Counteracting stigma
5. Controlled emotional involvement	5. Protection of vulnerable people
6. Confidentiality	6. Privacy and confidentiality within contextual limits
7. Self-determination	7. Promotion of choice

seeks to challenge and oppose it has, in many ways, become the main theme of radical social work. In the same period the inclusion of anti-discriminatory principles has been a major factor in shaping the recognised national qualification. Yet the limits of any convergence can be detected in a move in the early 1990s to launch a review of the DipSW precisely because of its specific stance on such issues (Jones 1993). This, it may be argued, if not inevitable was at least probable given the philosophical basis of other changes in ethical principles, for example from self-determination to the promotion of choice. This latter aim may be realistic (given the limitations to total freedom of self-determination for any member of society); however, it is an aim more closely associated with a free-market view of consumerism (Beresford 1988). The point is that the contemporary pantheon of ethical principles may be as internally contradictory as any which preceded it. Contention is inbuilt. We are left with the continuing need to question and explore the ethical dimensions to every aspect of social work. But on what basis are we to proceed?

RETHINKING SOCIAL WORK ETHICS

The difficulty with attempts to list the ethical principles that ought to inform social work practice – and the difficulty with any such list that we can imagine – can, according to MacIntyre (1985), be traced back to the failure of the philosophers of the late eighteenth-century Enlightenment to provide a rational basis for morality which would command general public assent. The principles of professional social work ethics are necessarily derived from more general ethical propositions, as Butrym (1976) made clear. MacIntyre argues that a genuinely shared morality requires a justification in a shared conception of the purpose and meaning of human life. Without such a conception (based, for example, on religious faith or a sense of the duties entailed by citizenship) principles of ethics are bound to lack universality, and there will be no way of conclusively resolving competing ethical claims. Ethical arguments – for example, the contradictory positions on the nature of justice advanced by Rawls (1972) and Nozick (1974) – cannot be settled by an appeal to higher authority or any general conception of what is good or right. The arguments may be equally logical and valid in their own terms, but their basic premises – the points from which they start – are incompatible or incommensurable, and there is no way in which the issues they raise can be settled within the term of conventional ethical debates.

This provides a general explanation of the internal contradictions of both Biestek's and the CCETSW's lists: they incorporate principles drawn from incompatible views of the purposes and functions of a human life. MacIntyre offers a way out of this impasse, and we shall discuss it shortly. The point we wish to make now, however, is that in the case of social work the general difficulty of constructing a set of principles which could be a useful guide to conduct is compounded because of the complexity of many of the situations in which social workers intervene. These situations involve conflicts of interest which cannot be resolved by an appeal to a general ethical principle. The expression of respect or care for one person in the situation may be seen by others as disrespectful or uncaring of their wishes and interests; the promotion of choice for one may restrict the choices of another; the protection of the vulnerable may entail the attachment of stigma to someone else (for example, the stigma of being an abusive or neglectful parent); and so on. Social workers have in practice to decide which ethical principle has priority, in respect of whom, in particular situations. Lists of principles are no help here, although other sources of guidance may be available, derived from the statutory framework within which social workers practise, such as the requirement to give priority to the welfare of children.

Our point, which is reflected in different ways in the chapters that make up this book, is that ethical decisions in social work are inevitably specific and contextualised. The question 'What is it right for me to do?' can only be answered with reference to the immediate situation which the worker has encountered. As Wise suggests in this volume, this stress on the concrete and contextual in thinking about ethics has been one of the major contributions of feminist moral philosophy (and also of feminist psychology, which has argued that there is a characteristically 'feminine' approach to ethical problems (Gilligan 1982; Noddings 1984)). Feminist ethics thus provide an example of how it is possible to move beyond the irresolvable dilemmas which MacIntyre identifies as our inheritance from the Enlightenment; the lack of a foundation for universal principles does not mean that there is nothing that can usefully be said, and in this volume the contributions of Wise and of Davis and Ellis show feminist ethics being applied to contemporary social work issues.

Furthermore, the lists of principles raise questions as to their scope. How broad is the context of which social workers need to take account in making morally informed decisions? In our view, it is a merit of the CCETSW's list when compared with Biestek's that it attempts to acknowledge the broader social dimensions of social work's responsibilities, particularly in its concern with anti-discriminatory practice. Inevitably, however, the 'personalist' focus of traditional views of the values of social work tends to suggest that it is clear in whose interests the social worker is acting, that we know who the 'client' is, and that it is to this person that the values of respect and so on are to be applied. A recurrent theme in the chapters which follow is that this is often problematic, and that, so to speak, we would do well to re-emphasise the 'social' in social work: we would not wish to promote every choice that someone might make (for example, a choice to continue to offend).

If attempts to state universal ethical principles are bound to fail because they cannot refer to a shared general conception of social and moral good, are we left with the kind of post-modernist relativism which suggests that there is no solid ground, no foundation on which we can build, as a basis for establishing ethical preferences? MacIntyre (1985) argues that we should indeed abandon the notion that we can rely on ethical statements of universal validity in order to make sense of particular situations. As a response to this 'post-modern' crisis, MacIntyre suggests that we should look back further than the eighteenth-century Enlightenment, to a conception of ethics which he identifies as Aristotelian. This entails a view of ethics which accepts that '[a]ll sources of moral authority can only provide principles which are rooted in a particular society at a particular point of time. There is no other kind of principle' (Donnison 1994: 28). And 'if our principles are derived from a robust, relevant and living tradition we must expect them to be constantly disputed and constantly evolving'.

As this reference suggests, MacIntyre's writing has had more influence on thinking about social welfare than most recent moral philosophy. One crucial implication of his argument, as we have seen, is that we should not expect ethical principles to be settled or be beyond dispute, because they are bound to be historically specific. Another, however, is that we can develop a framework for thinking rationally about what constitutes good social work, or what the virtues of a good social worker might be. Following Aristotle, MacIntyre argues that (contrary to a central position of Enlightenment philosophy) we can in some circumstances infer 'ought' from 'is'. When we speak of a 'good' farmer, or airline pilot or nurse, we have in mind some notion of what a farmer, pilot or nurse ought to do and be – what virtues, specific to their calling, their practice ought to express. These virtues can be expressed at the level of practices, in terms of an individual life, and by reference to the tradition in which this life is being lived. Mere 'competency' at the level of practice is not sufficient; it needs to be informed by a living sense of why skilled practice matters, how it flows from and expresses the meaning and purpose with which the individual interprets her or his life, and how that life is connected with a 'relevant and living tradition'.

This raises the tantalising question of whether we can specify what the virtues of social work are, what excellences go to make good social work practice. Without claiming that the pieces in this volume provide an answer, we believe that they may help to clarify thinking and advance the necessary debate. Husband's account of the 'morally active practitioner', for example, suggests some virtues for social work practice: care of others, the courage to accept responsibility for one's actions, scepticism about the claims of authority, self-criticism. Other chapters suggest, among others, the virtues of honesty (to oneself and others), a commitment to egalitarian relationships, perseverance, and clarity of thought. All demonstrate that to consider social work solely in terms of technical 'competencies', as has been the recent trend in thinking about training needs (not least, sadly, in statements from the CCETSW), fails to do justice to the moral complexity of social work practice. Not only does such thinking leave much out of account; it is also, arguably, dangerous. Social workers are statutorily endowed with important powers over those with whom they deal: they can deprive people of their liberty, remove children from their homes, and give or withhold services in ways which can have far-reaching effects on people's lives. Do we really want these powers to be exercised by people who have no vocabulary with which to ask ethical questions of their own practice, who are simply competent functionaries carrying out a range of tasks set for them by someone in authority (Bauman 1989)? Our view is rather that continuing ethical debate (even or perhaps especially when we know that agreement will not always be reached) is essential for the moral health of social work, and that ethically informed practice is essential if the rights and welfare of service users/clients are to be protected.

THE CONTENTS OF THIS BOOK

The chapters which follow cover a wide variety of topics: dilemmas of confidentiality, what constitutes ethically informed management, the implications for ethical choices of care in or by the community, the relevance of social work values as traditionally conceived to work with offenders, the interaction of organisational structures and the options open to social workers, the ethics of research and its uses, the problems of making sense of feminist ethics in real practice situations, and the moral stances required if anti-racist practice is taken seriously. The reader will find differences in emphasis among the contributions, and some outright disagreements; if he or she is logically consistent, he or she will therefore not be able to agree with everything in the book. In the light of our introductory comments, this is hardly surprising; and yet, as we have suggested, there are recurrent themes in the chapters which follow, despite their diverse topics and approaches, to which we want to draw attention here.

First, the contributors deal with ethical issues not in an abstract or idealised fashion but firmly within the real context of contemporary practice. Thus Shardlow explores issues of confidentiality and the ethical problems which attend it with reference to concrete situations rather than to general principles; Davis and Ellis situate their discussion of the ethics of community care in the context of current policy as it is actually being put into practice, rather than in terms of the ideals of normalisation or autonomy; Wise argues that much feminist writing on social work fails to help practitioners precisely because it neglects the problems which confront them in the settings in which most of them work; and Macdonald and Macdonald suggest that the ethical problems of social work research have often been misunderstood as a result of failures to consider the issues from the point of view of actors in the real world. For all the contributors, social work takes place within an organisational context which both makes it possible and sets limits to what it can achieve; and the organisation is itself subject to pressures and demands from external policy (and political) developments, which mean, for example, that the principles of consumer or user choice are heavily compromised by considerations of costs and resources (Davis and Ellis), or that efforts to make management more open and participative are contradicted by government expectations of tighter central direction (Vanstone).

A second recurring theme concerns the meaning of anti-discriminatory or anti-oppressive practice, and the related problem of the extent to which social work can be empowering to those who use its services, or have its services thrust upon them. Three of the pieces address these issues directly: Husband's account of how an active 'moral impulse' can help the practitioner to make critical connections between the ethics of professional practice and political interests and commitments; Patel's analysis of the difficulties of achieving authentic change in a hostile or indifferent organisational and political environment; and Browne's argument that if social work is to take the ideal of empowerment seriously the first people who may have to be empowered are social workers. All the contributors, however, address this theme in some way, and none takes it as unproblematic. For Nellis, anti-discriminatory practice has been promoted in social work in a way which has had the paradoxical effect of strengthening the managerialist tendencies of recent policy on social work organisation and training; for Macdonald and Macdonald, a rhetoric of anti-oppressiveness is too often compatible with an oppressive practice; for Vanstone, a key test of the ethics of management is the extent to which equal opportunities are actively promoted within social work agencies.

Third, and finally, these chapters are concerned with the social dimensions of ethical choices, and are sensitive to the inadequacy of a purely personalist ethics. Shardlow deals with the fine-grained issues workers must confront when face to face with service users, but the fact that confidentiality is a problem to be resolved reflects social work's responsibilities to people other than the immediate client. Both Nellis and Husband make connections between social work practice and broader social concerns; Nellis, indeed, argues that the guiding values for probation practice should be social and political, rather than individualised. Browne suggests the possibility of a transformation of the sources of power and influence over social work, in which social workers might begin to listen seriously to previously discredited and marginalised groups; and Patel discusses the entrenched social and cultural structures which sustain racism, and the inability of traditional ethical frameworks to provide a satisfactory guide to those who seek to change them.

A word about the organisation of the book. The chapters can be thought of as comprising three groups of three, within an overall structure which moves from issues of very general application towards greater specificity. The contributions of Patel, Macdonald and Macdonald and Shardlow deal with questions which are relevant to social work in any settings and with any service user/ client group; those of Husband, Wise and Vanstone, with the implications of various ideological and structural movements in contemporary social work; and those of Davis and Ellis and Browne with the issues raised for policy and practice by particular current concerns. All the contributions, however, raise questions which are relevant beyond a single agency context, and our hope is that together they will set a challenging and clarifying agenda for future debates and developments in social work ethics.

BIBLIOGRAPHY

Bailey, R. and Brake, M. (eds) (1975) *Radical Social Work*, London: Edward Arnold.

BASW (1975) *A Code of Ethics for Social Work*, Birmingham, British Association of Social Workers.

Bauman, Z. (1989) *Modernity and the Holocaust*, Cambridge: Polity Press.

Beresford, P. (1988) 'Consumer views: data collection or democracy?' in I. Allen (ed.) *Hearing the Voice of the Consumer*, London: Policy Studies Institute.

Biestek, F. (1961) *The Casework Relationship*, London: George Allen & Unwin.

Blom-Cooper, L. (1985) *A Child in Trust (Report of the Panel of Inquiry into the Circumstances Surrounding the Death of Jasmine Beckford)*, Wembley: London Borough of Brent.

Butrym, Z. (1976) *The Nature of Social Work*, London: Macmillan.

CCETSW (1976) *Values in Social Work (Paper 13)*, London: Central Council for Education and Training in Social Work.

———— (1991) *Rules and Requirements for the Diploma in Social Work (Paper 30)* (2nd edn), London: Central Council for Education and Training in Social Work.

Corrigan, P. and Leonard, P. (1978) *Social Work Practice under Capitalism*, London: Macmillan.

Donnison, D. (1994) 'By what authority? Ethics and policy analysis', *Social Policy and Administration* **28** (1): 20–32.

England, H. (1986) *Social Work as Art*, London: Allen & Unwin.

Galper, J. H. (1975) *The Politics of Social Services*, New York: Prentice-Hall.

Gilligan, C. (1982) *In a Different Voice*, London: Harvard University Press.

Halmos, P. (1978) *The Faith of the Counsellors* (2nd edn), London: Constable.

Horne, M. (1987) *Values in Social Work*, Aldershot: Wildwood House.

Hugman, R. (1991) *Power in Caring Professions*, London: Macmillan.

Jones, C. (1993) 'Distortion and resistance: the right and anti-racist social work education' in *Social Work Education* **12** (3): 9–16.

Jordan, B. (1990) *Social Work in an Unjust Society*, Brighton: Harvester Wheatsheaf.

Langan, M. and Lee, P. (1989) 'Whatever happened to radical social work?' in M. Langan and P. Lee (eds) *Radical Social Work Today*, London: Routledge.

MacIntyre, A. (1985) *After Virtue* (2nd edn), London: Duckworth.

McLellan, D. (1970) *Marx Before Marxism*, Harmondsworth: Pelican.

Noddings, N. (1984) *Caring: A Feminine Approach to Ethics and Moral Education*, Berkeley: University of California Press.

Nozick, R. (1974) *Anarchy, State and Utopia*, Oxford: Blackwell.

Pearson, G. (1989) 'Social work and unemployment' in M. Langan and P. Lee (eds) *Radical Social Work Today*, London: Routledge.

Rawls, J. (1972) *A Theory of Justice*, Oxford: Oxford University Press.

Shardlow, S. (1989) 'Changing values in social work: an introduction' in S. Shardlow (ed.) *The Values of Change in Social Work*, London: Routledge.

Simpkin, M. (1979) *Trapped Within Welfare*, London: Macmillan.

Timms, N. (1983) *Social Work Values: an Enquiry*, London: Routledge & Kegan Paul.

Wise, S. (1988) *Doing Feminist Social Work*, Studies in Sexual Politics No. 21, Manchester, University of Manchester.

Chapter 2

In search of the holy grail

Naina Patel

INTRODUCTION

In discussing the agenda for social work in the 1990s Hugman (1991) argued that the

> issues of sexism and racism can be seen as emergent, in that social work has yet to grasp fully their implications for organisation and professionalism. Whether or not a general council is created, social work is faced in the 1990s with the necessity of placing anti-racist and anti-sexist structures and practices higher on its agenda.

This article examines the issues, practices and consequences faced by personnel and organisations embarking on an anti-racism agenda. Inevitably the conduct of such personnel holds the key in understanding the complexity of racism and how it can be fought, in organisations, as part of a long-term struggle. In the process we can begin to understand what social work professionalism could mean in an anti-racist context based on the principles of social and racial justice.

To achieve this complex task, the article partly uses a narrative method. It focuses on a fictitious character, *She*, as a means to get to the end of understanding ethics and anti-racism. *She* could be a number of individuals (irrespective of 'race' or gender, though this will have an effect on the extent or degree of problems faced and success managed), working throughout the UK. The 'Firm' *She* works for is an organisation operating in the world of market-led services. Such personnel's task is to 'develop and implement' anti-racist work in social services, social work departments in colleges and universities and related organisations. Here begins the story.

*The worst betrayal of intelligence is finding
justification for the world as it is.*
                                                    Jean Guéhenno

STARTING ANTI-RACISM

There was much talk of fire and havoc. '*She* is a fiery sort. . . . *She*'ll
demand changes. . . . *She*'ll wreak havoc', they were whispering on
the rumour mill in the few short weeks following her appointment.
She carried that all-embracing title of 'Race Equality Officer', and
was responsible for 'race equality' changes in employment, training
and services for the Firm. *She* heard of these rumours and understood immediately what they meant. Racial stereotypes are a familiar phenomenon; they are to be fought against, not fulfilled.
'Besides,' *She* wondered, 'with what am I going to create a fire-
storm?' Her job was a specialised one, but her level of empowerment differed not a jot from that of any of her peers. *She* certainly
was not a director, or some such, of the organisation. Havoc was the
last thing *She* wanted to create.

An African saying goes: 'when your home is burning, it's no use
beating the tom-toms!' In the context of this chapter this means that
racism cannot be eliminated by hurling abuse or shouting slogans.
She wanted progress, not hype. *She* had come with particular ideas,
knowing that committed black and white workers had already done
some groundwork in the Firm. *She* sensed that the climate in the
Firm was now conducive to expanding the bridgehead in the fight
against racism. Perhaps this situation was temporary. Let her fellow
workers be disappointed if no blaze was created; after all, as the
Indian saying goes, 'People must not mess with Fire or Water.' This
made good sense as *She* began to make a preliminary assessment of
the Firm's culture.

There was much to be done in introducing policies and practices
on employment, training and services for minority communities: the
Firm had no policy in the fight against racism – anti-racism – and, in
its operations, much had to be accomplished to reflect anti-racist
practice. *She* was fired by a strong ideological commitment to fight
racism, but was aware of the limitations of individual workers and
their ability to challenge institutional racism. Underlying her commitment was a strong knowledge of racism, the reality of black
people's lives in the UK, and organisational and professional
behaviour in the Firm. Nevertheless there remained much to be

learnt: the practical implications of anti-racism policy would provide the *process* of learning for fellow workers on what anti-racist practice meant in employment and service delivery. Ethical considerations would guide the policy's implementation.

She also recognised the *context* in which *She* and others in this area were required to operate: many regarded the goals of anti-racist policies as a search for something unachievable. This attitude, *She* felt, by and large reflected a generalised (but fortunately not *en-masse*) resistance to change, as well as, in varying quantities, inertia, narrow-mindedness, short-term thinking and racism. As for her own position, marginalisation, work overload and colleagues' attitudes that anti-racism work is not *proper* work were all to be expected – a situation no different to the experience of many other black people. Thus, the degree of anti-racism progress *She* might be able to make depended on understanding the Firm's culture, contextualising it, anticipating all sorts of problems and barriers, and strategically applying her expertise at critical targets and junctures. *She* would need to couple all this with personal sacrifice and exceptional patience. Though *She* was no saint, *She* nevertheless recognised that posts such as hers could produce some change, albeit limited in extent. The limits arose because racism, *She* believed, is a structural phenomenon with a long history and ideology, developed and applied at a number of levels, interacting with class, gender and disability relations to produce differential psychological, socio-economic, cultural and political effects in society.

She foresaw difficulties in implementing anti-racism policies within the Firm. Much of this was to do with attitudes. 'The Germans needed all of Hitler's ranting and daily doses from Goebbels' propaganda machine to persuade them that they were better than other people. Englishmen simply take it for granted and rarely waste a syllable discussing it' (Scott 1945: 216). This wry remark carried some meaning for her in working relationships *She* recalled from her experience in other organisations. After all, centuries of exploitation and super-ordination, justified by racist claims (whether through the development of 'scientific' theories of racial superiority, or pseudo-religious propaganda or the dogmas of the 'new' racism), imprint heavily on people's consciousness: the individual sense of identity which is expressed in their 'normal' behaviour and practice. For instance, it is within a concept of 'British' identity and 'British' culture that white (and some black) social service workers practise in relation to white and black clients.

Black clients often find that their daily experience is omitted from the context of assessment of their social service needs. All clients are treated alike. Many a statement or principle echoes the sounds of equity and fairness, but is actually racism by default. The Christian maxim may state, 'Do unto others as you would have them do unto you', but the advice contains an assumption, as Bernard Shaw said: 'Don't do unto others as you would have them do to you – their tastes might be different.'

The Firm's intention to 'clean up its act on racism' was necessitated by the Race Relations Act 1976, which places a duty on employers on how they provide their services – which was where *She* came in. Guided by a conceptual framework on British racism (see Figure 1), *She* began to study the organisation. This was to determine what could be reasonably achieved in a certain timeframe. *She* heard that her colleagues, those who had previously expected her to generate fire, were now saying, 'Stick within your brief . . . do your bit . . . don't touch us . . . what about sexism, class, disability? . . . You know child care stuff is more important than all this political stuff.' Sometimes, when 'race' was lucky enough to be on the agenda, circular arguments were used as an effective tool 'to do nothing'. *She* wondered at these meetings whether her colleagues' liberal philosophical tradition, of which Kant's Categorical Imperative was one element, would now follow given the organisation's impetus and legislative duty: to act only as you would if you wished the principle of your action to become a universal law of human conduct, with the requirement of impartiality. This remained to be seen.

Anti-racism was now supported legally by the Race Relations Act 1976 in the UK and globally by the Human Rights enshrined in the United Nations Charter: 'You should fight racism and they should fight it too.' But instead of seeing Kant's maxim in practice, *She* encountered peer and professional resistance, circular arguments, sitting on the fence: What about sexism, disability, class, sexuality? . . . Are you ranking 'race' as an autonomous phenomenon? . . . We can't move on this . . . What about our feelings? . . . Well, we'll discuss this matter further at our next meeting, etc., etc. How can the categorical imperative of universalising an action be sustained when racism *is not even recognised by many*?

She thinks of, but rejects, the ethical egoist position that, as an epicurean, one should not participate in such struggles, since doing so would only lead to frustration and discomfort. Such things should

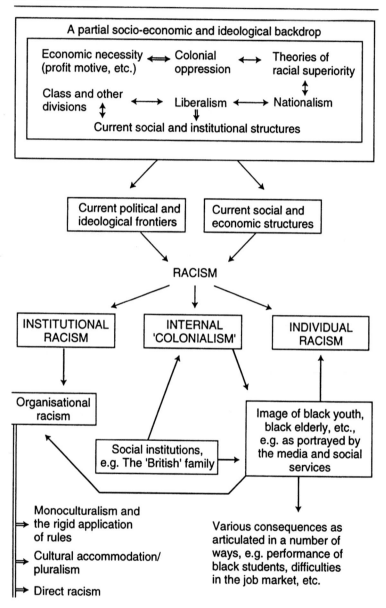

Figure 1 A conceptual framework for the analysis of British racism and its consequences, particularly at the organisational level. (From Patel 1990: 37)

be avoided. Walking away from such involvement is only maximis-
ing one's own pleasure – but *She* is sure that this view of self-
interest is a false one. Struggles can themselves create experiences
which give the greatest satisfaction, especially in the discovery of
humanity.

She considers a different brand of ethical egoism. A human's
moral purpose is the achievement of one's own rational interest,
and intrinsically one possesses certain basic rights by virtue of one's
nature as a rational human being. Rand (1964: 93) states in this
regard: 'A "right" is a moral principle defining and sanctioning a
man's freedom of action in a social context.' However, is the *right*
to engage (by virtue of being a rational being) in racist beliefs and
practices for the 'fulfilment' and enjoyment of one's life *ethically
acceptable*? The ethical egoist would probably say 'yes' because
that to him or her would be the meaning of right to life, liberty and
the achievement of happiness, for a racist. Such views are not often
expressed (or even understood) transparently, but are frequently,
She feels, the logical consequence of her colleagues' statements
and actions. Thankfully *She* has the armoury of the Human Rights
Charter and the Race Relations Act available to her . . . *as a starter.*

She considers again: given the long history of racism and racist
ideology, is it in her white colleagues' perceived interest to join in
the fight against racism in employment, education services and
working relationships within the Firm and its external activities?
Since, according to the rational egoist, one has the right to choose
one's own values and to pursue them, why should one choose
fighting racism as a value? Through self-discovery, by a process
of rational thought, one determines one's self-interest, and one's
actions are guided by this. This explains the actions of many colleagues. *She* understands: many have embraced anti-racism because
it is a good thing to do, or because they saw the climate of the Firm
changing. Better to follow the tide than to resist – but when it comes
to supporting action or taking a position, sitting on the fence or
fudging issues are the more common practices. Self-interest is
rationalised at the level of rhetoric to support anti-racism; self-
interest is rationalised to not engage in action: potential personal
costs put at risk 'safe' personal positions in the Firm. So risks are
not taken, a decision to seriously fight racism is not taken, or when it
is, it is limited for fear of reprisals from whites and suspicion from
blacks (Hacker 1993).

Beyond working relationships, *She* notices white workers have the luxury to choose in-service provision. In research conducted by the British Association of Social Workers, one worker argued, 'I do not accept this (ethnically-sensitive social work),[1] I prefer "culture-sensitive", which I feel does not segregate groups or individuals but acknowledges the differing cultures in all individuals and families and responds to them accordingly' (BASW 1990: 35).

The rationalisation that 'colour' does not matter is *only* the prerogative of a white worker, and translates itself into a 'colour-blind' service provision. A 'take it as it is or leave it' philosophy and views such as 'to cater for different needs is discriminatory and that would be unfair', or 'we cannot discriminate because that would be unethical, wouldn't it?' are common in many quarters of social work education and services. They are often compounded with a failure to recognise the *base* from which people start or the fact that existing institutional arrangements are culturally bound and need to be amended when the composition of society changes.

In contrast *She* recalls that some 'right-on' individuals who are 'ideologically sound' can conduct themselves in the most unethical manner in social and working relationships. *She* wonders how they reconcile their ideology with their personal behaviour of disrespect towards others, be this the oppression of women by men, or black women by white women. Their sole concern with own self-interest and advancement means that they dismiss and abuse workers committed to anti-racist progress in practice. Their quick willingness to rubbish fellow workers betrays the fact that their action may also be motivated by personal envy rather than a recognition of mutual interest in obtaining racial and social justice.

UTILITARIANISM

As part of her work responsibilities, *She* proposes specific measures to implement anti-racism policies. 'Act so as to bring about the greatest good possible', the act-utilitarian ethic in liberal philosophy, takes on a weak meaning when it becomes clear what the specific measures would cost: resources in financial and human terms, changes in staff conduct. Statements such as 'we must own the anti-racism policy and its implementation programme by setting examples ourselves' frequently take on a hollow ring in the general apathy and resistance which undermine change. Anti-racism policy may *ultimately* produce the greatest overall good, not least in utilitarian terms, but will the implementation of policy have the best consequences for all individuals, especially in the short term?

She knew from the practice elsewhere that any Firm serious enough in its commitment to move beyond rhetoric faces severe obstacles in showing that anti-racism progress is possible in the current context. These pressures, be they from political masters, related organisations, or in the form of internal staff resistance to change, produce heavy costs for Firms and individuals promoting anti-racism, especially when attempts at reversal are made with the cry, 'These policies have gone too far.' How far is *too* far? Inevitably it is asked whether these costs are worth it for the sake of a few black clients, workers, students, citizens, etc.

However, *She* tries to argue, should we not judge the rightness of an act (the adoption of anti-racism policy and its implementation in this instance) in relation to the consequences of adopting the *rule* under which a particular act falls rather than the act itself? If so, the costs of anti-racist policies are acceptable to the extent that all policies pursued under the rule 'Act so as to bring about the greatest good possible' incur costs. There may be an issue of prioritisation based on an array of cost-benefits for a range of programmes, but eventually the anti-racist programme *must* be adopted if one is to be true to the utilitarian principle of the greatest good.

It follows, also, from a consistent application of the utilitarian principle that the rule 'never be a racist' is an essential one, because there can never be degrees of racism which are acceptable: racist abuse against a black worker differs from a racist murder, and these require different means of censure and punishment, but whether there should be sanctions is not an issue. There can never be circumstances in which racism is acceptable. But *She* knows this is precisely the area where the Right and those of a liberal complexion find common ground in their actions against 'Political Correctness'.

Rule-utilitarianism also tries to address the issue of ethical relativism, i.e. that there are different moral *rules*, depending on conditions existing in various societies. The debate surrounding the 'black family's' duties towards the nurturing of the young and support of the old, for example, touches on this issue, especially to the extent that many white social workers (and indeed some black) impute 'undesirable' or 'problematic' moralities as the basis for pathologising the 'black family'. This debate has been widely covered (see Lawrence 1982; Harris 1991). Honeyford's comments (in the *Salisbury Review*) on black Caribbean and Asian families having low or poor morals (on parenting for example) as a result of a 'deficient' cultural fabric are an example. Honeyford argued that they lowered educational standards ('English is a second language' for Asians, and children from West Indian homes 'are fatherless') and contaminated others – presumably white society – through their values, customs, language and religion. In other words, 'your' (Asian, Caribbean) values are not as good as 'ours'. As such the issue is not just about different moral rules (ethical relativism), but about a racism which ascribes to these different ethics a lower value. In fact it makes them unethical.

The application of rule-utilitarianism can be considered in relation to the issues surrounding the case of Anita Hill v. Clarence Thomas in the USA in 1991. Briefly, Professor Anita Hill alleged that Judge Clarence Thomas (nominated to be appointed to the Supreme Court at the time and, like Anita Hill, black) sexually harassed her some ten years previously. At that time Hill was Thomas's assistant at the Department of Education and then at the Equal Employment Opportunity Commission in the Reagan administration, of which Thomas was the director. Hill claimed that Thomas had spoken to her of sex scenes from pornographic films and once asked, 'Who has put pubic hair on my Coke?' Thomas, it was alleged, had told Hill 'graphically of his own sexual prowess', 'referred to the size of his own penis as being larger than normal', and 'pleasures he had given to women with oral sex'. The denial from Thomas was 'unequivocal and categorical', that he had not 'had conversations of a sexual nature' or 'had a personal sexual interest in her'. 'This is a person I have helped at every turn in the road since we've met,' Thomas declared. Given the charges and the 'race' and gender mix, with an appointment to the Supreme Court hanging in the balance, the drama captured the public's attention on both sides of the Atlantic.

Kathleen M. Sullivan (1993: 15) cites the view of the African–American Harvard sociologist Patterson: 'Sexual banter in the workplace is taboo according to the "neo-Puritan" rules of gender relations enforced by "elitist" feminists and the "white upper middle class" . . . "the mass of the white working class and nearly all African–Americans" know that "raunchy things" are said in the workplace all the time. Strong women just talk back. Thomas, Patterson surmises, adhered in public to the "elitist" white feminist gender code, but on occasion he privately let "his mainstream cultural guard down" when he thought the setting was safe. He thought it was safe with Anita Hill because she was "aesthetically and socially very similar to himself". In what he thought was their shared "psycho-cultural context", regaling her "with his Rabelaisian humour" was a "way of affirming their common origins". Such sexual banter, Patterson writes, would have been "completely out[side] of the cultural frame of his white, upper middle-class work world, but immediately recognisable" as a common and unmalevolent language "to Professor Hill and most women of Southern working-class backgrounds, white or black, especially the latter" '. So Thomas's remarks to Hill were *ethically* acceptable given existing rules of conduct, according to Patterson, who divides the world into 'psycho-cultural contexts' by race and class.

Nevertheless, the Hill case illustrates the point that what is regarded as ethically acceptable is dependent upon cultural contexts and practices. However, the analysis offered by Patterson should caution us: cultural factors could be, and are, used as a smokescreen to obfuscate serious sexist practices. Indeed might not racists use the same 'logic' to justify racism as ethically acceptable on the grounds of its being part of one's 'culture'? Is this not the argument of the New Right (Barker 1981) under the guise of 'cultural difference'? Cultural contexts are extremely important in analysing conduct, but sole reliance upon them can open up dangerous precedents, as shown above.

Justice, legislation and human rights

So far *She* has considered western liberal theories of conduct based entirely on consequences – whether these arise from particular *acts* or *rules*. But it is not unusual to hear, 'Why am I against racism? Because it is just wrong, that's all'. This statement may appear simple, but the moral judgement is loud and clear. There are various types of moral obligations not recognised by the utilitarians. Among these are *Rights* – based ethics, where it is argued that people should be treated 'always as ends in themselves and never merely as means', as Kant argued, and principles regarded as defensible are those to which self-interested individuals would concur in ideal conditions. A good example is Rawls's (1972: 250) Equality Principle, according to which each individual has equal rights to basic liberties. The corollary to this is the Difference Principle, which declares that social and economic inequalities are justified only if the least advantaged are better off than they would be in conditions of equality (Rawls 1972: 83).

Although most would regard justice as a necessary virtue for human and institutional conduct, the two key points for Rawls are 'the reasonable' and 'public reason'.

> For example, the abstract persons will, as reasonable thinkers, all agree that the liberty of the individual should have an overriding importance. They will agree also that the worst-off members of society, whoever they may be, *must be protected against any worsening of their situation*; this principle must be built into the same structure of a liberal society from the beginning.
>
> (Hampshire 1993: 43, my emphasis)

And this is where a problem may lie: don't let black people's position get worse – in other words 'they must be protected against worsening of racial discrimination' – which means that racial inequality can be maintained, but not allowed to get worse. This effectively was the Scarman judgement after the rebellions of 1981,[2] and it can be seen in the policies surrounding equal opportunities, most notably in employment. Since the distribution of resources remains unequal and racial ideology intact, social reforms only allow entry to the workplace and economic rewards for a few. As for the Firm, it can claim that there is equality in the employment process, and that mobility is possible if only you 'choose' to progress.

The concept of justice must be embedded in human rights – to which we now turn. The practice of racism, according to UNESCO's declaration on 'race' and racial prejudice, 'has no scientific foundation and is contrary to the moral and ethical principles of humanity'. This is enshrined in Articles 1 and 2 of the Universal Declaration of Human Rights. At the national level in the UK, racism is legislated against in the Race Relations Act 1976 (except in Northern Ireland, though a consultative process may yield progress there in the near future). The legislation, in its various provisions such as direct and indirect discrimination (a recognition of institutional racism), segregation, detriment, and so on, places duties on employers and local authorities to eliminate unlawful racial discrimination and promote equality of opportunity and good relations between persons of different racial groups (S. 71). It further embodies principles of the legislation in its codes of practice, covering to date employment, health and education. In essence the code provides rules for organisations and individuals (including employees) on how they should conduct themselves in the management of racism in the spirit of the Act. A requirement to address issues of 'race', culture and religion is now also enshrined in the Children Act 1989, NHS and Community Care Act 1990 and the Criminal Justice Act 1991.

She knows, however, that legislation cannot in itself create the changes necessary to achieve compliance. This situation is also recognised by black people experiencing the effects of racism (to various degrees) as citizens, consumers, workers or students in all spheres of life in British society (Brown 1984). Bhikhu Parekh, once a deputy chair at the CRE, said, 'No European government has hitherto dared to follow wholly racist policies; none has dared to tackle racism head-on either' (cited in Essed 1991: 14). The effect of such legislation is often to provide protection or alleviation to individuals against racial discrimination rather than create major shifts within organisations.

Often changes within the organisation are prompted by successful action by individuals against racial discrimination rather than an enthusiastic commitment to implement the Race Relations legislation. An examination of individual cases illuminates particular conditions and trends: the commonplace, everyday nature of racism; the *ease* with which racist acts are perpetrated by individual workers and/or employers; and the fact that the casual nature of racism receives insufficient recognition. Most frequently, CRE cases (quoted at the end of the CRE's annual reports) show that calls for consistent (ethical) practice *vis-à-vis* white *and* black people are often (perhaps deliberately) misconstrued as calls for discrimination in favour of black individuals.

A recent illustrative case involved senior personnel at a large university. A unanimous tribunal decision found them guilty of sex and race discrimination by giving a senior lectureship post to a white woman in preference to a black man with more experience. One lecturer who was later on the interview panel had said that there was 'no need for the course to bear the brunt of employing black people as it was a Faculty-wide issue'. The Tribunal in its 20-page report (1993) found that the interview 'panel's approach to selection was almost entirely subjective, and that this was a significant factor which contributed to the unlawful discrimination'. The staff's reason for selecting the white woman candidate was that '[She] had better qualifications and preferred a ''facilitating'' approach towards students rather than a ''directive'' one which they felt

Mr. Patel would adopt.' 'The Tribunal concluded that Marion
Charlton, the course leader, and Susan Palmer, the professional
group head, had given evasive, unsatisfactory and not entirely
honest replies during evidence' (M. Wainwright, *Guardian*, 30 July
1993).

Courtney Hay, of the Northern Complainant Aid Fund which
supported Mr Pravin Patel, said, 'Senior staff in this case ignored
their own written policies and did as they pleased with apparent
impunity' (*ibid.*). The *Yorkshire Evening Post* (23 September 1993),
commenting on the compensation decision a few months later, was
quite frank on the nature of racism: 'Mr. Patel . . . was no victim of
casual, red-neck bigotry on the shop floor. Quite the contrary. The
discrimination was by supposedly liberal, middle-class professionals
at Leeds Metropolitan University. The case casts a terrible slur on an
institution whose very ethos aims to be untainted by such irrational
prejudice.'

She knows that such acts are not of a one-off nature, nor restricted
to a particular geographical area, institution or sector. Nor, as the
above case illustrates, are they the acts of misguided or nasty
individuals (though such people of course exist). Racism has a
particular dynamic where, by virtue of colour, identity, history,
organisational evasiveness and failures to act (in the above case
Leeds Metropolitan University did not discipline any of its staff
found in breach of the Sex and Race Discrimination Acts, despite all
the negative publicity), acts of race discrimination become *routine*.
And what of the human, personal, economic (job-wise) costs to
those, such as Pravin Patel, who take a stand against such behaviour?

This takes us to the heart of how black professionals conduct
themselves and organisations' responses to black professionals who
are in the system. Black professionals with an anti-racism remit are
a nuanced subset of this group. After many months, *She* reflects on
the context in which *She* arrived in the Firm. '*She*'ll set the place
ablaze.' 'Do we need such posts when there are more pressing
things to be done, such as child care work?' '*She*'s only been
employed because *She*'s black.' '*She*'ll soon run out of steam.' 'I
am against racism, but all this is political stuff – what we need is
common sense.' *She* also knew that in the organisation the majority
of black workers, as elsewhere, were to be found at lower levels in
the organisational hierarchy; whereas black professionals such as
herself were expected to be Jacks of all Trades (with immense
consequences for their workloads). '*She*'ll soon run out of steam'

seemed to be built into the structure! All this, of course, was to be expected. More importantly, *She* recalls that her position (middle management) was not simply due to her skills and knowledge. It owed much to the *openings* created through many struggles over the years, in particular (in her case) the activity following the rebellions of 1981 and 1983, when many ordinary black and white people fought for improvements in all walks of life. The rebellions of 1981, in particular, created an attitude in political circles permitting the 'toleration' of the fight against racism, provided it was essentially restricted to the individual psyche. Lord Scarman, reporting after the 1981 rebellions, fell short of recognising institutional racism as a fundamental problem in Britain and the source of the *systematic* nature of racism over a long period – not just during the late 1970s recession, but throughout the history of black people in Britain (see Smith 1977; Brown 1984).

Institutional racism

Thinking of this, *She* remembers that Carmichael and Hamilton (1967) first offered an explanation of the consequences of institutional racism in the United States. This led Jones (1993) to define it as 'those established laws, customs and practices which systematically reflect and produce racial inequalities in American society. If racist consequences accrue to institutional laws, customs or practices the institution is racist whether or not the individuals maintaining those practices have racist intentions.' Those 'established laws, customs, practices' cannot be reduced and explained purely as individual or group actions. They are firmly rooted in relations of production based on exploitation and racial subordination, reproducing inequalities (Figure 1). Williams (1985) offers an important model of institutional racism to explain various institutional processes which generate 'racial' inequality through the interplay of 'racial', class, cultural, political and professional ideologies. As Figure 1 shows, institutional racism encompasses the social institutions as well as organisations *per se*, with direct and indirect interrelationships with other 'forms' of racism.

In reality, it is difficult to overlook or deny the fact that racism is a prime factor in explaining:

1 Why, on the employment front, the rate of unemployment is double (or higher as there are variations within black groups)

for black people compared to white people, after controlling for qualifications, sector and location. Although the economy has significantly changed since the 1970s, the disparity between black and white unemployed appears to be regular (Smith 1977; Brown 1984; Jones 1993).

2 Why, in education, the Eggleston Report (1984) found black students more active than whites in pursuing educational goals, but being held back by the low expectations of teachers and lack of challenge put to them by schools.

> In 1988 the report of a survey by the CRE in eight education authorities found that only 2% of the 20,246 teachers were from ethnic minorities. They tend to be on lower pay scales than their white colleagues, are steered into shortage subjects and are passed over for promotion. Nearly two-thirds of white teachers surveyed and 81% of ethnic minority teachers thought there was racial discrimination in schools.
>
> (Cited in CARJ 1994)

3 Why, according to the Council of Legal Education in 1992, 'Black students at the Bar's Law School had three times the failure rate of white students, a disparity that could not be dismissed on the grounds of ability' (*The Times*, 3 November 1992). Similarly in social work, black students have complained of their experiences on CQSW, CSS and DipSW courses, leading a higher proportion of them to leave the course/programme and with a higher failure rate than white students (Reports in 1993).

4 Why black people appear disproportionately in the mental health system (Sashidharan and Francis 1993); among children in care (Barn 1993); in the criminal justice system (NACRO 1992); while being under-represented in the welfare services for older people (Patel 1990; Atkin and Rollings 1993). Experiences of disadvantage and discrimination are also to be found in housing and health (Ahmad 1993).

5 Why, 'out of 75 cases of black deaths in custody recorded, only one has resulted in a prosecution (of the police) and only in one has the family of the deceased received compensation' (Sivanandan 1991).

6 Why, according to the Runnymede Trust, it has been estimated that there are '70,000 incidents [of racial violence and harassment] a year – 1,400 each week, 200 each day, one every seven or eight minutes', leading them to conclude in its submission to the

Home Affairs Committee (1994) that 'racial harassment is endemic in British society' (Runnymede Trust 1994: 1).

7 And, finally, on immigration, why *The Economist*, hardly recognised as an enthusiastic supporter of anti-racist work, could not help but make the following comments on the 'bungled deportation' by the 'extradition' squad on 28 July 1993, of Joy Gardner, which led to her death four days later:

> Laws on immigration have been tight for 30 years – the trickle of people now let in are almost all closely related to British citizens. . . . It has become fashionable to tighten rules on immigration. . . . In June, EC interior ministers agreed to expel illegal immigrants more readily. The French Government has been talking about 'zero immigration'. Britain provides a lesson in keeping out and booting out foreigners. It is a lesson in efficiency, not justice.
>
> (7 August 1993: 26)

She knows that institutional racism is often dismissed as a phenomenon because it is claimed that this means that *every* white individual and every white institution is racist (see also the later discussion on political correctness). This is a flagrant misrepresentation of an analysis which seeks to show that racism is deeply rooted in (British) society and therefore difficult to flush out. This does not mean that every individual, organisation or action is racist. The argument is no different to that about institutionalised sexism: can one deny that women have had to struggle for their rights in Britain over the years? Why was the vote for women such a hard struggle? Even in the darkest recesses of the nineteenth century not every male was a sexist; nor was every white a racist: but the deep-rooted nature of the problem, perhaps reducing in intensity, cannot be denied.

She reflects that some liberal or black movements are themselves guilty of the misrepresentation 'deep-rooted=100%', as in the case of the Race Awareness Training (RAT) thesis imported into the UK from the USA and employed, in its mind-numbing simplicity, to devastating effect by those (including Liberal and Labour authorities) who should have known better. RAT reduces the complex process of racism into a formula: 'Racism=Prejudice+Power' (no one would dare to define, say, *poverty* in such a way); and racism is defined as 'a white person's problem'. Attempts to change their attitudes through Race Awareness Training programmes have done much harm to serious anti-racism work. It has allowed the Right and New Right to manipulate the public into regarding anti-racism as a 'loony, left-wing' cause and reduced analyses of racism to 'cultural differences' and 'common sense' (Barker 1981; Sivanandan 1988; Macdonald Report Enquiry 1991). Moreover, the climate has been generated where it is shameful to be seen to support racial justice through serious anti-racism work, however limited, in organisations in the business of serving *all* sections of the community. Racial marginalisation knows no frontiers.

DIFFERING GOALS

She as a professional black worker is expected to bring, often alone, major changes in the Firm's employment practices and services. Broadly speaking, professionals with anti-racism remits (and/or black workers elsewhere in the system without such briefs) are required to initiate many policy changes within their organisations, including: strategic 'marketing' policies; appropriate developments in employment, services and training; the strengthening of their own area by creating structures, building alliances and entering networks; the enhancement of colleagues' understanding on 'race'; acting as buffers against community and pressure groups; and, broadly speaking, enlarging the boundaries wherein anti-racism change is accepted. The task may seem endless. Commonly the organisation expects *minimal* changes to pacify community pressures or, if it is genuinely committed, its own structures can limit progress.

Inevitably, differing goals between the organisation and black professionals/workers result in a degree of conflict. *She* and others support anti-racism initiatives and fulfil various duties, embracing commitments made to serve 'all sections of the community'. In the process they seek to produce tangible results, establish credibility for themselves as workers and professionals, and, furthermore, establish credibility for the area of anti-racism itself. *She* recognises that the process of bringing about changes often dehumanises her within the context of the Firm, constructs her into a 'nasty personality'. Her high-quality work and competence to juggle competing agendas in a highly politically charged climate, while maintaining her passion for change, are undermined by charges of being 'emotional'. Standards of debate, engagement and analysis which

She has striven to set can evaporate without leaving a trace. Meanwhile the *struggle* to maintain the results of anti-racist actions continues.

Such struggles amid diversity require more than an ethical person guided by self-interest – as an ethics of rational self-interest would suggest. At the heart of *Her*/black workers' action lies a deep commitment to fight racism – unreservedly. '[If] you have known racism, if you have felt racism, felt it like an incubus on your brain all the time and had to liberate yourselves . . . ' (Sivanandan 1991: 44). This does not mean that *all* black professionals and workers are acting in the interests of racial and social justice or for the greater good, acting ethically in the communitarian sense.[3] The culture of individualism over the last decade or two has had a sharp impact on all sections of British society. Responsibilities placed on black workers by themselves ('felt racism like an incubus on your brain') or by job descriptions, should guide their conduct – ethics – and, in the process, build professional ethics around anti-racism principles and approaches. Instead, for some, 'equal *opportunities*' have become 'equal *opportunism*'. Such *individuals* act on self-interest as the ethical egoist would do. Worse still, some clothe their activities in the language of liberation, externalising all problems when it comes to 'doing' what they preach, and use their professional power for their own advancement. This does not represent even personal liberation since the system can use them against fellow workers active in serious anti-racism work (Sivanandan 1993).

Leaving such 'equal opportunists' aside, since *She* regards racism as a structural phenomenon, the ethical strategies *She* follows must be those which engage with 'people's most obvious, uncomplicated, unreflexive apprehension of the problem . . . and show that these are social and historical processes . . . not written in the stars, [but] handed down . . . [and that] they are deep conditions which are not going to change if we start tinkering around with them' (Hall 1980: 6). *She* also recognises that racist ideologies and practices do not leave a segment of the population free of them.

Racism in our society is in part sustained by the defensive institutions of the working class as much as the rampant and offensive institutions of the capitalist class. The fact that certain forms of working class and trade union racism differ in their extent, in their modality, in their grip on people's imagination from other types, say National Front racism, the fact that it is quite significantly different in its articulation, is not the same thing as saying that it would be possible to make a cut through the British population and come out with goodies on the one hand and baddies on the other. . . . In fact the history of the period [the 1950s onwards] is the history of the continued internal segmentation of the labouring force and one of the principal ways in which that segmentation has expressed itself politically and ideologically is around questions of race . . . racism of a virulent kind has been able to provide a kind of adequate explanation, not so much for people at the top of the society but more for people at the bottom of the society, as to what it is they are experiencing and why it is that a kind of racist politics makes sense.

(Hall 1980: 12–13)

An example of these processes, in the 1990s, might be the case of a white woman manager in one of the Firm's cost centres offering a job to a white woman, in an intra-Firm transfer, without notifying the latter's black (woman) manager or following organisational procedures. Hall's explanation fits the white manager's action in that it is quite permissible to do this. Her conduct is 'in the best interests of all' – a utilitarian ethic with no inkling of justice at its core. Such actions represent the culture of racism, made more respectable recently, and the racial politics, racial divisions and racist ideological and historical relations which make these and other practices in organisations 'normal'. On housing estates and on streets racial harassment, racial attacks, racial murders intensify and are seen as 'normal', casual, not to be registered.

Indeed at the organisational level, *She* regards racist incidents at work as so routine that *She* often disregards them. To be preoccupied at this level would mean that the changes and shifts necessary in employment, education and services would be sacrificed. To be surprised at their frequency would be to underestimate the complexity of racism. Instead the philosophies of *Her* cultural background come into play: 'They say that the power of senses is great. But greater than the senses is the mind. Greater than the mind is Buddhi reason; and greater than reason is He [sic] – the Spirit in man and in all' (Gita: 3, 42: 60). So *She* must use her knowledge, resources, network of family, friends and allies, and her ingenuity, to challenge racism and other injustices.

Professional ethics demand that *She* (and others) must set new boundaries on professionalism. The achievement of this is no easy route. Frederickson, a highly respected black American historian, writing about a black scholar in 1963, says,

> he must remain true to the rigid requirements of equanimity, dispassion and objectivity. . . . He *must* pursue truth in his own field. But in the face of forces that deny him membership in the mainstream of American scholarship and suggest that he is unable to perform creditably, the task of remaining calm and objective is indeed a formidable one. There is always the temptation to pollute his scholarship with polemics, diatribes, arguments. This is especially true if the area of his interests touches on the great questions in which he is personally involved as a Negro. If he yields to this attractive temptation, he can by one act destroy his effectiveness and disqualify himself as a true and worthy scholar. He should know that by maintaining the highest standards of scholarship he not only becomes worthy but also sets an example that many of his contemporaries who claim to be the arbiters in the field do not themselves follow.
>
> (Frederickson 1993: 31)

It must be recognised that a black social worker's professional ethical appraisal is based on the ideological and political context of 'race' and racism. *She* works with, but also widens, existing professional ethical codes.[4] In the process of establishing a wider, fully fledged code of ethics, some existing practices are challenged and changed (for instance views that one should simply 'treat clients as individuals' – thereby excluding the forces of class, poverty, racism and gender which shape people's reality as individuals and *in* these groups). In other words, because of black professionals' commitment to the goals of racial and social justice, professional ethics are *extended* (and altered) as can be seen by the following examples.

Black professionals in businesses, in the USA, perceive an ethical need to have a wider professional perspective. 'There is a tremendous sense of obligation to serve as a mentor,' says Frank Savage, a Senior Vice President of Equitable Company. 'I can't be like a normal white executive and just do my job and go home.' For M. Alexis at Northwestern University, 'Our greatest challenge is finding a way to make opportunities for the people in inner cities.' But not all share an ethical prescription that blacks have a wider duty, wherever they are, to their community. The first black governor of the Federal Reserve Board, A. F. Brimmer, believes that holding blacks to such a standard is unfair: 'I do not see why black businesses should have any more responsibility than anyone else to improve life for blacks' (Lesley and Mallory 1993).

A parallel can be drawn for black workers in social work agencies and colleges in the public sector in the UK. The emergence of black staff groups is based on the belief that there is 'strength in numbers' and that a 'survival network' is needed to combat individual and institutional racism. In practice these groups may be rendered ineffective through employers' lack of a positive response. Sometimes the group may reduce its own potency where, for example, issues are purely restricted to black workers' conditions within the organisation rather than the wider context.

The differing ethical perspectives among black business professionals, illustrated above, are indicative of a continuing tension among black individuals throughout the public and private sectors. What *She* and like-minded people have attempted to show is that their ethical appraisal is founded on principles of obtaining racial and social justice, not for themselves 'in jobs', but also for their black clients (poor white clients also benefit) and workers in the community (expressed as a share of the organisation's power base and resources, translated into services and jobs) (Rooney 1987). They do not lose sight of the ultimate aim, which is to build anti-racism politics in relation with class, disability and gender, to deconstruct, not reform or tinker with, the 'cake' based on exploitative relations which maintain racism, sexism and class division and thus an unequal society.

At this point *She* recognises the deficiency of the Kantian position, and indeed of Rawlsian rights-based ethics of justice in operation. Bloch (1938), taking a critical look at the Categorical Imperative, argues:

> never to regard man merely as a means but always as an end at the same time is not exactly bourgeois; it cannot be fulfilled at all in any class society. For each of these societies was based, though in different forms of association, on the master–servant relationship, on the use of people and their work for ends which are by no means their own. Man as the only end: however general this humane element and especially the abstract notion 'humanity in man' may be in Kant, . . . exploitation is absolutely denied by it. Only morally denied, of course . . . it follows precisely for the Kantian moral proposition: it sketches a should-be *which,*

against the grain at that time and place, is not even approachable in any class society. Kant cited the freedom from contradiction as a criterion in order to be able to conceive a maxim of behaviour as a generally followed law. . . . But if the contradiction is not covered in the *concept* and especially in concepts of mere business ethics, . . . if it appears instead in one *volitional maxim itself*, then it actually does become a criterion which can decide the moral enforceability or non-enforceability of an action as a generally valid one. And this decision then makes it impossible to obey the *categorical imperative as a whole*, and hence not just its individual trial problems, in the class society. For no proletarian can want the maxim of his behaviour to be able to be conceived as the principle of a general legislation, which also includes the capitalists; that would not be morality but betrayal of his brothers.

(Bloch 1938: 872–3)

The limits of organisational change

Given this, in the context of racism, *She* recognises the *internal limits* of fighting racial disadvantage and discrimination. Solutions to racism which marginalise black communities along poverty and 'race lines', dehumanise people, play off one 'oppression' against another,[5] and casualise life so that a racially motivated murder victim is just another 'Asian' (Gordon 1989), have to be fought outside the system, while doing the utmost to enlarge the internal perimeter. The confusion between the two realms of action by black professionals provides a useful tool for organisations and classification of individuals into 'good' and 'bad' black social workers (Stubbs 1985: 17).

She knows, however, that the *internal limits* mean that tackling racial disadvantage and discrimination through organisational policies and procedures is not without problems. This is particularly so when individuals responsible for the enactment of policies lose sight of what racism is and how it reproduces itself. Instead they sanitise it into neat procedures – *procedural anti-racism* becomes the practice. On 'difficult anti-racist or management-related questions involving black and white staff', take the application of grievance procedures in an organisation as an example. In our scenario, after over three years of service, a white secretary alleges that her black (woman) manager is intimidating, racialist, etc. She initially does this covertly by making these allegations to her manager's white line-manager (also a woman). Half truths and outright lies appear. No allegation can be substantiated and the issue is really of insubordination and defamation – a familiar one for many black managers. The organisation, through its grievance procedures, hears the secretary's 'case', but fails to safeguard the black manager. Instead it chooses to see the 'case' in the white secretary's terms, and omits to ask fundamental questions such as: *where* is the racialism? Where is the intimidation? Why is the secretary having difficulties following legitimate work requirements? And why *now*? Most seriously it treats libellous statements blithely. It fails to detect that racism (on the part of the secretary and the institution) guides the entire process. So what ethical lessons can be learnt here? First, the organisation fudges and, like a utilitarian, regards both positions with equal respect, and sees the entire issue in terms of 'holding different perspectives'. Charges of 'racialism' and other lies remain unanswered. The black manager insists that such charges be examined. Insistence on her right to demand justice turns her into a demon, not a victim, for an organisation intent on expediency in its procedures. In other words, liberal procedures and their enforcement not only fail to arrive at a just verdict, but senior management abdicates its managerial responsibilities, partly because 'race', it argues, has impaired its ability to conduct the 'case' properly. Consequently incompetent, unprofessional and unethical practices result.

And what of the black manager? She is told to be a 'good' black worker, to shut up and put this experience behind her. Meanwhile the white secretary obtains promotion elsewhere in the organisation! Where, then, should the black manager obtain justice: not in the organisation's procedures, given her experience, clearly, so should it be in courts? We should remember the hundreds of cases which come before Industrial Tribunals whose outcomes are not as satisfactory as in the earlier-cited case at Leeds Metropolitan University. Instead, understandably, the black manager feels like Qiu Ju (Spence 1993): 'something wrong has been done. Something unfair. There need not be financial redress – that is not necessary, and when proffered, rejected – but there must be an apology. Then the world can get back to its regular business.' But the art of fudging does not produce such justice, and 'regular business' cannot return because 'the punishment is . . . without significance. The true crime is one of callousness against human dignity, and for that no one has any redress' and so she 'shouts the truth that no one wishes to hear' (Spence 1993: 13).[6]

Guilt and political correctness

In thinking about her work, *She* knows that she may have to counter the charge of creating *guilt*. Many white workers, challenged by requirements to change or an analysis of racism markedly different to their perspective, cry out and claim that black workers make them feel guilty of their past and present. These white workers have failed to understand how each one of us *connects* to our history, and to the prevailing culture and ideological conditions (Scott 1945). For some white workers, the use of guilt is a useful mask for their 'passive racism'.

The 'creation of guilt' charge has received much support from the media and elements of the academic world. The kinds of practice experienced by certain white workers do not help. Sivanandan (1988) explains:

> Maureen McGoldrick, for instance, was suspended from her school headship by Brent Council on suspicion of being a racist (on the basis of a remark she is said to have made in a telephone conversation) and therefore in contravention of the anti-racist policies that the council wished to carry out in education. . . . The fact remains that the council, in its anxiety to do right by black children, did wrong by Ms. McGoldrick. Whereas the fight for racial justice, if rightly fought, must of its very nature improve and enlarge justice for all. . . . As a result Ms. McGoldrick was handed over as a *casus belli* to the genuine racists in our midst and to the racist media in particular, who were only too willing to espouse her cause in order to discredit the cause of anti-racism.
>
> (*ibid.*: 16)

> Consequently, with 'fascism personalised', the 'personal guilt' which characterised the event at Brent 'has begun to replace shame as a moral value in society at large. . . . To be guilty of racism is to have transgressed someone else's standards, to be ashamed of it is to fail one's own.'
>
> (*ibid.*: 18)

In this connection, *She* thinks of the recent press campaign against the CCETSW in the UK over its anti-racism policies, which focused on the organisation's so-called 'political correctness'. Is the attempt to get anti-racist practice into a professional code of ethics for *all* social workers a 'politically correct' act? The media campaign reflects a culture of racism in which eminent academics use emotional language (which, ironically, anti-racists are often mistakenly charged with) to charge a UK Validating Body, the CCETSW, with 'obsession' and 'a lethal kind of looniness' (Phillips 1993; Appleyard 1993; Pinker 1993). This is because the CCETSW, as part of its Requirements, has asked that *all* social workers trained in the UK must be competent to work in a multiracial society. They need to be taught to understand racism and develop skills in anti-racist social work. Nowhere in the six columns of Professor Pinker's article in the *Times Higher Education Supplement* (1993) does he state his position on racism, or what would be an acceptable approach in the fight against racism. From elsewhere we get rhetoric and hyperbole:

> in our University social work departments . . . the urge to stop oppression has itself become oppressive. Indeed, it would hardly be an exaggeration to describe what is going on as totalitarian. . . . University tutors are abandoning social work teaching because they say they are being forced to teach 'political correctness' attitudes on race and gender in a climate of intimidation and fear.
>
> (Phillips 1993)

As mentioned before, some serious mistakes have been made in the implementation of anti-racism programmes and these should be highlighted and changed. However, the many articles during the anti-CCETSW campaign of August/September 1993 go beyond this. They have a number of themes in common: (1) there is an explicit denial that racism, and particularly institutionalised racism, exists (despite overwhelming evidence to the contrary); (2) amazingly, it is claimed that because anti-racism declarations have been made (and surely these law-abiding professors and journalists would want the Race Relations Act to be honoured – of which anti-racism policies are but one product), the *power balance has shifted so completely* that the 'anti-racism zealots' (presumably many of them black) are able to 'do things' to white tutors, practitioners and students;[7] and, finally, (3) 'the declarations are fine, but why do you want to implement them?' is a view which can be read between the lines of these articles. All the articles talk about how the requirements are '. . . inimical to open-minded inquiry and free speech', of how a 'climate of fear' is generated.

Sivanandan (1988; 1993) is rightly critical of those on the Left who 'accepted the spurious equation of individual growth with

individualism and confuse personal moralism with socialist morality' (1993: 18). In the process their 'right-on' thinking led them to
stress 'Politically Correct' language and behaviour, only to see their
efforts hijacked by the Right and used as a vehicle for reactionary
politics. Now those who stood for progress, for justice against
racism and sexism, were openly charged with a 'PC' label: a
new form of McCarthyism had arrived, and the Right had found
'an enemy within'. Anti-racism is regarded by the Right as the
preoccupation of a fanatical minority but as Moore (1993: 5) asks:

> Western civilisation is not so fragile that it will crumble under the
> weight of a few black writers in the reading list, the odd exhibi-
> tion by a female artist, a gay movie star – is it? Those who pit
> themselves against PC act as if they themselves had no agenda, as
> if they were entirely neutral forces simply protecting 'our culture'
> from extremists. But ask yourself, as Mark Twain once did, 'Who
> are you neutral against?'

Inevitably, the route to incorporating anti-racism in professional
ethics is long and hard. To practise it in the context of real understanding of the human condition so that we can change and trans-
form that which currently sustains it, is even more difficult. *She*
must believe, with Cox (1959: 37) that since 'morality is a function
of the social system, a better system can change both morality and
human nature for the better'. But *She* knows that in the meantime,
for many black workers, the search for the holy grail has been
(hopefully only temporarily) abandoned, at least within organisations. Many have left, or have been forced to leave, organisations
which once relied upon them to give direction on implementing
serious anti-racism work. Such workers accepted a 'buffer' position
in social work education and/or practice (it came with the job). As
Raj Palasoorir, a black community worker in social services, says, 'I
have eaten a lot of humble pies in my life, but no longer.' The
exhaustion, the dehumanisation suffered and bigotry experienced
leave little space for such workers to remain in organisations
committed to caring.[8]

She begins to feel the same and recalls how her parents and their
generation arrived in the UK in the 1950s from countries colonised
and left undeveloped. To quote Bloch (1938):

> this glance therefore confirms that man everywhere is still living
> in prehistory, indeed all and everything still stands before the

creation of the world, of a right world. True genesis is not at the beginning but at the end, and it starts to begin only when society and existence become radical, i.e. grasp their roots. But the root of history is the working, creating human being who reshapes and overhauls the given facts.

But to do nothing, whether as individuals or organisations, is to accept the world as it is (see the quote at the beginning) and that cannot be acceptable either. Meanwhile, our society is experiencing rapid socio-economic, political and technological transformations, with market-mimicking reforms being introduced to the world of social work. Consequently, an impact on anti-racist progress is felt. To respond to these changes, new strategies are needed without compromising the principles of racial and social justice, in spite of daily grind and rising pessimism. So *She* reminds herself of Bloch's book *The Principle of Hope*, which encapsulates the concept of hope for her and others in the field. *Hope*, that there will be improvements in employment, education and welfare services for black and minority groups. *Hope*, that there will be recognition, understanding and participation in the fight against racism and other injustices by black and white women and men, collectively and individually. *Hope*, that although the changes are relatively small, they will constitute a good beginning towards a better life for all:

> Once he [sic] has grasped himself and established what is his, without expropriation and alienation, in real democracy, there arises in the world something which shines into the childhood of all and in which no one has yet been: homeland.
>
> (Bloch 1938: 1375–6)

ACKNOWLEDGEMENT

My thanks to Hafiz Mirza for critically reading this chapter and suggesting some revisions.

NOTES

1   'Ethnically-sensitive social work' is debatable (Gambe *et al.* 1992; Humphries *et al.* 1993). Many argue that it unduly emphasises culture to the detriment of understanding the impact of racism. This view leads to a preference for anti-racist social work over ethnically sensitive social work.

2   Lord Scarman's inquiry into the rebellions of Brixton in 1981 con-

cluded that racial disadvantage was a 'fact of current British life' and called for 'positive action' to overcome it, but fell short of recognising institutional racism.

3   In *communitarian* ethics appraisal takes place in the *context* of relations to others. Such a view represents a criticism of both utilitarian and Kantian assumptions that ethical appraisal is to be based on the view that individuals and their interests are to be given equal respect, irrespective of context.

4   The Code of Ethics for the British Association of Social Workers, adopted in 1975, states: 'as individuals and as part of their professional responsibilities . . . they will not act selectively towards clients out of prejudice, on the grounds of their origin, race . . . ; they will not tolerate actions of colleagues or others which may be racist, sexist or otherwise discriminatory . . .' (10, iii).

5   See the media coverage of Jane Brown, a white gay woman, Head of Kingsmead Primary in Hackney, who refused to accept an offer of tickets at Royal Opera House for the play *Romeo and Juliet* because it was 'entirely about heterosexual love', and the criticism of her by Gus John, a black man, Director of Education at Hackney. Here the homosexuality and 'race' cards were played, turning John into a demon by virtue of his 'race' and Brown into a poor white victim (Hugill 1994).

6   There is some anecdotal evidence which suggests that black professionals are leaving the system. In some cases this is through 'constructive dismissal'; and others are just burnt out – a worrying trend. Nor are these individuals leaving organisations for many lucrative contracts.

7   This situation must have completely passed me by! From experience we know that anti-racism issues generate a lot of feelings and emotional response – but which area of the human condition does not?

8   On principles of ethical resistance and racism see Richardson's excellent chapter (1992: 57–71).

BIBLIOGRAPHY

Ahmad, W. I. U. (1993) *Race and Health in Contemporary Britain*, Milton Keynes: Open University Press.

Appleyard, B. (1993) 'Why paint so black a picture?', *The Independent*, 4 August.

Atkin, K. and Rollings, J. (1993) *Community Care in a Multi-racial Britain: A Critical Review of the Literature*, London: HMSO.

Barker, M. (1981) *The New Racism: Conservatives and the Ideology of the Tribe*, London: Junction Books.

Barn, R. (1993) *Black Children in the Public Care System*, London: Batsford.

BASW (1990) *Obstacles to Progress – Report of the Action Research Project into Ethnically Sensitive Social Work*, Birmingham: BASW.

Bloch, E. (1938) *The Principle of Hope*, vols 2 and 3, English edition 1986, Oxford: Blackwell.

Brown, C. (1984) *Black and White: The Third PSI Survey*, London: Heinemann.

Carmichael, S. and Hamilton, C. V. (1967) *Black Power: The Politics of Liberation in America*, Harmondsworth: Penguin.

CARJ (1994) *Racism in British Society*, London: Catholic Association for Racial Justice.

Coulson, M. (1993) *Catalysts or Victims of Change? The Pattern of Student Failure on Social Work Courses*, London: CCETSW.

Cox, O. (1959) *Caste, Class and Race*, New York: Monthly Review Press.

Essed, P. (1991) *Understanding Everyday Racism*, London: Sage.

Frederickson, G. M. (1993) 'Pioneer', *New York Review of Books*, 23 September.

Gambe, D., Gomes, J., Kapur, V., Rangel, M. and Stubbs, P. (1992) *Improving Practice With Children and Families*, London: CCETSW.

Gordon, P. (1989) 'Just another Asian murder', *The Guardian*, 20 July.

Hacker, A. (1993) 'Diversity and its dangers', *New York Review of Books*, 7 October.

Hall, S. (1980) 'Teaching race', *Multiracial Education* 9 (1): 3–13.

Hampshire, S. (1993) 'Liberalism: the new twist', *New York Review of Books*, 12 August.

Harris, V. (1991) 'Values of social work in the context of British society in conflict with anti-racism', in *Setting the Context for Change* (Northern Curriculum Development Project), Leeds: CCETSW.

Hospers, J. (1967) *An Introduction to Philosophical Analysis* (2nd edn), London: Routledge & Kegan Paul.

Hugill, B. (1994) 'Plague descends on all their houses', *Observer*, 30 January.

Hugman, R. (1991) 'Organisation and professionalism: the social work agenda in the 1990s', *British Journal of Social Work* 21: 199–216.

Humphries, B., Pankhania, H., Seale, A. and Stokes, I. (1993) *Improving Practice Teaching No. 7 – A Training Manual* (Northern Curriculum Development Project), Leeds: CCETSW.

Institute of Race Relations (1991) *Deadly Silence – Black Deaths in Custody*, London: IRR.

Jones, T. (1993) *Britain's Ethnic Minorities*, London: Policy Studies Institute.

Lawrence, E. (1982) 'In the abundance of water the fool is thirsty', in *The Empire Strikes Back*, London: Hutchinson.

Lesley, E. and Mallory, M. (1993) 'Inside the black business network', *Business Week*, 29 November.

Macdonald Report Enquiry (1991) *Murder in the Playground*, London: Longsight Press.

Moore, S. (1993) 'Gets politically correct', Preface, *Observer Magazine*, 27 June.

NACRO (1992) *Statistics on Black People Working in the Criminal Justice System*, London: NACRO.

Nussbaum, M. (1992) 'Justice for Women!', a review of *Justice, Gender and the Family* by S. M. Okin, *New York Review of Books*, 8 October.

Patel, N. (1990) *A 'Race' against Time? Social Services Provision to Black Elders*, London: Runnymede Trust.

Phillips, M. (1993) 'Anti-racist zealots "drive away recruits" ', *Observer*, 1 August.

Pinker, R. (1993) 'A lethal kind of looniness', *Times Higher Education Supplement*, 10 September: 19.

Rand, A. (1964) *The Virtues of Selfishness*, New York: New American Library.

Rawls, J. (1972) *A Theory of Justice*, Oxford: Oxford University Press.

Richardson, R. (1992) 'Rottweilers and racism – notes and stories towards ethical resistance', in M. Leicester and M. Taylor (eds) *Ethics, Ethnicity and Education*, London: Kogan Page.

Rooney, B. (1987) *Racism and Resistance to Change: A Study of the Black Social Workers Project*, Liverpool: Merseyside Area Profile Group.

Runnymede Trust (1994) *Submission on Racially Motivated Attacks and Harassment to the Home Affairs Committee*, London: Runnymede Trust.

Sashidharan, S. and Francis, E. (1993) 'Epidemiology, ethnicity and schizophrenia', in W. I. U. Ahmad (ed.) *Race and Health in Contemporary Britain*, Buckingham: Open University Press.

Scarman, Lord (1981) *The Brixton Disorders 10–12 April 1981: Report of an Inquiry* (Cmnd 8427), London: HMSO.

Scott, J. (1945) *Europe in Revolution*, Boston.

Sivanandan, A. (1982) *A Different Hunger*, London: Pluto Press.

———— (1988) 'No such thing as anti-racist ideology', *New Statesman*, 27 May.

———— (1991) 'Black struggles against racism' in *Setting the Context for Change No. 1* (Northern Curriculum Development Project), Leeds: CCETSW.

———— (1993) 'Race against time', *New Statesman and Society*, 15 October.

Smith, D. J. (1977) *Racial Disadvantage in Britain: The PEP Report*, Harmondsworth: Penguin.

Spence, J. (1993) 'Unjust desserts – the story of Qiu Ju', a film by Zhang Jimou, *New York Review of Books*, 24 June.

Stubbs, P. (1985) 'The employment of black social workers: from "ethnic sensitivity" to anti-racism?', *Critical Social Policy* 12: 6–27.

Sullivan, K. M. (1993) 'The Hill–Thomas mystery', *New York Review of Books*, 12 August.

The Times (92) 'Bar faces action over bias against blacks', *The Times*, 3 November.

Tribunal Report (1993) The Industrial Tribunals *Case No. 60199/92*.

Wainwright, M. (1993) 'University guilty of sex and race bias', *Guardian*, 30 July.

Williams, J. (1985) 'Redefining institutional racism', *Ethnic and Racial Studies* 8 (3): 323–48.

Yorkshire Evening Post (1993) 'The taint of prejudice', *Comment*, 23 September.

Chapter 3

Ethical issues in social work research

Geraldine Macdonald and Kenneth Macdonald

'nam et ipsa scientia potestas est'
for knowledge itself is power
Francis Bacon (1597)

INTRODUCTION

There is no shortage of material regarding the ethics of social work or social work research, but the subject matter has interesting biases: we seem to enjoy discussions of the ethics of 'doing' to the exclusion of the ethics of 'not doing'; some things come in for scrutiny (behaviour therapy, the abuse of power by researchers) whereas others do not (doing what feels right, even if it lacks supporting evidence). The decision-making rule used to select topics for this chapter was to focus on more neglected issues, and areas which would benefit from rethinking. We begin with the fundamental issue of the relationship between research and social work, before turning to more familiar territory: the ethical dilemmas inherent in undertaking research in social work. Research might be viewed as the continual battle against the bewitchment of our senses by immediate experience. A question worth returning to is: What constraints are imposed by the particular activity of *social work* research?

SOCIAL WORK AND RESEARCH

A recent review of social work effectiveness research (Macdonald and Sheldon 1992) unearthed a plethora of articles claiming the near impossibility of undertaking research in social work, on the grounds that (i) much as one should be wiser than to look for the sacred Emperor in a poor teahouse, one will not unearth the verities of social work in the results of scientifically directed research; (ii) given that – it is said – science itself has now eschewed some of the major tenets of empiricism,[1] to build on this foundation would be to compound one error with another; (iii) the power difference between practitioners and clients,[2] and, *ipso facto*, researchers and clients, means that, unless great care is taken, any research can reinforce this difference, leaving clients and workers disempowered.

Broadly speaking, two kinds of research are pertinent to social work: (i) research concerning the problems which social workers are expected to address, how these arise, the factors that maintain them or inhibit their resolution; (ii) research regarding the interventions available to social workers – effectiveness research. The relationship of social work to both has had a chequered history, distinguished by apathy and conflict. If this is thought to be a harsh view, or one that is out of touch with the current ethos in the profession, the reader is invited to examine a random sample of social work curricula, or departmental training programmes. There you will find two things: (i) a dearth of empirically based studies; (ii) an array of alternative viewpoints and theories, most of which are mutually exclusive, presented to students on a 'take your pick' basis. The consequences are serious for those at the receiving end of the efforts of would-be helpers. For example, despite the considerable body of evidence testifying to the complex range of factors implicated in the onset of schizophrenia and its patterns of relapse, students are still offered a 'range of perspectives' from which to choose, including the work of Laing and others, whose theories resulted in what amounts almost to the persecution of the families of schizophrenics, with mothers attracting especial opprobrium. Again, thousands of children were affected by decisions made deploying Bowlby's theories of maternal deprivation (1951), the precarious basis of which was little known by those who used his arguments. Bowlby's views still have currency, and often people are unaware of the work of Rutter and others (Rutter 1972), which offers a critique and contrary evidence (we return to questions of research interpretation later). The critical question is: On what basis should one choose between accounts of social problems? More particularly, should the tenets of empiricism ('the scientific method') have a casting vote, or indeed, any vote at all?

Similar problems and questions arise in respect of the relationship between effectiveness research and the methods of intervention used by social workers. Here is an example of the dangers inherent in this 'take your pick' approach when applied to intervention, this time from the field of child sexual abuse:

> In the constant search for 'tools' which aid the therapeutic process with abused children and adults, we have found a new medium which seems in many ways ideal for post-disclosure therapy. This medium is ice. It can be very cheaply made in large amounts, and sustains a child's interest, especially in large quantities. If the room and the child are hot and the child is asked to touch the ice quickly, the experience is refreshing, exciting and meets the need of the hot child.
>
> (Zelickman and Martin 1991: 16)

Such 'innovative approaches' rarely raise shouts of 'foul' from those concerned with ethical groundrules. Yet, how ethical is it to operate a programme, with little rationale, and no inbuilt attempt to at least make sure we are not doing more harm than good? While speculation and good ideas inevitably precede research, taken alone they provide a very slender basis on which to intervene in other people's lives.

Debates about the relevance of empiricism in the physical and social sciences (Heineman 1981) make little sense when considering the effectiveness of alternative strategies of intervention (how else are we to make informed decisions, but via identifiable differences?) and it is difficult to envisage how we could make informed decisions between competing theories without recourse to disconfirmable claims. Empiricism does not provide an escape route from theory to 'truth' – observation is never theory-free, it cannot be. However, it offers a way of making explicit the theoretical underpinnings of our conceptualisations, hypotheses or assumptions about problems (and solutions), and the possibility of controlling for some of these influences when seeking to test their relative usefulness. Without such self-imposed checks we shall not be able to develop our knowledge base beyond the anecdotal and fashionable, or answer with any degree of confidence questions about 'What works best with these sorts of difficulties and these constraints?'

A minimal set of ethical requirements (for individual action or the organisation of services) might be to make sure that what one is doing is (i) not harmful (to the client or others), (ii) is legitimated, and (iii) is the course of action most likely to be effective. When we get things wrong, vulnerable people, notably children, die (London Borough of Brent 1985; London Borough of Greenwich 1987);

families break up (Palmer 1993; Butler-Sloss 1987); black children are over-represented in care (Batta and Mawby 1981), black people in prisons and psychiatric hospitals (Bolton 1984; NACRO 1991); and so on. Research is integral to social work, not an optional, second-order accessory of interest only to those wishing to pursue their career in academia. Our argument is that social work is essentially a skill-based activity informed by understanding, rather than something intrinsically 'ethical' (contrast, for example, Reamer 1982). The claim that social work decision making is intrinsically ethical would entail (if it is to be other than vacuous) that the decisions properly differ with the differing ethical principles of the decider; it is not at all clear where this would leave the interests of the client. Put it another way: power is ineluctably part of social work interactions – no amount of moral emphasis can dissolve that away – but to see social work as knowledge-based introduces a strong accountability, and such a move can clarify many seeming-moral disagreements (Macdonald 1980). Licensing bodies such as the CCETSW should be in the business of certifying competences, not moralities. CCETSW's failure to make this distinction is in large part responsible for bringing into disrepute a focus on anti-discriminatory or anti-oppressive practice. As a licensing body, the CCETSW can legitimately require that qualifying students demonstrate competence. The legitimation is practice-based. Certainly in many areas it is difficult to imagine practice being divorced from comparable attitudes or beliefs – consider the probability of a fundamentalist Christian counselling young gays or lesbians, or members of the British National Party empowering black families – but we should monitor the practice, rather than the belief. The corollary, which is sadly more familiar, is of many people and organisations purporting to share certain anti-oppressive views and behaving oppressively.

RESEARCH METHODS AND SOCIAL WORK

Random-controlled trials (RCTs), in which large numbers of subjects are randomly allocated to groups only one of which receives the help under scrutiny (others receive either no help, something different, or help later), provide the only sure-footed way of piecing together a picture of what works; other (perhaps more user-friendly) methodologies provide evidence of diminishing certainty. RCTs were a prominent feature of early evaluations of social work and are what we, as a profession (and as taxpayers), should be aspiring to. Rather than the numbers of these studies steadily increasing and diversifying with the changing roles and tasks of social workers, and the methods they use, RCTs are found less frequently, and when undertaken often use such small groups that the results are less certain than they should be. Why this decline? A number of hypotheses present themselves.

1 Allocating clients randomly is not considered ethically accept-able. Consider the following: an inner London borough asked one of us, together with a colleague, to evaluate the work of a family centre working with parents whose children were considered to be at risk. This borough, like many at the time, had a long list of unallocated cases – some of whom would be admitted to the project (partly because they had no allocated social worker). When we suggested undertaking a RCT instead of the pre-post test (before and after picture) they were seeking, we were told that it would be unethical to allocate clients randomly, with no discussion of ways in which this could be approximated while taking into account their concerns about leaving very vulnerable clients without help. Personal social services are delivered daily in the context of a large-scale, random-uncontrolled trial. We are, it seems, only beset with ethical qualms when asked to formalise arrangements which we happily operate as long as they arise by chance or due to organisational constraints, and as long as we do not attempt to learn anything *en route*.

Also, the worry over leaving clients 'unhelped' may be exag-gerated; in many social work RCTs we will wish the control group to have some intervention (else our trial will measure only the impact of 'being attended to', not the content of our inter-vention) and we are seldom so prescient as to be secure that our intervention will be markedly better.

2 Another reason for the demise in random-controlled trials is certainly their cost. They are often long-term and/or complex endeavours requiring considerable organisation. But this impli-cates another issue, that of available funding. If one examines the research output of social work academics, particularly those funded by the Department of Health (DoH) and the major fund-ing bodies such as the ESRC, one will notice two things: (i) a relatively small cartel of people who are in receipt of research grants – indeed the DoH declines to circulate its research agenda

to all but a handful of 'trusted' academics; and (ii) a preponderance of descriptive, retrospective research, much of it concerned with process variables of social work, or the organisation of social services, rather than with the relative effectiveness of either in terms of bringing about desired change. We typically work with the very vulnerable and needy and wield considerable power which can be legitimated only by knowledge and competence, whence we must heed Cabot's exhortation, made in 1931, to 'measure, evaluate, estimate, appraise your results in some form, in any terms that rest on anything beyond faith, assertion, and the "illustrative case" '.

3 Doubt and uncertainty about their assessments or proposals are not characteristic of social workers, who often simply *know* something works, or is right. This disinclination to be disturbed out of a lifetime's allegiance to a world view, often decided on at the outset of professional training, if not before, is both arrogant and dangerous (and may lead to an overestimate of the dangers of trials – see above).

4 Anti-oppressive critiques of practice have also been influenced by perceptions of our knowledge-base, including research. Emphasis has been placed on ways in which the 'scientific method' has promoted a predominantly masculinist construction of knowledge. Elshtain (1981), Rose (1983) and other writers have argued the need to develop a model of research that reflects the experiences and world-views of other oppressed groups, rather than that constructed by others, for example, disabled people (Morris 1991), black people (Lorde 1984) and gay and lesbian people (Kitzinger 1992). But by equating the masculinist, racist, or heterosexist assumptions underpinning much research with the methodology, the proverbial baby has often been thrown out with the bathwater. Engage in a quantitative approach to research or evaluation and you are unlikely to be seen to be on the side of the angels:

> Qualitative methods . . . are seen to be more suited to the exploration of individual experiences – the representation of subjectivity within academic discourse and to facilitate (in practice if not in theory) a non-hierarchical organisation of the research process. . . . Conversely, quantitative methods . . . are cited as instituting the hegemony of the researcher over the researched, and as reducing personal experience to the anonymity of mere numbers.
>
> (Oakley 1989)

Oakley's study indeed demonstrates how research, even the random-controlled trial, can be deployed in such a way as to benefit those with little power. In the case of maternity care, it offers the possibility of calling a halt to (or at least evaluating) the rise in unevaluated technology. There is nothing intrinsically incompatible in conducting scientific research from an anti-oppressive perspective. Oakley's summary of the tenets of a feminist perspective towards the process of research as (i) not employing methods oppressive either to researchers or to the researched, and (ii) 'oriented towards the production of knowledge in such a form and in such a way as can be used by women themselves', offers a guide to good research generally, particularly in a field where the nature of the task is, in part, to address oppression and its consequences.

   It is not difficult to generalise the reasons for the paucity of RCTs in social work to research generally. If we add in the stressful nature of the job and the near-impossibility of performing satisfactorily in statutory settings, then the failure of agencies and staff to evaluate their work routinely becomes understandable, if indefensible. But far from adding to stress-loads, routine feedback might alleviate it (Macdonald 1990); a systematic approach to evaluation would provide clients with an opportunity to comment on their experiences and seek appropriate changes; a rigorous approach to evaluation would provide agencies and policy makers with the data they need if they are to provide effective services, including the effective deployment of staff and staff time. Research, we repeat, is not an extra, but an integral part of the activity of social work.

   Choice of research method has ethical implications; but, as we next argue, interpretation also imposes its own obligations.

RESEARCH INTERPRETATION

In the interpretation of research it can be too easy to claim knowledge, and hence power, whence we have obligations to ensure that the information is correctly understood. When these obligations are not met, we add to our problems, as this example from the inquiry into the death of Jasmine Beckford illustrates:

> Professor Greenland told us . . . that it seemed prudent to classify all non-accidental injuries to young children as 'high risk' cases, since 80% of all children unlawfully killed by their parents had been previously abused.
>
> (London Borough of Brent 1985: 288)

It does not follow from the fact that 80 per cent of unlawfully killed children have been previously abused by their parents, that any serious percentage of non-accidentally injured children are at risk of being killed or seriously injured by their parents. What we need before we can say anything is the percentage of non-accidentally injured children later unlawfully killed. Careless interpretation leads to misplaced prudence.

Even when correctly presented, prediction may be less secure than at first might seem. For low-incidence conditions (of which child abuse is one) even a small diagnostic error can lead to disconcertingly high misattributions. Suppose, for a medical condition that occurs in one per thousand of the population, that we have a diagnostic test which produces a 5 per cent incidence of false positives, and a zero incidence of false negatives (which would make it quite a good diagnostic test). Suppose that X is diagnosed on our test as positive; what is the chance that X actually suffers from this syndrome? The answer is around a 2 per cent chance. Applied over one thousand cases from the population, a test with the above characteristics would on average locate one true positive and generate fifty false positives. We do not know which of these fifty-one positive reports (one true, fifty false) is X; whence the approximately 2 per cent probability that she is a true positive. Admittedly the narrative shifts as the population incidence of the event increases (whence the debate, for example, over population or only 'at risk' screening for HIV), but the incidence in this example is already quite high (in social work terms one per thousand would yield more than one case to each social worker). When we turn to the problems of assessment and prediction facing child protection social workers, these difficulties multiply – as is well brought out in Dingwall's (1989) dissection of Blom-Cooper's simple recommendation that 'Research designed to refine the techniques for predicting accurately those children who will continue to be at risk is urgently required' (London Borough of Brent 1985: 289). False positives are devastating for all parties (putative 'victims' as well as putative 'perpetrators') and, as the responses to Cleveland and Orkney (Asquith 1993) have demonstrated, socially unacceptable. Increasingly in certain areas of social work it is being suggested that prediction is a matter within our gift, and that mistakes are made because we fail to attend to lists of 'risk indicators' there for the taking. This is not the case, as scrutiny of the methodologies used in the generation of such lists makes clear (McDonald and Marks 1991). The point is that information is not a simple good. For social work research in particular, it must be assessed in terms of its utility for action.

While our bias is manifestly towards stressing the pertinence of information and research in general, it may be worth noting that it is possible to envisage situations in which the garnering of information may be counter-productive. Elster (1989) argues persuasively that – subject to constraints of minimal parental adequacy – disputed child custody cases might be best settled randomly. Casual information is unhelpful; the generation of requisitely detailed information (on parents, and child–parent interactions) would impose unacceptable waiting costs (children age rapidly); and many decisions are so intrinsically indeterminable (we are fundamentally unclear on which of two viable parents 'ought' to have the child) that the more rational, and just, decision-making strategy may be an information-free one. Our guess would be that most readers would prefer a wrong decision made with good intentions, than the random selection of one of two equally justified courses. Why? Answers are likely to presuppose a view of social work as intrinsically ethical.

The role of information in decision making provides part of the answer to one of our opening questions: What are the ethical issues peculiar to social work research, as distinct from research in general? The nature of social work should perhaps also influence our perceptions of statistical errors. In research generally the major sin is to fall into the trap of causal attribution where none exists (Type 1 errors – rejecting the null hypothesis when it is true), and much of inferential statistics is geared to preventing this. However, the price of avoiding this is also to reduce the chances of 'seeing' something that is there (i.e. increasing Type 2 errors – accepting the null hypothesis when it is false). As Crane (1976: 237) puts it: 'type 2 errors have no special claims to grace'. When making policy decisions (for example, about what approach to take to a particular problem) we rarely have the option of agnosticism – to do nothing is still to act; and appropriate significance levels should be chosen with this in mind. Similarly we should not confuse statistical significance with professional significance.

Finally, because social work research entails consequences for people, the price of another common researcher's sin comes much higher, viz. that of reporting as '*the* narrative that accounts for the research data' what is in fact but *one* narrative which fits the data. Take as an example the influential work of Brown and Harris (1978) on the social origins of depression. The researchers skilfully circumvent the potential distortions that the subjective interpretation of depressed people might introduce, and convincingly demonstrate a connection between the occurrence of severe life events and the onset of depression. They then locate a set of factors (whether the subject has a mature adult relationship, whether she lost her mother before some specified early age, whether she has several young children at home) which mediate between the events and depression, and identify the common element among these factors as 'self-esteem'. But at the technical level the data can as readily be fitted by a model in which the factors are concurrent effects, not mediating interactions (see, for example, McKee and Villhjalmsonn 1986), which attenuates the claim of the factors to be regarded as causal. Substantively we could argue that the factors are a measure of available social resources (adult companion and – inversely – young children at home are straightforward; mothers, we know from the textbooks, mediate kinship networks). These two interpretations (poor self-esteem increases vulnerability to depression; poor social resources help precipitate depression) entail very different consequences for the social work task. But the reader of Brown and Harris comes away from the book with a sense that the data entail the first, with no hint that the second is also, on their data, tenable. The temptation of presenting *an* account as *the* account is common; we have taken the Brown and Harris volume as our example because it is otherwise a model of competent research.

The issues in this section are in part technical issues, but they are technical issues with moral implications – implications which become sharper as we attend to the consequences of research in social work practice. Our own bias is the Wittgensteinian one ('that whereof we cannot speak thereof should we be silent'), which again – and that is part of its echoic strength – is both a logical and a moral prescription.

Underlying much of the preceding discussion of research method and interpretation have been questions of the choice of issues researched; we consider these next, before turning to a popular issue – client protection – from perhaps an unpopular perspective.

RESEARCH TOPIC CHOICE

Research topics follow diffuse concerns over social problems, which as we know (e.g. Hilgartner and Bosk 1988) are socially generated. Even after disregarding the influence of particular political orientations (for example, research agendas striving to show the dangers of single parenthood, the inadequacy of African-Caribbeans, or the superiority of Asians), variations remain in what research attracts funding, and these merit scrutiny. Why do we spend large resources to avert high-cost, low-probability outcomes (e.g. child mortality), rather than low-cost, high-probability outcomes (e.g. chiropody services for the elderly)? Why, for example, the stress on *non*-accidental injury to children?

> There are about 22,000 [accidental] injury deaths each year for children and adolescents in the United States. . . . This rate is more than the number of fatalities in the Vietnam War for the two bloodiest years of fighting, 1968 and 1969. . . . Yet there are not many marches on the streets to stop these deaths. . . .
>
> (Roberts and Brooks 1987: 11)

The apparently simple answer – that intentional injuries are in principle preventable while accidents, being accidents, are not – does not survive inspection. As Roberts *et al.* (1987) demonstrate, there are straightforward interventions which would sharply reduce the incidence of the latter. Our instinctive reactions – which may well do us credit as compassionate individuals – may mislead us when we begin to allocate scarce resources. By influencing available funds, large policy emphases affect the nature of the research that is perceived as worth doing.

Some research (participant observation at the soup kitchen) is easier than others (observation of Directorate meetings), and it is not accidental (nor a matter of malevolence or malfeasance) that power and information often echo each other's distribution; there exist consistent impediments to the study of sensitive topics (Lee 1993: 18ff.). In addition to the vagaries of the funding process, the dictates of short-run efficiency (find costlessly a researcher to deliver results promptly) may tramline research and run counter to long-run knowledge acquisition. Absurdly short-term follow-up rates, evidenced in much effectiveness research, are also evidence of this unfortunate trade-off.

We referred earlier to the theory-laden nature of research. This raises ethical concerns about the consequences of imposing value-sets. A classic example would be research on the family structure of black Americans in the 1960s, which, starting from a traditional definition of 'family', perceived a strongly matrilineal structure with peripheral males as pathological. In criticism it was argued that the pathology was a definition of the observer; the research was flawed by its ideological stance. But the successful navigation of these issues may also be more technical than at first blush it appears. The concept of the 'family' is not an analytic concept, but derived from the common language of a particular culture at a particular time, and so unlikely to prove a fruitful analytic tool. An important prophylactic against value-biased research is, therefore, our scrutiny of its technical quality, as well as the search for biasing values, the most insidious of which are, almost by definition, difficult to disinter as values.

Discussions about the importance of empowering those on the receiving end of research activity often presuppose that the self-reports of actors have privileged epistemological status. But our clients are just as much theorisers as we; hence at least as given to attending disparately to positive and negative outcomes, and to making inferential errors. Therefore, while clients' views should play an important part in effectiveness research, they are not in a uniquely privileged position to assess benefits – and in some settings may be particularly disadvantaged. Some assessments of what optimum practices are – or what counts as effective intervention – can only be answered by systematic acquisition of outcome information. This is nowhere more clearly illustrated than in the many studies which reveal client satisfaction, but no change.

A tension also exists between the pursuit of knowledge *simpliciter*, and focused knowledge for decision making. For example, our social incompetence may reflect an horrendous narrative of historical deficiencies; but acquisition of simple social interaction skills may most readily improve quality of life. More generally, if, as Lipsky (1980) persuasively argues, the time-pressure of social work decision making is an ineluctable consequence of its structural position, not a transient aberration of a particular political domination, then perhaps research topic choice should focus on obtaining the kind of information that enables choices in such constrained situations.

This does not entail an endorsement of 'needs led' research as against fundamental research; epistemologically we cannot simply identify what we need to know, since by definition we lack sufficient knowledge. There exist, at any one time point, specific questions to which answers would be useful, but the general historical record suggests we do not recognise the truly interesting question until we know at least the shape of its answer. And as MacIntyre (1982: 179) reminds us, the insight that individually rational decisions do not necessarily cumulate into collective rationality may well apply to social research. Indeed some – with this in mind – have suggested the random allocation of research funding (subject to minimal competence) as a rational choice strategy (it might well increase the number of RCTs). Which is not to endorse research for the sake of research. Though collective mythology regards research as a high-powered intellectual endeavour, much is pedestrian – a straightforward garnering of information that might well have been the task of a junior manager, had the world of social work been better organised. It requires therefore some justification beyond just 'doing research': some puzzle to be addressed, some suggestion that the answer, if located, will affect something. Costs and benefits are a proper part of the discussion (though cultural variations exist in their interpretation). Which leads naturally to our next section, on the interests of respondents.

CLIENT PROTECTION

The interests (or autonomy, or rights – the language varies) of research participants are of central concern. Neglect or disregard of these range from the horrendous example of biomedical experimentation under the Third Reich (there are harms to which it would be immoral to subject persons, irrespective of any potential benefit), to lesser ills such as the invasion of privacy (clients/colleagues requiring protection from yet another questionnaire with no purpose but the passing of an examination). The power asymmetry between clients and social workers matters, for while in most survey-research respondents can vote with their feet if they do not wish to be interviewed, it is more problematic when researchers come with a penumbra of authority: 'I am gatekeeper of resources (or connected to gatekeepers): would you agree to answer a few questions?' Research indicates that clients characteristically over-perceive the powers of social workers, so seeking their consent may not provide protection.

   Obtaining informed consent in social research is no less complicated than in medical contexts (King 1986). When we permit researchers to attend our case-conferences, to what have we given consent? If they wish to test the hypothesis that medical staff make improper appeals to 'authority' as a way of settling arguments, do we need to give assent to *that* (and remember that it requires some disregard of the issue by the observed for the accounting to work)? And what if they are interested in turn-taking and non-verbal cues in discussion; or the conceptualisation of inter-agency boundaries; or the dynamics of the Jungian primal horde as a tool for conceptualising authority discussions within the case-conference? Few of us would be equally sanguine about these various descriptions of our behaviour. Is our consent required before their adoption? Are we consenting to the (political) consequences of this research once published? Some of the answers are most appropriately anchored in a consideration of who is accountable for the phenomenon in question and who will be affected by the consequences of research. In the case-conference example, the purpose of these meetings is the protection of children and the provision of help to families. We may appropriately refuse observation on the grounds of increased distress to parents in attendance (though parents are much less likely to decline such requests than professional staff) but insofar as such research has the aim of providing information which will assist the development of competent practice, the reluctance of individuals seems precarious as a basis for refusal. And the issue becomes more complex when the research affects the interests of groups, but these groups themselves are split as to what is in their best interests; who then should decide? Participating agencies should certainly have an opportunity to comment on the data, and may wish to influence the parameters of research at the outset, but some of the problems about consent arise from the absence of routine evaluative research conducted by agencies themselves.

Where explicit harms are not at issue, the nature of the research intrusion is not always straightforward to assess. Consider the following: On arriving at the labour ward I am introduced to X who, white coated like the rest of the medical personnel, I am told, is there to observe labour ward practices. I – my mind very much elsewhere – agree to X's presence. In the subsequent hours, as much normal 'privacy' is routinely disregarded, and actors come and go, the presence of X seems small intrusion. If I later learn that X's real interest was in patients' reactions to stress and uncertainty, and that throughout labour it had been *my* reactions, hesitancies, and fears which were being recorded, I might feel – and at first blush you might agree – justifiably aggrieved. X's research is unlikely to benefit me, and she now has personal information about me that I might not have chosen to give – indeed might not have been capable of giving if I had known I was being observed. As indicated earlier, some harms are indefensible, but is this an example of such a harm? Possibly not. We have good grounds for wishing to deny neighbours or colleagues intimate information which they might subsequently use against us; and such intuitions are not entirely out of place – even those in professional roles might be connected to others who know us. But safeguards against the misuse of personalised information cannot depend on consent or its absence. Nor does explicitness always minimise the cost to others: asking the grief-stricken 'Can I come and observe you because I wish to understand the process of grieving?' also incurs costs. The answer perhaps lies in the purpose of the research, and therefore its potential consequences; whether this is helping to improve grief counselling or simply satisfying personal curiosity/obtaining a higher degree may differentially affect our evaluation of research procedures.

Some writers wish to retain privacy as an intrinsic good ('Invasion of privacy . . . can be subsumed under the category of . . . "moral wrongs" . . .' (Kelman 1982: 48)), but we would wish to argue for a consequentialist position. Arguments against such consequentialist accounts often hinge on allegations that they entail means–ends justifications. But on further inspection the arguments are not so straightforward. The standard objection to a consequentialist position is that it can produce absurd answers – as when the devil offers happiness to all for the cost of damnation to one, and the consequentialist says 'accept'. But absurd answers arise from absurd questions; it is not accidental that we do not encounter omnicompetent devils. Consider another example, from Williams's (1973: 98) deft critique of one variety of consequentialism, where a situation is so defined that an individual is faced with the choice of killing one innocent to save nineteen. While accepting that utilitarianism provides an answer, perhaps the right answer in this case, Williams argues that it fails because it dissolves the moral issues, our sense of unease. The consequentialist's reply is that as actors in any real-world situation we will also experience uncertainty and unease (in the example the consequences of participation in an act of terrorism are incommensurable), and the particularism of the world we inhabit is a potent factor in our moral evaluations. Certainly the consequentialist position would be untenable had the Third Reich, by its experimentation on Jews, found a cure for cancer, and were that experimentation a necessary route to that finding. But that is precisely not the world we inhabit; the route to knowledge does not of necessity lie through human exploitation. The facts of the world save consequentialism from folly (which is not accidental since it was devised to deal with the facts of the world), and its advantage in relation to the issue of privacy is that it gives us a tool to balance protections and benefits, and frees us to consider other protective devices.

The protection of those researched is important, but we should be clearer about what we are protecting them from. Involving clients, those with experience of being on the receiving end of our good intentions, or those who represent them (locally elected representatives), is desirable, and particularly in the context of random-controlled trials there is evidence that clients are beginning to see these issues very differently, as mechanisms to protect professional interest rather than empowering users of services (Chalmers 1983). The protection afforded by standard intentionalist defences (particularly informed consent) is flawed, and we perhaps need to develop other, 'external' consequentialist assessments of harms and benefits as providing a better safeguard. Research, on this approach, would be undertaken as part of social work; and the protections would be those which in any case should be put in place to monitor that activity. Many questions remain unanswered – this is a short chapter – but they are, we would argue, on this approach in principle answerable. It is not accidental that ethical behaviour has survival value. 'It is sloppy research, but ethical' is at one level intelligible (badly designed questionnaire, but cleared by the ethics committee), but at a deeper level absurd. Research which fails in its purpose is a waste of time and space; not ethical.

CODA

We concur with others that there are real dangers in the conduct of research in social work – dangers of the exploitation of clients and of the values biases of the researcher, both in selection and execution. There exist useful practical checklists (e.g. APA 1982); our suggestions-for-action, however, run somewhat counter to some prevailing orthodoxies. The best protections, we have argued, do not come from ceaseless scrutiny of our own values, nor just from empowering clients and seeking informed consent. They come – more prosaically but more effectively – from technically better research.

NOTES

1   Such as the claim that the meaning of a particular theoretical statement is directly reducible to particular empirically testable consequences (though note that – as the science research budgets amply demonstrate – this still leaves much room for science to continue to be concerned with the business of attempted empirical disconfirmation).

2   Given the power imbalance in many of the relationships people are constrained to 'enjoy' with social workers, we persist in the use of the term 'client' rather than 'customer' or 'user'. Although we appreciate that these terms are themselves intended to address this issue, and are sometimes apposite, there is still a preponderance of cases – not least of all due to current 'targeting' – in which individuals simply cannot be accurately identified as 'customers' except by endowing the term with properties that would suffice to describe inmates of HM Prisons.

BIBLIOGRAPHY

APA (1982) *Ethical Principles in the Conduct of Research with Human Participants*, American Psychological Association.

Asquith, S. (1993) *Protecting Children. Cleveland to Orkney: More Lessons to Learn?* London: HMSO.

Batta, I. D. and Mawby, R. I. (1981) 'Children in local authority care: a monitoring of racial differences in Bradford', *Policy and Practice* 9 (2): 137–50.

Bolton, P. (1984) 'Management of compulsorily admitted patients to a high security unit', *International Social Psychiatry* 30: 77–84.

Bowlby, J. (1951) *Maternal Care and Mental Health*, Geneva: WHO; London: HMSO.

Brown, G. W. and Harris, T. (1978) *The Social Origins of Depression*, London: Tavistock.

Butler-Sloss, Lord Justice (1987) *Report of the Inquiry into Child Abuse in Cleveland*, London: HMSO.

Cabot, R. C. (1931) 'Treatment in social casework and the need for tests of its success and failure', *Proceedings of the National Conference of Social Work*.

Chalmers, I. (1983) 'Scientific inquiry and authoritarianism in perinatal care and education', *Birth* 10 (3): 151–64.

Crane, J. A. (1976) 'The power of social intervention experiments to discriminate differences between experimental and control groups', *Social Service Review*, pp. 224–42.

Dingwall, R. (1989) 'Some problems about predicting child abuse and neglect', in O. Stevenson (ed.) *Child Abuse: Professional Practice and Public Policy*, London: Harvester Wheatsheaf.

Elshtain, J. B. (1981) *Public Man, Private Woman*, Oxford: Martin Robinson.

Elster, J. (1989) *Solomonic Judgements. Studies in the Limitations of Rationality*, Cambridge: Cambridge University Press.

Heineman, M. (1981) 'The obsolete scientific imperative in social work research', *Social Service Review* **55**: 371–97.

Hilgartner, S. and Bosk, C. L. (1988) 'The rise and fall of social problems: a public arenas model', *American Journal of Sociology* **94**: 53–78.

Kelman, H. C. (1982) 'Ethical issues in different social science methods', in T. L. Beauchamp *et al.* (eds) *Ethical Issues in Social Science Research*, London: Johns Hopkins University Press.

King, J. (1986) 'Informed consent', *Bulletin of the Institute of Medical Ethics, Supplement No. 3*, December.

Kitzinger, J. (1992) 'Sexual violence and compulsory heterosexuality', in S. Wilkinson and C. Kitzinger (eds) *Heterosexuality*, London: Sage.

Lee, R. M. (1993) *Doing Research on Sensitive Topics*, London: Sage.

Lipsky, M. (1980) *Street-Level Bureaucracy. Dilemmas of the Individual in Public Services*, New York: Russell Sage Foundation.

London Borough of Brent (1985) *A Child in Trust: The Report of the Commission of Inquiry into the Circumstances Surrounding the Death of Jasmine Beckford*, London: Borough of Brent.

London Borough of Greenwich (1987) *A Child in Mind: Report of the Commission of Inquiry into the Circumstances Surrounding the Death of Kimberley Carlile*, London: Borough of Greenwich.

Lorde, A. (1984) *Sister Outsider*, New York: Crossing Press.

Macdonald, G. M. (1990) 'Allocating blame in social work', *British Journal of Social Work* **20**: 525–46.

Macdonald, G. M. and Sheldon, B. (1992) 'Contemporary studies of the effectiveness of social work', *British Journal of Social Work* **22**: 615–43.

Macdonald, K. I. (1980) 'Time and information in political theory', in M. Freeman and D. Robertson (eds) *The Frontiers of Political Theory*, London: St Martins Press, pp. 140–72.

McDonald, T. and Marks, J. (1991) 'A review of risk factors assessed in child protective services', *Social Service Review*, March: 112–31.

MacIntyre, A. (1982) 'Risk, harm, and benefit assessments as instruments of moral evaluation', in T. L. Beauchamp *et al.* (eds) *Ethical Issues in Social Science Research*, London: Johns Hopkins University Press.

McKee, D. and Villhjalmsonn, R. (1986) 'Life stress, vulnerability and depression: a methodological critique of Brown *et al.*', *Sociology* **20**: 589–600.

Morris, J. (1991) *Pride against Prejudice. Transforming Attitudes to Disability*, London: The Women's Press.

NACRO (1991) *Race and Criminal Justice, NACRO Briefing*, London: National Association for the Care and Resettlement of Offenders.

Oakley, A. (1989) 'Who's afraid of the randomised controlled trial? Some dilemmas of the scientific method and "good" research practice', *Women and Health* **15** (4).

Palmer, A. (1993) 'Guilty when proved innocent', *The Spectator*, 14 August: 9–10.

Reamer, F. G. (1982) *Ethical Dilemmas in Social Service*, New York: Columbia University Press.

Roberts, M. C and Brooks, P. H. (1987) 'Children's injuries: issues in prevention and public policy', *Journal of Social Issues* **43**: 1–12.

Roberts, M. C., Fanurik, D. and Layfield, D. A. (1987) 'Behavioral approaches to prevention of childhood injuries', *Journal of Social Issues* **43**: 105–18.

Rose, H. (1983) 'Hand, brain, and heart: a feminist epistemology for the natural sciences', *Signs* **9**: 73–90.

Rutter, M. (1972) *Maternal Deprivation Reassessed*, Harmondsworth: Penguin.

Williams, B. (1973) 'A critique of utilitarianism', in J. C. Smart and B. Williams *Utilitarianism: For and Against*, Cambridge: Cambridge University Press.

Zelickman, I. and Martin, J. (1991) 'Feeling the way forward', *Community Care*, 16 May: 16–17.

Chapter 4

Confidentiality, accountability and the boundaries of client–worker relationships

Steven Shardlow

> What need we fear who knows it, when none can call our power
> to account.
>
> (Shakespeare, *Macbeth*, Act V, Scene i)

INTRODUCTION

A central question in the study of ethics in social work has been to ask how social workers ought to behave towards clients. Which kinds of behaviour are acceptable and which are not? Is it acceptable, for example, for a male social worker to physically touch a distressed female client to offer comfort? It is not so much the answer 'yes', 'no', or 'it depends' that is important as the reasons and the understandings that give us clues about the nature of relationships between male social workers and female clients. The boundaries of what is acceptable in a relationship between a social worker and a client are defined by such questions and the answers.

Ideas about what constitutes acceptable, permissible and desirable behaviours are subject to change as ideas of professional relations and the nature of social work shift over time. In constructing the boundaries of acceptable behaviour between clients and social workers much emphasis has been given recently to the effects of socially structured difference – age, race, sexuality, etc. What is acceptable with one person may not be acceptable with another who has a totally different personal biography. The boundaries of the relationship have to be defined by the dynamic between the social worker and the client. This will vary according to who has the power to define that boundary and how that power is employed in any given situation. There is a broad range of concepts in the social work firmament that serve to delineate and define the nature and quality of aspects of relationships between social workers and clients. Two concepts, confidentiality and accountability, will be examined here. They are interesting because they are generally located in that part of the relationship that the social worker usually defines. So, how these two concepts are expressed can tell much about acceptable and unacceptable relationships between social workers and clients. Interestingly, these ideas are often approached theoretically in isolation, yet confidentiality and accountability interact in practice!

To examine and reveal some of the tensions in the interaction of confidentiality and accountability a rather unusual methodology is adopted: three fictional dialogues between a client and a social worker discussing aspects of confidentiality and accountability in practice.

DEFINING CONFIDENTIALITY AND ACCOUNTABILITY

Before mixing a compound, the chemist is always careful to understand the properties of each element to be used in an experiment. Dangerous and poisonous gases can be given off when two elements are mixed, and the resulting compound may also have dangerous properties – a strong acid or alkali may be produced. These potentially hazardous consequences are an everyday problem for the chemist. Similarly, in the realm of ideas, before uniting and joining concepts their individual properties need to be examined. So before 'confidentiality' and 'accountability' are joined in a rich mixture we shall define them separately.

These are brief working definitions and are not intended as extended conceptual explorations. They serve the purpose of delineating the area of interest. For both confidentiality and accountability, the major difficulties do not seem to arise in definition but in their operation.

Confidentiality

When applied to social work practice, confidentiality may be taken as an exhortation to social workers to keep secret both written and verbal communications from clients. Social workers are given information by clients in the full expectation that this will be kept secret by the social worker. Timms (1983) suggests that confidentiality is a rule or a norm regulating the behaviour of social workers and that it operates in a fairly straightforward manner. As a requirement it can be grounded in one of three ways: prudentially, we tend to keep the confidences of those who we think will keep our trust; technically, because not keeping some information confidential will generate problems in providing social services to the public; morally, because to treat confidential information as being available to others would be an act of discourtesy and demonstrate that the individual was seen as having little moral worth (Timms 1983). Timms also suggests that confidentiality may be in either a weak or a strong form. In the strong form all information obtained by virtue of being in a particular role (e.g. being a social worker) should be treated as confidential. In the weak form only information specifically identified as confidential should be treated as such.

> *Confidentiality* is then a system of rules and norms applied to information given by clients to social workers: it is expected that social workers will not divulge this information to others except in certain specified circumstances.

Accountability

As for confidentiality, a working definition of accountability appears to be fairly simple and straightforward: to be accountable is to be in a position to give an explanation for one's actions – with reasons and justifications. Clark states that in conventional usage the terms *accountability* and *responsibility* are synonymous – with the requirement that somebody has to be responsible to someone else for something (Clark with Asquith 1985: 41). It is in deciding what social workers are responsible for, and to whom, that the problems arise – the practical problems deriving from the principle. However, Coulshed, following Wareham, distinguishes between accountability and responsibility: the former is organisational and derives from the position held, while the latter is personal and derives from being a citizen and human being and therefore responsible for one's actions (Coulshed 1990).

> *Accountability* is where social workers give an explanation and justification of their actions to somebody else who might reasonably expect to be given such an explanation.

CONFIDENTIALITY AND ACCOUNTABILITY: THREE DIALOGUES

There are three dialogues between an imaginary social worker (SW)[1] and an imaginary client (C)[2]. Both have been stripped of the usual attributes of human identity: they have no gender, race or age. Nor does the social worker represent any particular form of social work practice. They are both representative and idealised. The questions put do not relate to any particular social work agency. The dialogues can be extended by giving the participants particular identities and asking questions based on their personae. The dialogues serve to illustrate various difficulties in realising notions of confidentiality and accountability.

The first dialogue

C   Do you mind if I ask you some questions about things that have been on my mind?

SW   No, go ahead.

C   Suppose I tell you about myself, my innermost thoughts, can I be sure that you will keep them to yourself?

SW   Yes, of course I will.

C   Would it matter what I told you? I used to go to the priest, he never told anybody, you could rely on the priest to keep things secret . . . some of the things he must have heard in his time. . . . He always said it was between him and God . . . telling him was just telling God.

SW   Well it couldn't be quite like the priest, you know.

C   Well could it be like with my solicitor? She told me that whatever I told her was absolutely private – no court in the land could make her tell. She told me that anything I said to her was 'privileged' or something like that.

SW   No, I'm afraid it wouldn't be quite like that either.

C   Why not? Tell me why it would be different.

SW   You see, a lawyer belongs to a recognised profession with special rights which are guaranteed by the law. Social work isn't quite like that.

C   You mean it's not a profession?

SW   Possibly it is . . . possibly it isn't . . .

C   . . . that's not much of an answer!

SW   The real point is that social workers are not recognised in the way that lawyers are. If a court asked me what you had told me, I would have to tell them. I would protest of course, and say that it was unfair, but in the end I would either have to tell the court or go to prison. It would be different if we lived in New York in the United States. They have a law which makes social workers and lawyers equal in this respect. Whatever is said to a social worker is treated in the same way as what is said to a lawyer.

C   But that isn't really much of a problem, I shall just have to be careful about not telling you anything that I don't want the court to hear! I can't imagine that most of what I want to tell you would be of any interest to the courts. So that's it then! Whatever I told you, you would keep secret unless for some reason you had to tell a court? I suppose that's fair enough.

SW I still couldn't absolutely guarantee that *everything* you told me could be kept secret.

C   Why not?

SW If you told me about a crime that had been committed I might have to report it to the police.

C   Would that be only if *I* had committed the crime?

SW No, if you told me about a friend or someone in your family I might still have to report it.

C   What sort of a crime would it have to be?

SW If you told me you had murdered someone, or stolen a large amount of money, then I would have no choice.

C   Do you mean that there is a law that makes you do this?

SW No, I just think it would be my professional duty.

C   But why? A priest or even a doctor might just tell me that it was my responsibility to report the matter to the police, if and when I chose. I can see that in a very serious case it would be difficult.

SW Yes, even a doctor would have little choice if they thought that somebody else was in danger; this is the duty to warn. Suppose a doctor knew in confidence from conversations with a patient that the same patient harboured murderous desires towards another person – say it was a social worker! Then the doctor would, if he or she believed the threat to be genuine, have the responsibility to inform the social worker and the police.

C   That seems fair enough, if somebody presents a real danger to others then I can see that it is reasonable to break a confidence. That is not bothering me so much as . . . as the kind of crime.

What if it wasn't as serious as murder? What would happen if I told you I was growing some cannabis plants for my own use? That doesn't really affect anybody else.

SW That is a more difficult question, I'm not sure what I would do. I know some of my colleagues who disapprove of illegal drugs would feel obliged to report this to the police; others . . . they might, as the saying goes, 'turn a blind eye'.

C That's not fair, it depends on who you have as your social worker, whether or not you are reported to the police.

SW Yes I suppose you are right, but there is no law or code of practice to tell social workers what to do.

C So how do you decide in these cases?

SW I use my discretion.

C What's that? I'm not sure I have any discretion.

SW It means that I take account of all of my training and experience to help me decide what to do. I might talk to other social workers, but I would certainly do a lot of thinking about social work knowledge, skills and values.

C So in the end it would be your decision – based upon your views – what you would do with information about me that I had told you. Would you even ask me what I thought?

SW Yes, I would ask, some social workers might not – but the final decision would have to be mine.

C You would exercise your power to decide. It seems as if you would not be on my side but would be working for somebody else. Who is that? Yourself, your loyalty to your employer, or to a romanticised ideal of what a professional does?

SW No, it's not like that.

C It seems to me that you are more accountable to your boss than to me if you can't keep my little secrets. When the chips are down it's not my interests that you are going to protect.

The second dialogue

C Hello, I've been thinking about our last conversation: I've a few more questions I would like to ask – is that OK?

SW Yes, that's fine with me.

C I think I understand about when you would keep what I tell you secret, but how would I know that you had done it?

SW I suppose you would just have to accept my word that I had not told anybody.

C   That's OK, I think I can trust you, so if you told me you wouldn't tell anybody else then I would believe you. I am right, aren't I, you wouldn't tell anybody else except in the cases we talked about? So I can trust you?

SW   I'm very pleased to hear you say that.

C   What if I had the kind of social worker that I didn't trust: could I find out if the social worker had kept my secrets?

SW   It is very difficult to check up on what a social worker does.

C   Why? Surely it shouldn't be?

SW   But you want to know how to make your social worker account to you for how that person behaves in handling your confidences.

C   Shouldn't the social worker have to tell me if my information is given to someone else?

SW   Well yes, of course, but I don't think the law makes this absolutely necessary. If the social worker told the police you wouldn't have to be told that this had happened.

C   But that is unfair, it is my information. I am the one who can give permission for the social worker to tell somebody else. Surely I ought to be able to say if I wanted to release a part of the information that I had given to a social worker?

SW   Yes, you ought.

C   If something goes wrong with an operation that a doctor has done I can complain to the Medical Council – I think it's called that. Is there anything like that for social workers?

SW   No, not yet. There has been some talk about setting one up. The idea was first suggested almost 20 years ago. It is closer to being created now than it ever has been before . . .

C   That's not much use to me, I need something now – is there nothing else?

SW   If you were lucky you might be part of a social work project that was managed locally.

C   What do you mean and how would that help me?

SW   Some social workers are managed by local groups of clients and interest groups who decide on general policy and advise professional social workers what needs to be done and how to do it.

C   That's all very interesting and worth while, I'm sure – but how does it help me?

SW   Usually where social workers work in this way they would be expected to give a regular report to the management committee.

C   Yes, but I still don't see how this could help me.

SW It could. Suppose your management committee, in discussion with the social workers, had strong feelings about keeping information confidential; you could agree a local policy about it. You could agree that no information would be divulged without the committee's approval or the agreement of whoever the information was about. Then you and anybody else in your part of the city would know that information was not being given to others.

C   That sounds fine, but what would happen about what we were talking about last time?

SW What do you mean, exactly?

C   Suppose the courts wanted information?

SW I'm afraid the social worker would still have to tell them what they wanted to know, but you would have more information about what the social worker was doing.

C   How?

SW As well as the reports that the social worker gave to the management committee you would also be able to ask the social worker questions about what that person was doing.

C   If I didn't live in an area that had one of these committees, what could I do then?

SW You can complain about your social worker; you could complain that he or she was giving away your secrets and breaking your confidences. All social services departments have to have a complaints procedure.

C   That would be rather a serious step to take. Besides which, it depends on the social worker having done something wrong – and also I've got to find out first that something has happened.

SW Yes that would be very difficult to do, because, as you say, it is quite possible that you would not know what is being done with information about you.

C   So social workers have all the power; they can decide what to do with information about me and there is no way that they can be controlled. Surely there must be something that stops social workers behaving just as they please?

SW Yes, of course there is. Many social workers work for local government and so they are responsible to the elected officers of the council. So by going to the polls you have some influence over these social workers in your city.

C   It's not very much is it? It doesn't help me with my problem in bringing social workers to account for how they use information about me.

SW Perhaps it does. Many social workers have to justify their actions to the elected councillors. It's rather like how it was with the locally managed project that we were just discussing.

C You might say that, but councillors have a lot to think about. They won't have the time to worry about my little concerns. Besides, you can't tell me that it is the same to have someone answer to somebody else. Don't you think it's better if the social worker can be responsible directly to somebody like me – somebody who makes use of social workers?

SW Yes, I agree that would be best but it's not always possible.

C There is one more thing that I don't understand.

SW Tell me and I will try to explain if I can.

C Is there no other way that social workers have to explain their behaviour than to elected councillors? They have so many other things to do.

SW Yes, you are quite correct. Social workers have managers who are responsible for what the social workers do.

C Do the managers tell social workers how to behave and what to do with information about me?

SW It's not quite as simple as that. The social worker asks the manager for advice, and if things are really difficult they will often decide what to do together.

C I keep thinking about the information about me. If the social worker and a manager were going to talk about me then the social worker would have to give the manager a lot of information about me – without me knowing anything about it.

SW Yes, you are quite right!

C But that's not fair! I thought that if I had given information to a social worker it wouldn't be discussed with anyone else.

SW Yes, but the social worker might need to share the information with other people in the agency where the social worker works. There could be many reasons to do this, to get resources for you, to get advice or perhaps if what you had told the social worker was very serious the social worker might need a more senior person's agreement to decide how to help you.

C This all seems very unfair. I gave some information to an individual, and now you tell me that many different people where the social worker works might be able to see the information and that I have no control over who sees the information inside the social worker's agency.

SW It must seem like that – but remember your information is still being treated confidentially.

C How do you mean?

SW Well when you told the information to the social worker, you didn't just give it to the one person, you gave it to the whole organisation. It's a bit like when you tell a priest you are also telling God.

C No, it's not! God already knows. I thought I was telling one person not a hundred.

The third dialogue

C I was very angry at the end of our last conversation.

SW Why was that?

C It seemed as if I had been cheated; I expected some things and when we talked I realised that I had been wrong. I have some more questions, is that OK?

SW Yes, go ahead.

C I know that social workers keep files on people like me. Can I at least see what is in the file? Then I would know what my social worker thinks about me – I feel as though I would have some control if I could see my file. Do I have the right to see it?

SW Yes, you can see it, the government has passed a law allowing you to see your file.

C Can I see all of it?

SW No, you can only see those parts of the file that contain information about you; there might be information about other members of your family. It would not be fair for you to see that information. Just as you might want to keep information about yourself from them, so information about them is kept from you.

C Is that the only kind of information I can't see?

SW More or less. Some information given by other people, such as doctors or the police, may not be available for you to see.

C If the information they have is incorrect can I change it?

SW Yes, if it is factual information about you, but if it is that you have one opinion and your social worker has another opinion then this can't be changed.

C   This is good. I know that a lot of information is on computer these days – can I still see what is kept about me on a computer?

SW Yes.

C   I can't believe that you are giving me as much good news as this – after the previous conversations when I seemed to have very little influence over social workers. Using my powers to see my files I can really call the social worker to account, can't I? But I suppose it might not be as rosy as all that. If people know that the files are open I suppose they will be very careful about what they write down?

SW Yes, I think you are correct.

C   I have been thinking about what you are saying, and it's not enough just to be able to see what is written about me after it has been put in the file.

SW How do you mean?

C   I mean I want to be able to control what goes into the file in the first place. If I've got to go to the City Hall to see my records and then check them I won't want to do that very often, will I? I bet a lot of people would never do that because it would be too much trouble. So the social workers still win, don't they? If they say they have a system to let people see their files, well they have, but it's not giving people much is it, if it's hard for them to use the system. A lot of people around here couldn't get to the City Hall could they?

SW I suppose you are right, it would be difficult for some people.

C   What I want is something that will give me control over what is written about me all the time. Is that a possibility then?

SW Yes it is in some places. Again it depends on where you live.

C   Why? Tell me more about this!

SW Some social workers are experimenting with different ways of keeping records about people. They would decide with the person what would be put in the record and might even write it jointly. This gives people as much control as possible over what information is kept about them. Of course it can't work where children are too young to understand what is written about them or where other people can't understand for whatever reason, such as substantial intellectual impairment.

C   This sounds like the kind of system that I want to use with my social worker. It seems so unfair that it is only available in some parts of the country. How do I influence my social worker to follow this kind of approach?

SW Now you are asking very difficult questions indeed! I don't
think I have an answer. But the first step must be to get
information about what is happening to your case, what your
social worker is doing.

C The next step is to change it.

COMMENT

Throughout the dialogues several themes can be traced:

Power

In the dialogues, the attitudes and behaviours adopted by the social
worker defined the nature and texture of the relationship between
the social worker and the client. This was not a relationship where
both had equal access to information, or to decisions about what
happened to information, nor were there easy mechanisms for the
client to hold the social worker to account. The social worker had
the power to define the boundaries of the relationship between them.
Part of the reason for this is that the nature of the relationship
between the client and the social worker is as much a relationship
between an individual (the client) and an organisation (the social
work agency). Partly it is also because social work is not a profession
that enjoys statutory guarantees about privileged information.

In the dialogues, the nexus that unites confidentiality and accountability in their operation in practice is power. During the dialogues it
is evident that the social worker usually has the power to define
what information will be treated as confidential, just as the means
for the client to hold the social worker accountable are defined
through social work processes. Oddly, if social workers were paid
by their clients, the client would have a mechanism to make the
social worker accountable. However appealing this might be to
sections of the New Right, it is highly implausible, given that a
substantial proportion of clients are living at, or below, the poverty
line. Nonetheless patients, without payment, are able to choose the
doctor with whom they wish to register, so perhaps there is an
argument to suggest that clients should have stronger rights to
choose their social workers and to change them if dissatisfied. All
too often, however, social workers are acting as representatives of
their employing agency, and enabling the client to change to another
social worker may lead to a change in presentation rather than of

substance. The dialogues illustrate that there are some other mechanisms to increase the accountability of the social worker to the client, but these are not widespread. Ways to give clients power to define and defend their interests need to be developed.

Inadequacy of the literature on confidentiality and accountability

This is mostly framed in terms of the dilemmas for the professional, not in terms of how attitudes to confidentiality and accountability have a place in structuring the relationship between clients and workers.

Confidentiality

The dialogues present a conventional view of confidentiality which appears to be shared by both client and social worker. Confidentiality is seen to be about the social worker keeping information that the client has provided, and the difficulty of not divulging that information. Commenting about the operation of confidentiality in practice, Hudson, on the basis of his work in a residential unit, considers that most of the problems with confidentiality arise not with serious life-threatening cases and high-order moral dilemmas, but rather with what he terms the 'middle ground' where there are different expectations about who will have access to not particularly personal information (Hudson 1985).

A body of literature grounded both in social work and other therapeutic professions (much of it from the United States) outlines the rules that govern how information given by clients should be handled: from the general overview of legal and professional rules and regulations (Wilson 1978); to the more specific circumstances when confidentiality should be breached (Oppenheimer and Swanson 1990); or, among other aspects, the impact of new technologies on the storage of confidential information (Reamer 1986). Typical of this literature is an article by Schwartz describing the operation of a law passed in New York State in 1985 which placed communications between social workers and their clients on the same footing as those between doctors and patients, lawyers and their clients (Schwartz 1989). This article provides practical guidance for the practitioner based upon recent examples of case law. In much of this literature confidentiality is presented as a problem for the practitioner trying to ensure that professional ethics and legal requirements coincide; as Gutheil (1990: 606) writes:

> What does one do if the law (statute regulation) dictates one path, and one's ethical mandates point another way: e.g., when the law compels a disclosure of sensitive information and one's ethical promptings urge silence?

We may ask where the client's interests are in defining the operation of the principles of confidentiality. There is in this literature little evidence of joint decision making between clients and social workers about issues of confidentiality. By locating the problem as an issue for the social worker, professional power is maintained and reinforced, with implications for the nature of the relationship between social workers and clients. Using confidentiality in this way forces 'distance' between the client and the social worker, enhancing the status of the professional as being the competent person in the relationship to decide on such issues. It reinforces the power that the social worker has over the client.

A critique of the traditional view of confidentiality can also be found in the literature – much of it British. Following Bill Jordan's widely quoted address to the 1975 BASW conference, 'Is the client a fellow citizen?', which criticised the way in which clients were often denied access to information (Jordan 1975), and the much publicised Gaskin case (where a man who had been in care had to fight through the courts to gain access to his file), a debate was fuelled, which led ultimately to changes in the law giving clients access to information stored about them by social workers (Department of Health and Social Security 1983; Department of Health 1988). An important preoccupation of the British literature has been how to make records open to clients and the implications of so doing (Øvretveit 1986; Raymond 1989). In one account of a small-scale experiment with open records, Doel and Lawson (1986) reported that making the record open began to challenge existing social work practices and could begin to promote a more equal partnership between client and social worker. Yet it is evident from the dialogues that being able to see information is not synonymous with having power over that information. A client might be able to see the information that was stored about him or her and yet the social worker might, for whatever reason, feel compelled to discuss that information with some other party. Opening up the records is one step: it makes the social worker accountable to the client over the content of the records but not necessarily over their disposal. Another step would be to share control with the client and to develop a partnership in jointly deciding what material is included and what happens to that material. Following Rooney, Dominelli (1988: 135) suggests that black social workers may be more disposed to include their clients in the 'circle of confidentiality' on account of their close links with black communities.

Accountability

Literature about accountability in social work tends to be located in works which focus on social work management and, as Terry Bamford remarks in his introduction to Coulshed's book, *Management in Social Work*: 'The literature of social work management is sparse' (Coulshed 1990: xi). It might be added that the focus on accountability is as often as not confined to discussion of how managers can ensure that their staff are accountable to them for the actions they perform in the course of their duty. Bamford's own book differs in this respect. He follows the British Association of Social Workers in identifying five different forms of accountability – personal accountability, accountability to employer, professional accountability, accountability to other agencies, and public accountability – but he adds perhaps the most important, *accountability to the client* (Bamford 1982: 25). It is this form of accountability that helps to define the nature of relationships between clients and workers. Accountability seems to come to the forefront following social work scandals, the prime examples being in the field of child abuse; for example, the Cleveland affair generated calls for social work to be more accountable following reports of social workers removing children from their families in the middle of the night. As a direct result the Children Act introduced considerable changes in practice, requiring that social workers involve children and families in decision making and provide more information to them. However, despite these changes Ryburn has commented:

> The ability of children and families to exercise their voice in the services they need and in their delivery, will continue very often to depend upon the willingness and the capacity of professionals and agencies with the power to let them do so.
>
> (Ryburn 1991: 76)

The question should not be how can staff be made accountable to managers but how can they be made accountable to the clients with whom they work; and will social workers allow themselves to be accountable in that way?

CONCLUSION

In examining ethical and moral concerns both within social work practice and more generally, it can be problematic to develop clear and unambiguous conclusions. Partially, this is because the nature of these issues is highly elaborate, intricate and complicated; partially, because the enterprise of ethical and moral enquiry is to reveal this complexity rather than to provide definitive answers; and also, because different individuals will draw differing conclusions from similar material. There can be no sense of creating a moral hegemony that defines correct conclusions. This should not be taken to imply that no effort should be made to frame conclusions, only that they may be relatively general and contested and, as such, may leave us feeling dissatisfied. Some key conclusions drawn from the dialogues might be:

1 Accountability and confidentiality as abstract concepts and ideals are not too difficult to conceptualise. It is only when examined in practice that the difficulty of meeting these ideals is illustrated. Moreover, by examining the two ideals together the interaction between their operation in practice can be demonstrated. This is important because they are most often considered separately.
2 It is evident in most forms of social work practice, illustrated through the dialogues, that the social worker occupies a powerful position in his or her relationship with the client. This allows the social worker to define the limits of that relationship in terms of confidentiality and accountability. If that privileged position is regarded as being unacceptable, then social work as a profession and social workers as individuals, working together with clients, need to take action to bring about change.
3 The selection of a dialogue form emphasises the need for social workers to be able to justify to clients why they behave as they do. In the dialogues the social worker often seems to have difficulty in meeting the client's expectations: for example, proposals made by the social worker do not always seem to accord with commonsense notions of fairness or justice – but have more

to do with the needs of bureaucracies. If there is a difficulty evident for the social worker in defending much of current orthodox practice, that practice must be questioned. If social workers were actually put into positions of having to defend their actions to clients, would their practice be adjusted, and in what direction?

4 Even if individual social workers were able to redefine their practice with clients, the dialogues illustrate that the structural nature of many of the difficulties would remain. A close examination of the arguments suggests that there is much to gain from clear statutory regulations governing social work and the establishment of structures and systems such as a social work council and proper and enforceable codes of practice. At their best, such systems give clear guidance about what may legitimately be expected of social workers and how these expectations may be enforced. Not that a social work council is a panacea to regulate all that is dubious in relationships between clients and social workers.

Perhaps all can accept that there is a need to define acceptable practices in the way in which social workers and clients relate to each other and work together mediated through notions of accountability and confidentiality.

CODA FOR PRACTICE

The myth of social workers as autonomous professionals free to structure relations between themselves and their client was first punctured by the bold step of asking clients what they thought about social work and social workers (Mayer and Timms 1970). We now need to create dialogues between clients and social workers to define mutually desired and desirable relationships around key points such as confidentiality and accountability and to promote structural developments in social work practice. Here are some questions for practitioners to consider about their practice which may help to both define the boundaries of relationships with clients and to create dialogues:

1 In my work with clients how am I accountable to the person I am working with? Is there a mechanism that makes me directly accountable to that individual?

2 How do I see myself as being accountable to the client?

3 Do I keep information from the client? If so, what sort of information and why, and, most importantly, does the client know that I keep information to myself?
4 How do I treat the information that a client gives to me? What are the rules that I operate? How far does the client have a say in what happens to the information?
5 In the final analysis where does my loyalty lie: to my client or to my employer? If the client gave a piece of information about a serious matter to me in strict confidence, would I be able to keep and maintain that confidence?
6 What changes would I like to see in this aspect of practice?

NOTES

1 The term 'social worker' implies any practitioner who works in any social work agency.
2 The term 'client' is used to describe the person who uses social work services. It does not find universal favour; some prefer terms such as 'user'. In the absence of a universally acceptable term, the conventional word 'client' is used.

BIBLIOGRAPHY

Bamford, T. (1982) *Managing Social Work*, London: Tavistock.
Clark, C. L. with Asquith, S. (1985) *Social Work and Social Philosophy*, London: Routledge & Kegan Paul.
Coulshed, V. (1990) *Management in Social Work*, Basingstoke: Macmillan.
Department of Health (1988) *Personal Social Services: Confidentiality of Personal Information LAC(88)17*, London: Department of Health.
Department of Health and Social Security (1983) *Personal Social Services Records: Disclosure of Information of Clients LAC(18)14*, London: Department of Health.
Doel, M. and Lawson, B. (1986) 'Open records: The client's right to partnership', *British Journal of Social Work* 16 (4): 407–30.
Dominelli, L. (1988) *Anti-Racist Social Work*, Basingstoke: Macmillan.
Gutheil, T. G. (1990) 'Ethical issues in confidentiality', *Psychiatric Annals* 20 (10): 605–11.
Hudson, J. R. (1985) 'The ethics of residential social work', in D. Watson (ed.) *A Code of Ethics for Social Work: The Second Step*, London: Routledge & Kegan Paul, pp. 141–53.
Jordan, B. (1975) 'Is the client a fellow citizen?', *Social Work Today* 6 (15): 471–5.
Mayer, J. and Timms, N. (1970) *The Client Speaks*, London: Routledge & Kegan Paul.

Oppenheimer, K. and Swanson, G. (1990) 'When should confidentiality be breached?', *Journal of Family Practice* **30** (2).

Øvretveit, J. (1986) *Improving Social Work Record and Practice: Report of the BASW/BIOSS Action Research Project into Social Work Recording and Client Participation*, Birmingham: BASW.

Raymond, Y. (1989) 'Empowerment in practice', *Practice* **3** (1): 5–21.

Reamer, F. G. (1986) 'The use of modern technology in social work: ethical dilemmas', *Social Work* **31** (6): 469–72.

Ryburn, M. (1991) 'Making the Children Act work: professional attitude and professional power', *Early Child Development and Care* **75**: 71–8.

Schwartz, G. (1989) 'Confidentiality revisited', *Jewish Board of Family & Children's Services* **34** (3): 223–6.

Timms, N. (1983) *Social Work Values: An Enquiry*, London: Routledge & Kegan Paul.

Wilson, S. J. (1978) *Confidentiality in Social Work*, New York: The Free Press.

Chapter 5

The morally active practitioner and the ethics of anti-racist social work

Charles Husband

INTRODUCTION

In this chapter I have tried to contextualise anti-racist social work within its historical context, and in relation to the broader politics of anti-racism. I shall develop my argument by distinguishing between a personal capacity to act morally, which is a property of the individual; and the existence of external ethical frameworks which are social and political in their origin and nature. In developing this argument I draw centrally upon Zygmunt Bauman's (1993) *Postmodern Ethics*. In doing this I make no claims that his analysis is 'true'. I start from a position which finds his vision of human moral identity personally appealing, and his arguments persuasive. I am moved by his analysis and its centring of moral responsibility within the individual, and I share his scepticism about the universality and objectivity of ethical frameworks.

Through invoking a hypothesised *morally active practitioner* I have sought to expose the normative nature of ethical frameworks, and to indicate their function in the service of professional regulation. And, when looking at the potential foundations for the ethics of anti-racist social work, I conclude that they lack universality; but that they may yet be rescued to inform practice. In essence my argument pivots around Bauman's vision of 'the moral impulse': of being for the other, of acknowledging one's responsibility for them in advance of their demands. I propose that such a moral impulse is a necessary basis for anti-racist social work, and that the ethical framework which may legitimate this commitment is always subsequent and may have a variety of forms.

ETHICS AND MORAL RESPONSIBILITY

In addressing the issue of the ethics of anti-racist social work I am very conscious of the highly contested nature of the philosophy of ethics, and equally of the lack of consensus in the definition and practice of anti-racist social work (Dominelli 1988; CCETSW 1991a; Gilroy 1990). Consequently, I shall address this topic from an unashamedly personal perspective; first, as someone who has been, and is, actively involved in the promotion of anti-racist professional practice (Husband 1991, 1992). Second, given my lack of professional training and competence in the philosophic analysis of ethics, I make no claims for the philosophic adequacy of my argument, as I seek to problematise the relationship between ethics, codes of practice and anti-racist social work. In approaching this task I find myself greatly influenced by my response to Bauman's conception of the moral impulse. It is essentially an emotional response in that I am moved by his assertion of the truly fundamental nature of human autonomous morality. This chapter is intended as an appreciative adoption, and adaptation, of Bauman's provocative argument in order to develop our understanding of anti-racist social work.

For Bauman, morality is found within the individual and is driven by a wish *to be for* the Other. He argues that this recognition of our responsibility for others predates our recognition of the demands others may legitimately make upon us. Nor is this morality a utilitarian expression of a rational recognition of the coercion, and compromise, which is attendant upon our coexistence with others. Bauman offers a vision of moral behaviour which necessarily makes ethics a heterogeneous, external, law-like system of rules. Additionally, he points to the necessity of such rules in modernity's pessimism regarding human goodness.

> Throughout the modern era, echoing the concerns of the order-builders, philosophers deeply distrusted the moral self. That selves cannot be left to their own resources, that they have no adequate resources to which they can be, conceivably, left – was an assertion which did not depend for its truth on empirical findings; it did not generalise from reality, but defined the way in which (in the case of the guardians of order) reality was to be shaped and (in the case of the philosophers) was to be thought about and interpreted.
>
> (Bauman 1993: 63)

In rejecting the possibility and reliability of a human moral impulse the condition was created for the external imposition of ethical guidelines and their coercive institutional regulation. Ethics cannot stand as self-evident codes of conduct but must themselves be legitimated in relation to claims about principles which allow for the recognition of right and wrong in human conduct. And thus we find ethical prescriptions being themselves embedded in, and legitimated through, paradigmatic assertions relating to the universality of sound judgement, the nature of sociality and the possibility of cohabitation. In the modern world such ethics and the validating paradigms are themselves normalised via the institutions which police and regulate their 'law-like' prescriptions in the interests of a state, a specific *polis*, or indeed a profession.

Ethics then are always subject to normative pressures, and in a plural society we might reasonably anticipate ethical pluralism. And here indeed lies one of the primary struggles which must impinge upon an ethics of anti-racism; for in Britain there is an active and highly charged struggle over the admission that Britain is a plural society. The New Right (Gordon and Klug 1986) has been forced to recognise the multi-ethnic nature of Britain, but has been vigorously asserting the primacy of an imagined 'British' culture, which renders the cultures, and hence values, of ethnic minority communities marginal and subordinate to the political project that is the British Nation. The corollary of this assertion is that draconian immigration regulation and time, will resolve the contemporary aberrant situation. Where through political institutions a homogeneous polity is asserted and defended then the reality of cultural pluralism must attract exclusionary moral judgements, and practices, which seek to expunge the deviant values from society. For the New Right, and many British nationalists, the anti-racists' assertion of this pluralism as a *de facto* reality and future certainty is in itself heretical. Hence the frequent assertion that anti-racists are 'political'. In essence this means that they stand outside the norm, and being aberrant must be negated. Consequently, we cannot assume an ethical neutrality, nor a common ethical framework, to apply in discussions of the nature and implications of social work in contemporary multi-ethnic Britain.

Following Bauman, and others, it is apparent that moral responsibility cannot be synonymous with conformity to ethical prescripts, which are social, but must always reside with the individual. This is an invigorating and challenging perspective from which to begin to examine the ethics of anti-racist social work. For those who, like me, have found the reliance on reason and rationality in the philosophy of ethics counter-intuitive in an existential sense, and sterile and improbable intellectually, then Bauman provides an impetus to struggle with the ambiguity of being, rather than seeking resolution, and absolution, in rationalist cognitivism.

The morally active practitioner

It follows from the argument above that a 'morally active practitioner' would recognise *all* the prescriptive 'professional-ethics' of social work for what they are, namely, a reasoned and legitimated set of externally prescriptive guidelines, backed by the coercive pressure of a regulatory body, which is itself an agent of the state. Recognising this external foundation of prescriptive guidance in ethical matters in social work as inherent in the 'professional' regulation that legitimates the powers and practices of social workers is significant. First, it indicates that the CCETSW's requirements and guidance in the area of non-discriminatory and anti-racist practice are *not* a unique extension of its regulatory powers. However, given what has already been said above about the contested recognition of multi-ethnic Britain, we may choose to view it as a surprising application of those powers to an aspect of practice that was, and is, highly contentious.

Second, the morally active practitioner would recognise the implementation of professional ethical guidelines as desirable, and as being permanently irreducible to routine. Doing one's duty may not be the same as being morally responsible. Doing one's duty may be mere compliance: an habitual and ultimately habituated application of generalised responses to a particular instance. Morally engaged practitioners could not hide within this professional ethical anaesthesia, but would retain their responsibility for their professional practice and its implications. Such a stance would be potentially, and perhaps fundamentally, at odds with the current technicist trend in social work: where articulating a personal moral concern with the other, as person and not client, is so often labelled 'political'; and responsibility to the employer precedes identification with and *being for* the client. The professional social worker is primarily an agent of an external state authority, rather than an empowered, autonomously moral, carer. Social workers' *ethical status* is defined and limited by the employing agency which legitimates their actions as professional intervention, rather than personal caring. In arguing that following convention calls for neither thought nor involvement Bauman quotes Løgstrup thus: 'No one is more thoughtless than he who makes a point of applying and realising once delivered directions. . . . Everything can be carried out very mechanically; all that is needed is a purely technical calculation' (Løgstrup 1971: 121, quoted in Bauman 1993: 79).

The moral impulse, as conceived by Bauman, as the prime determinant of social work intervention would recognise needs which cannot be politically admitted and would prescribe intervention which cannot be cost limited. It would challenge the arbitrary delimitations of need definition and the equally arbitrary institutional allocation of care provision. Denied the anaesthetic of professional structures and routines, with their temporary imperatives and certitudes, social workers would be conduits for the expression of need rather than vehicles for its management and containment. Practising as autonomous moral agents they would be politically dangerous; and professionally anarchic.

Clearly the practice which follows from the ethical anarchy of autonomous morality challenges socially constructed professional ethics, and the institutional structures which normalise them. This would apply to 'consensual' guidance, as in the CCETSW's Paper 30 and its anti-racist requirements, as to everything else. For morally active practitioners can never be complacent and assured that they have acted in the right manner, although they may know that they have done their professional duty. This, for such practitioners, would always be a source of ambiguity and anxiety. How much more so when their moral impulse exposes the shallowness of professional practice, at a time when the language of the market and the neo-liberal economics of the minimal state characterise their professional context. In a political environment which has defined away poverty, denies racism, and celebrates individualism within a politics of contentment (Galbraith 1992), this personal recognition of moral responsibility is terrifying in the burden of knowledge it makes possible. Denied the comfort of externally ratified ethics, and the 'professional practice' which is their behavioural expression, practitioners are exposed to the reality of the clients' needs and the open-endedness of their responsibility to address it. This recognition is in itself painful, but when placed in relation to an understanding of the paucity of contemporary resources for the caring professions, the technicist panaceas of management, and the de-skilling of social workers, this stance is potentially unbearable and likely to result in burn-out. Seen in this light, a detached professionalism practised in relation to an explicit ethical code, and its subordinate and complementary practice guidelines, may be regarded as a shelter from the 'excessive responsibilities' of moral autonomy. Perhaps this may be particularly so as social work seeks to confront the complexity of racism in contemporary Britian. Denial of the phenomenon and a retreat to professionalism may in this context be highly attractive, and politically rewarding (Jones 1993).

One of the impacts of the development of anti-racist social work has been to challenge the fragile ethical base of contemporary social work (Harris 1991; Naik 1991). It has challenged the political hegemony by asserting a plural *polis*. It recognises a cultural heterogeneity which, through the experience of racism and other exclusionary practices, has been shaped into a variety of differentiated politics. It has challenged the Eurocentric value base of social work education and problematised a rights-based approach to ethics as also being culturally myopic. At a conceptual level anti-racism has not been able to exist as a simple add-on to existing social work theory, nor has it been able to present itself in a manner which has not elicited a sense of confrontation. This is partly a consequence of the expression of anti-racism as politics where it has on occasions borne some of the characteristics of a social movement. But more fundamentally it is because, at its core, anti-racism has indeed challenged consensual values and dominant political interests (see CCETSW 1991a and 1991b).

In considering the relation between ethics and anti-racist social work I am arguing that we must begin by recognising the normative nature of ethics and their relation to socially structured interests. This leads me away from an immediate attempt to legitimate the 'newcomer' – anti-racist social work – by an unproblematised identification of its linkage with established social work ethics. By invoking Bauman I have sought, rather, to initially problematise all social work ethics by reference to a hypothesised 'morally active' practitioner. And subsequently I have begun to suggest that the political, and individual, resistance to anti-racist social work has a reality in the radical challenge which it has presented to existing interests and values. The time has come to discuss anti-racist social work more fully.

ANTI-RACISM AND SOCIAL WORK

CCETSW believes that racism is endemic in the values, attitudes and structures of British society, including those of social services and social work education. CCETSW recognises that the effects of racism on black people are incompatible with the values of social work and therefore seeks to combat racist practices in all areas of its responsibilities.

In exercising its statutory remit throughout the UK, CCETSW will address issues of racism within its own organisation, the structures and content of courses it validates and its developmental activities. It will require programme providers and expect agencies to take effective action to combat racism at institutional and individual levels.

The effectiveness of a policy is the real test of a statement; therefore CCETSW is committed to ensuring that its equal opportunities and anti-racism policies are implemented and their effectiveness monitored and evaluated.

This robust statement is not, as some would wish to present it, the rabid manifesto of the 'Central Committee of Extremely Truculent Social Workers'; but is in fact the CCETSW's official policy statement on anti-racism approved by its Council in November 1988. Importantly, it is a statement which has been matched by action in the form of anti-racist requirements for practice set out by the CCETSW and backed by potential sanctions from the professional regulatory body. As Tony Hall, the Director of the CCETSW, noted in 1991:

In the list of key features of the Council's new Diploma in Social Work (Dip SW) appears the statement: 'Students will be required to recognise, understand and confront racism and other forms of discrimination and to demonstrate their ability to work effectively in a multiracial society.' This requirement is codified in CCETSW Paper 30 both as the basis for Council approval of Dip SW programmes and in the specification of knowledge and skills against which students will be assessed. Similar provision is made in CCETSW Paper 26.3 which governs the Council's approval of agencies for practice learning and its requirements for the accreditation and training of practice teachers.

(Hall 1991: 6)

Placed within the political context of the times in which the statement and the requirements were developed, they do appear anomalous and in need of specific explanation. The late 1980s saw the racialised nationalism of radical Thatcherism operating in an unambiguous and strident manner (Husband 1994), and with the moral certainties of 'British values' being defended against the polluting treason of 'the enemy within' (Levitas 1986; Gilroy 1987; Gordon and Klug 1986). The post-war consensus of the one nation had been violated by the conflictual politics of Thatcherism (Jessop *et al.* 1988); and within the New Right fusion of neo-liberal economics and neo-conservative politics there was a radical promotion of possessive individualism. This was given a collective expression in xenophobic nationalism. British nationality legislation in conjunction with the draconian anti-immigrant politics of 'Fortress Europe' ensured that ethnic minority communities remained marginalised and demonised (Bunyan 1991; Murray 1986; Searle 1989; Egan and Storey 1992; Fernhout 1993). Government policies and rhetoric maintained a programme of ethnic nationalism in which 'our' identity and 'our' traditions were defined in terms which invoked an imagined cultural homogeneity and presented minority ethnic citizens as a problematic aberration. The theme of Britishness (read Englishness) was sustained through processes as diverse as Norman Tebbit's 'cricket test' and the curricular prescriptions of the 1988 Education Act, with its definition of canonical British culture and history. For minority ethnic British citizens these politics, coupled with their personal experience of British racism, have ensured that their ethnic and community identities have remained fundamentally important and qualify their experience of being British (Gilroy 1987, 1993; Modood 1992). Britain has, through the Thatcher years, become a country characterised by the politics of narrow self-interest, expressed in individualism and egocentric in-group preference. It has become a two-nation state of the haves and have-nots, in which complacency in the face of others' impoverishment has become a predominant trait. How then can the CCETSW espouse anti-racist requirements which were so at odds with the sentiments of the time, and thus likely to be contentious and resisted?

Part of the answer lies in the history of anti-racism. Anti-racism, as an analytic perspective and a paradigm for policy formulation, has emerged from the past experience of British policy responses to becoming a multi-ethnic society. The initial government policy and popular expectation in response to the arrival and settlement of ethnic minority persons in post-war Britain, was assimilation. Assimilation as a policy, and an aspiration, operated on the belief that over time immigrants would adopt 'British' values and behaviour, and that they would merge into the dominant community. The social psychology of identity presented one form of resistance to this process, but a critical factor in guaranteeing its failure was the racism of British society. Adopting British ways was not sufficient to ensure the acceptance of migrant persons settled in Britain. Their ethnicity and their labelling in terms of 'race' remained a marker which led to exclusion and discrimination (Daniel 1968; Smith 1974). Given the emergence of settled immigrant communities in Britain throughout the 1960s, themselves partly an unintended consequence of British immigration policies, the *de facto* pluralism of British society became politically inescapable, and multiculturalism emerged as the new policy paradigm. Multiculturalism was premised upon the recognition of cultural diversity within a conceptual framework wherein tolerance was promoted as the primary social virtue. As I have argued elsewhere (Husband 1988 and 1994) the promotion of tolerance requires that there be something to tolerate, and it assumes that one person has the dominant position which allows him or her to demonstrate a generous forbearance towards someone who is intrinsically objectionable and not deserving of the privilege being allowed. The paternalism inherent in the politics of multiculturalism was heavily criticised (e.g. Bourne 1980; CCCS 1982), and from such critiques there emerged the perspective called anti-racism. In recognising the limits of liberal multiculturalism, anti-racism went beyond the recognition of cultural diversity in order to expose the bases of power in society, and the processes which reproduced inequalities. Politically, anti-racism represented a shift from requests for respect for difference to a confrontational claim for power: a move from invoking tolerance to claiming rights.

These paradigms did not replace each other but continued as competing perspectives, and indeed the broad consensus that emerged around multiculturalism in the 1980s has itself been driven back towards qualified assimilationism by the very vehemence of the assault upon anti-racism during the late 1980s and early 1990s (Gordon and Klug 1986; Gordon 1990; Murray 1986). These paradigms have operated as broad and unsystematised perspectives, which have to different extents informed a wide range of policy; from education, to housing, to social work. Hence part of the answer as to how the CCETSW came to adopt anti-racist requirements lies in the fact that anti-racist policies had, in certain local authorities and particular professions, already established themselves as viable and defensible, although always contested.

Within social work itself there was already a long and very varied critique of social work's response to operating within a multi-ethnic society. Cheetham (1972) and Triseliotis (1972) presented essentially multicultural critiques of 'colour-blind' practice; while Jones (1977), the Commission for Racial Equality (1978) and Baker and Husband (1979) identified the relative absence of any organisational response to the new multi-ethnic reality by social care providers and social work training. And throughout the 1980s the critiques, and proposals for innovation, were sustained (Cheetham 1982; BASW 1982; Ohri et al. 1982; Ahmed et al. 1986; Stubbs 1985; Coombe and Little 1986; Rooney 1987; Ely and Denney 1987; Connelly 1988 and 1989; Dominelli 1988; Ahmad 1990). This is a long list, but with a purpose: it indicates that, while these texts had a highly varied approach and reflected different perspectives, 'race', ethnicity and social work were very much on the professional agenda. Indeed, by the early 1980s the received orthodoxy of professional social work bodies such as the BASW, the CCETSW and the Association of Directors of Social Services reflected a multiculturalism which was comfortable with advocating cultural sensitivity in practice. However, they remained happier with considering 'equal opportunities' issues in employment, rather than engaging with a broader anti-racist exploration of racism and power relations within social work. The implications of the ethic of equity were more containable, though problematic enough, when applied to employment practices. Applying the same ethic to social work practice would have opened up generic issues of accountability which the social work profession struggled with in the 1960s and 1970s and has since been encouraged to view as navel-gazing, futile and/or 'political'. The concern with moral responsibility has been neutralised in favour of demonstrating professional competence (see Bauman 1993: 125–32 for a discussion of the general phenomenon).

One of the factors which must have contributed to the context in which the CCETSW could adopt its anti-racist commitment was the recruitment of ethnic minority personnel into social services. Their experience of direct racism, paternalism and institutional racism has generated an internal critique of the social work profession (Stubbs

1985; Rooney 1987). While often experienced individually, its implications have been understood and explored collectively through the formation of Black support groups in the work place, and Black and Asian professional bodies. To their experience might be added the experiences of marginalisation and exclusion of Black minority students in social work training institutions (de Gale 1991; Pink 1991; de Souza 1991). The presence of African–Caribbean, Asian and other ethnic minority persons within the institutions of social work generated a critique of racism within the profession which could not be dismissed lightly; particularly as the critics had access to the internal grievance mechanisms of the profession as a minimal point of leverage. Also, drawing on the precedents in local government and elsewhere, they were able to exploit their collective experience through their own informal and formal groups. That the CCETSW established its own Black Perspectives Committee was symptomatic of this process. Subsequently it would seem to be the case that the Black Perspectives Committee was central to the development of the CCETSW's policy statement on racism and its anti-racist requirements. (Those wishing to understand anti-racism in British social work might fruitfully explore the processes which led to the establishment of this committee, and its proposed demise.)

At this point it is necessary to recognise an inevitable complexity in the terminology which is used in relation to ethnic identities. In the politics of British 'race relations' the category 'Black' became a politicising category which was widely inclusive in incorporating all those who recognised themselves as having a commonality of existence in being subject to white racist oppression. As such the identity of being Black allowed for an oppositional alliance of people of different ethnicities but with a common context of struggle (see Mohanty et al. 1991: 7). However, more recently the political adequacy of blackness as 'an idea transcendent of colour' (Grewal et al. 1988) has been subject to mounting criticism (e.g. Modood 1990), and there has been the emergence of ethnically distinctive and exclusive professional and political groups. Hence in this chapter, in speaking of Black and Asian professional bodies, I am pointing to these political developments. And in speaking of African–Caribbean, Asian and other ethnic minorities I am using flawed generalisations to indicate the ethnic diversity within Britain and the social work profession (Ahmad and Husband 1993).

We should not, however, see anti-racism in social work as solely the product of the struggle of African–Caribbean, Asian and other ethnic minority persons. Many white, ethnic majority social workers have sought to interrogate their own prior training, and critically explore the cultural roots of their own ethnicity, in order to expose their ethnocentrism as practitioners. For many, this enables them to become conscientious multiculturalists concerned to develop ethnically sensitive practice. For others this sensibility is informed by a consciousness of power relations within society and social work institutions; and they have become anti-racist practitioners. However, it cannot be said that they are a homogeneous collectivity. They, like their Black colleagues, employ a variety of theoretical frameworks to articulate their anti-racism. Some employ a neo-Marxist analysis which, for example, might locate both racism and social work in a framework defined in terms of hegemony. Some focus their anti-racism through a concern with institutional and bureaucratic power and effectively come close to reducing anti-racism to equal opportunities policies. And yet others come to their anti-racism through an empathetic sense of outrage arising from their understanding of the inequities of racism: an understanding informed by a theism or humanism which nourishes their moral impulse towards good in the absence of a socio-political analysis. All of these people may be called anti-racist in the sense that they reject a paternalistic ethnic pluralism within a framework of tolerant multiculturalism. They all seek to expose and confront power relations and the processes of reproducing inequalities directly. And they have a dual capacity to disagree and to fail to understand that they are not in agreement. Their differing ways of theorising their anti-racist commitment mean that inevitably they will have different priorities and nuances in identifying the foundational basis of their anti-racist ethics.

This diversity within anti-racist social work may constitute a problem for those who wish to adduce a definitive ethical basis for anti-racist practice; but it is not necessarily an impediment to the political development of anti-racist strategies within social work. It should be noted that Paper 30, in paragraph 2.2.1, states a general value base for social work thus:

> Competence in social work requires the understanding and integration of the values of social work. This set of values can essentially be expressed as a commitment to social justice and social welfare, to enhancing the quality of life of individuals,

families and groups within communities, and to a repudiation of all forms of negative discrimination.

The generic commitment to repudiate *all forms* of discrimination is echoed in paragraph 2.2.3, which specifies *inter alia* that social workers must be able to:

- develop an awareness of the inter-relationship of the processes of structural oppression, race, class and gender;
- understand and counteract the impact of stigma and discrimination on grounds of poverty, age, disability and sectarianism;
- recognise the need for and seek to promote policies and practices which are non-discriminatory and anti-oppressive.

The generic non-discriminatory and anti-oppressive aspirations of Paper 30 sit comfortably with the non-exclusive, non-essentialist ethos of anti-racist social work which seeks always to locate an understanding of racism in relation to other modes of oppression (e.g. Bradford Post Qualifying Partnership 1991). Within the politics of Black struggle there has been an eloquent resistance to essentialist notions of an authentic 'Black' identity putting boundaries *within* the struggle against oppression (hooks 1991). And in reality those entering into a struggle against gendered, class and race oppressions have had to recognise the dangers of such fracturing of resistance to oppression (Anthias and Yuval-Davis 1993). Individuals enter into a struggle against oppressions from the unique existential vantage point of their own oppression, and dominance. Hence, to continue as a programme for change, anti-racism must recognise both the unique point of entry into opposition to racism which each person possesses, and the consequent diversity of experience people have of the interaction of oppressions. From such a standpoint the list of *values* identified in Paper 30, paras 2.2.1 and 2.2.2, can only offer the most minimal of foundational *universals* for an ethical basis for anti-racist social work. The diversity of understandings that individuals bring to being anti-racist is a proper reflection of lived experience. An attempt to discern an exclusive and unproblematic ethics of anti-racism might reasonably be considered an act of intellectual hubris.

CODES, ETHICS, PRACTICE

Codes of practice, examples of good practice and guidance notes are, within the structures of recognised professions, a means of guaranteeing regularity and uniformity of action in the behaviour of those licensed by the regulatory body. For those agents such codes offer a degree of certitude about the adequacy of their actions as professionals. To the extent that these codes are adopted and followed primarily because they have been determined by 'those in authority', they have no ethical substance. To the extent that these same codes are legitimated by an appeal to shared norms of moral action they have at least an ethical reference. We may consider the Values of Social Work outlined in Paper 30 as having such a function. Beyond their general depiction in paragraph 2.2.1 quoted above, they are specified in greater detail in paragraph 2.2.2, thus:

Qualifying social workers should have a commitment to:

- the value and dignity of individuals;
- the right to respect, privacy and confidentiality;
- the right of individuals and families to choose;
- the strengths and skills embodied in local communities;
- the right to protection of those at risk of abuse and exploitation and violence to themselves and others.

Read in isolation, each of these 'values' may seem constitutive of an ethical basis for anti-racist practice; and yet they are not unproblematic. The value and dignity of individuals may fit happily with the liberal individualism of European social work. It is certainly compatible with the New Right politics and philosophy of Thatcherism. However, an unproblematised acceptance of the primacy of the individual may be a highly ethnocentric basis for practice in multi-ethnic Britain. In non-European cultures the self-evident primacy of the individual in relation to the collective cannot be assumed. Similarly, the rationale behind the right to privacy and confidentiality takes a different form, depending upon who is the beneficiary: the individual or the family. Protecting an individual's right to privacy may compromise a family's honour, and respecting a family's right to choose may qualify an individual's rights. Nor can we be complacent about the self-evident nature of the abuse and exploitation that persons shall be protected from. Indeed, the families of Black and Asian communities in Britain have been patholo-gised by white social science and the caring professions, and whole cultures have been characterised as abusive and exploitative of *their women* (CCCS 1982; Carby 1982; Gambe *et al.* 1992).

The problem here is two-fold. First there is the generic issue that values may conflict and constitute an ambiguous ethical basis for action. Second, in a multi-ethnic society values are not culturally neutral, and hence when they are presented as universalistic values within a system which articulates the world view of a dominant ethnic group they cannot provide the basis for fair and equitable treatment. In a multi-ethnic society values such as those listed in Paper 30 may provide an approximate template for informing action, when accompanied by a critical reflexivity and self-conscious awareness of their historical and cultural relativity. In these circumstances such values may be *accepted as adequate* for an ethics of practice. This would not require a flight to the ethical free-fire zone of post-modernist excess where subjectivity is all. Recognising difference does not require the denial of structure and shared experience.

Additionally we may note that anti-racism has a close affinity with equal opportunities policies in its commitment to equality. Yet equality as a foundational basis for anti-racism is not without its difficulties. As Jewson and Mason (1986) have shown, there is no consensus regarding the determination of equality. They have distinguished between radical and liberal conceptions of equal opportunities, with the latter being defined by a processual concern with equality of opportunity to compete for a resource, and the former by a concern with the manifest achievement of equality of condition. Baker (1987), as a philosopher, has argued the necessary inadequacy of the liberal position. And while it should not affect the ethical status of equality as a value, it has been argued that the promotion of equal opportunities for the disadvantaged discriminates against the advantaged in arbitrarily qualifying their access to their normative privileges. And, of course, in a zero sum game, where there is, in a society pursuing equality, no compensatory expansion of wealth and opportunity, this must be the case. This doubtless accounts for much of the opposition to equal opportunities, and to anti-racist social work.

Anti-racism has benefited significantly from its ability to draw upon a rights approach to formulating an ethical basis for its policies. The existence of such international instruments as the Universal Declaration of Human Rights, the European Convention on Human Rights and the Declaration against Racism and Xenophobia provide an apparently universalistic framework for grounding anti-racist practice. Regrettably, human rights law is itself culturally relative (e.g. Newman and Weissbrodt 1990), and, for example, Keba

Mbaye (1985), in his foreword to the African Charter on Human Rights, critiques the Eurocentrism of the Universal Declaration. Thus while international instruments on human rights may valuably inform anti-racist philosophies and practice, they do not provide an unproblematic foundation for them.

CONCLUSION

Looking back at the argument presented in this chapter, it is apparent that I have concluded that ethical frameworks for behaviour are always flawed and partial as a consequence of their social determination. It may then seem that I have also concluded that ethics have no social, or indeed professional, merit. However, this is not the case.

Following upon my conception of the morally active practitioner, I would argue that Bauman's 'moral impulse' may be seen as a necessary basis for responsible social work intervention. By its untrammelled innocence and generosity it is the creative core of caring. However, the pure individuality of the moral impulse would render it an anarchic basis for organised systems of care in contemporary society. Moral autonomy is always resistant to the regulation of social order, and it is that anguish in the social regulation of caring which must be nurtured and valued, rather than eliminated through professional ethical certitude.

Systems of state welfare and care are, by their very nature, dependent upon the political will present in the state to pursue such policies. And the ethical values which legitimate these policies at the societal level are fundamentally expressed in the formulation and regulation of welfare systems. What I have argued here is for making explicit this ethical framework for practice and hence make it continuously problematic. Through knowing such ethical frameworks to be always plural and 'political' we may thus recognise their limitations and transitory nature. This is true of social work *per se*, and anti-racist social work differs only in the array of ethical foundational claims which have been associated with it. And like any other sub-field of social work, this analytic process must lead us to make the necessary link between the domains of ethics and political philosophy. This is a linkage made all the more necessary by the nature of anti-racism.

I have argued that anti-racism is a political programme, and consequently its ethical claims are a reflection of the politics which inform it. Having rejected racism as personal pathology, anti-racism must address the structural determination of racism in society. Anti-racism aims to change social structures as much as it aspires to produce non-racist practitioners. Indeed, the latter would inevitably be only a tactical intervention since it is the structural reproduction of oppression and racism which is fundamentally seen an issue. Thus I have argued that anti-racism is a political practice informed by an understanding of racial oppressions; driven by a commitment to the values of justice and equality rather than of toleration and paternalistic concern. As such it may not sit easily with the consensual professional ethics of British social work, and it will certainly expose the limitations of codes of practice premised upon monocultural assumptions. The antipathy which has been aroused by the visible development of anti-racist social work has been precisely because it exposed the linkages between professional ethics and political philosophy. The campaign of vilification in the national press amply demonstrated the political agendas of its critics.

My argument, as it has developed from the conception of the morally active practitioner, has been for a permanently reflexive practice. Through nurturing the empathy of the morally active practitioner as a carer we render permanently explicit the pragmatic and heterogeneous legitimacy offered by professional social work ethics. In such a context these ethical guidelines may be heuristically accepted as adequate. Anti-racist social work, as a permanent challenge to the structural reproduction of racism, happily has a degree of such self-conscious reflection thrust upon it by the system within which it operates.

BIBLIOGRAPHY

Ahmad, B. (1990) *Black Perspectives In Social Work*, Birmingham: Venture Press.

Ahmad, W. I. U. and Husband, C. (1993) 'Religious identity, citizenship and welfare: the case of Muslims in Britain', *American Journal of Islamic Social Sciences* **10** (2): 217–33.

Ahmed, S., Cheetham, J. and Small, J. (1986) *Social Work with Black Children and their Families*, London: Batsford.

Anthias, F. and Yuval-Davis, N. (1993) *Racialized Boundaries*, London: Routledge.

Baker, J. (1987) *Arguing for Equality*, London: Verso.

Baker, L. and Husband, C. (1979) 'Social work for a multi-racial society: How has social work education responded?', *Social Work Today* **10** (25): 24–6.

Ball, W. and Solomos, J. (1990) *Race and Local Politics*, London: Macmillan.

BASW (1982) *Social Work in Multi-Racial Britain: Guidelines for Preparation and Practice*, Birmingham: British Association of Social Workers.

Bauman, Z. (1993) *Postmodern Ethics*, Oxford: Blackwell.

Bourne, J. (1980) 'Cheerleaders and ombudsmen: the sociology of race relations in Britain', *Race and Class* 21 (4): 331–52.

Bradford Post Qualifying Partnership (1991) 'Antiracism requirements and the Diploma in Social Work', in CCETSW (1991b).

Bunyan, T. (1991) 'Toward an authoritarian Europe State', *Race and Class* 32 (Jan–March): 19–27.

Carby, H. V. (1982) 'Schooling in Babylon', in CCCS (1982), pp. 183–211.

CCCS (Centre for Contemporary Cultural Studies) (1982) *The Empire Strikes Back*, London: Hutchinson.

CCETSW (1991a) *Setting the Context for Change: Anti-Racist Social Work Education*, London: Central Council for Education and Training in Social Work.

—— (1991b) *One Small Step Towards Racial Justice*, London: Central Council for Education and Training in Social Work.

Cheetham, J. (1972) *Social Work with Immigrants*, London: Routledge & Kegan Paul.

—— (1982) *Social Work and Ethnicity*, London: George Allen & Unwin.

Commission for Racial Equality (1978) *Multi-Racial Britain: The Social Services Response*, London: Commission for Racial Equality/Association of Directors of Social Services.

—— (1981) *Probation and After-Care in a Multi-Racial Society*, London: Commission for Racial Equality.

Connelly, N. (1988) *Care in the Multiracial Community*, London: Policy Studies Institute.

—— (1989) *Race and Change in Social Services Departments*, London: Policy Studies Institute.

Coombe, V. and Little, A. (1986) *Race and Social Work*, London: Tavistock.

Daniel, W. W. (1968) *Racial Discrimination in England*, Harmondsworth: Penguin.

de Gale, H. (1991) 'Black students' views of existing CQSW courses and CSS schemes', in CCETSW (1991a).

de Souza, P. (1991) 'A review of the experiences of black students in social work training', in CCETSW (1991b).

Dominelli, L. (1988) *Anti-Racist Social Work*, Basingstoke: Macmillan.

Egan, S. and Storey, A. (1992) 'European asylum policy: a fortress under construction', *Trocaire Development Review*: 49–65.

Ely, P. and Denney, D. (1987) *Social Work in a Multi-Racial Society*, Aldershot: Gower.

Fernhout, R. (1993) 'Europe 1993 and its refugees', *Ethnic and Racial Studies* 16 (3): 492–507.

Galbraith, J. K. (1992) *The Culture of Contentment*, London: Sinclair-Stevenson.

Gambe, D., Gomes, J., Kapur, V., Rangel, M. and Stubbs, P. (1992) *Improving Practice With Children and Families*, London: CCETSW.

Gilroy, P. (1987) *There Ain't No Black in the Union Jack*, London: Hutchinson.

—— (1990) 'The end of anti-racism', in W. Ball and J. Solomos (1990).

—— (1993) *Small Acts*, London: Serpents Tail.

Gordon, P. (1990) 'A dirty war: the New Right and local authority anti-racism', in W. Ball and J. Solomos (1990).

Gordon, P. and Klug, F. (1986) *New Right New Racism*, London: Searchlight Publications.

Grewal, S., Kay, J., Landor, L., Lewis, G. and Parmar, P. (1988) *Charting the Journey*, London: Sheba Feminist Publishers.

Hall, T. (1991) 'Foreword' to *Setting the Context for Change*, CCETSW (1991a).

Harris, V. (1991) 'Values of social work in the context of British society in conflict with anti-racism', in CCETSW (1991a).

hooks, b. (1991) *Yearning*, London: Turnaround Press.

Husband, C. (1988) 'Racist humour and racist ideology in British television, or I laughed till you cried', in C. Powell and G. E. C. Paton, (eds) *Humour in Society: Resistance and Control*, London: Macmillan.

—— (1991) ' "Race", conflictual politics and anti-racist social work', in CCETSW (1991a).

—— (1992) 'A policy against racism', *The Psychologist* 5 (9): 414–17.

—— (1994) *'Race' and Nation: the British Experience*, Perth, WA: Paradigm Press.

Jessop, B., Bonnett, K., Bromley, S. and Ling, T. (1988) *Thatcherism*, Cambridge: Polity Press.

Jewson, N. and Mason, D. (1986) 'The theory and practice of equal opportunities policies, liberal and radical approaches', *The Sociological Review* 34 (2): 307–34.

Jones, C. (1993) 'Dishonesty, distortion and demonisation: the right and anti-racist social work education', *Social Work Education* 12 (3): 9–16.

Jones, C. J. (1977) *Immigration and Social Policy in Britain*, London: Tavistock.

Levitas, R. (1986) *The Ideology of the New Right*, Cambridge: Polity Press.

Mbaye, K. (1985) 'Keynote address on the African Charter on Human and People's Rights' in *Human and People's Rights in Africa and the African Charter*, Geneva: International Commission of Jurists.

Modood, T. (1990) *Muslims, Race and Equality in Britain*, Birmingham: Centre for the Study of Islam and Christian–Muslim Relations.

—— (1992) *Not Easy Being British*, Stoke on Trent: Trentham Books.

Mohanty, C. T., Russo, A. and Torres, L. (1991) *Third World Women and the Politics of Feminism*, Bloomington: Indiana University Press.

Murray, N. (1986) 'Anti-racists and other demons: the press and ideology in Thatcher's Britain', *Race and Class* 27 (3): 1–20.

Naik, D. (1991) 'An examination of social work education with an anti-racist framework', in CCETSW (1991a).

Newman, F. and Weissbrodt, D. (1990) *International Human Rights*, Cincinnati, Anderson Publishing.

Ohri, A., Manning, B. and Curno, P. (1982) *Community Work and Racism*, London: Routledge & Kegan Paul.

Pink, D. (1991) 'Black students' views of existing CQSW courses and CSS schemes', in CCETSW (1991a).

Rooney, B. (1987) *Racism and Resistance to Change*, Liverpool: Department of Sociology, University of Liverpool.

Searle, C. (1989) *Your Daily Dose: Racism and The Sun*, London: Campaign for Press and Broadcasting Freedom.

Smith, D. J. (1974) *Racial Disadvantage in Employment*, London: PEP.

Stubbs, P. (1985) 'The employment of black social workers: from "ethnic sensitivity" to anti-racism?', *Critical Social Policy* 12: 6–27.

Triseliotis, J. P. (1972) *Social Work with Coloured Immigrants and their Families*, Oxford: Oxford University Press.

Chapter 6

Feminist ethics in practice

Sue Wise

INTRODUCTION

How realistic is it in mid-1990s Britain to expect the social work profession to contribute to the revolutionary programme of feminism? I shall argue in this chapter that current dominant views of 'feminist social work', while promoting an ethic of 'empowerment' for service users, paradoxically run the risk of disempowering and de-skilling female workers, as well as masking the coercive elements of much social work practice. These unintended consequences arise, I suggest, from the use of universalised instead of contextualised ethical principles which disguise the often extremely complex and difficult ethical dilemmas involved in everyday social work practice. I argue that it is more realistic, more honest and perhaps *preferable* for feminist women and pro-feminist men in social work to eschew the notion of 'feminist social work' as currently defined in favour of the less radical, more liberal feminist aproach of providing non-discriminatory services based on informed theoretical knowledge (including feminist knowledge) provided by a genuinely sexually unsegregated labour force.

The perspective from which I explore these issues is that of 20 years' involvement as a feminist in social work: in voluntary self-help organisations and statutory settings; in direct work with service users and in supporting those doing direct work; in researching, writing and teaching about social work; and last, but by no means least, as a (rather disillusioned) service user myself. Clearly, these different roles offer differing perspectives on the phenomenon of social work, but one thing has remained a constant for me. Throughout these many involvements with social work, I have struggled to understand from a feminist perspective my own role and the roles of those with whom I have worked, and I have followed (and contributed to) with interest and sometimes dismay the development of feminist theorising about the enterprise of social work.

Feminist commentators who have attempted to evaluate the status of feminism in social work have ranged between pessimism on the one hand (Hudson 1985), and optimism on the other (Dominelli 1992) about its impact in the last 20 years. There are, of course, real problems about how to measure such a phenomenon since social work is located in different constituent groups – students, practitioners, service users, managers, academics, the CCETSW, professional associations and so on. Typically, however, evaluations of the mark of feminism in social work focus on only some of these areas, and particularly on the academic level with its easily accessible 'data' of publications.

There exists a growing, and impressive, collection of books dedicated to the discussion of feminist ideas in social work, both in this country (Brook and Davis 1985; Hanmer and Statham 1988; Hallett 1989, Dominelli and McLeod 1989; Langan and Day 1992) and elsewhere (Norman and Mancuso 1980; Bricker-Jenkins and Hooyman 1986; Marchant and Wearing 1986; Van den Berg and Cooper 1986; Burden and Gottlieb 1987). It is also the case that mainstream texts on social work theory now include 'feminist social work' as a method or perspective (Howe 1987; Rojek *et al.* 1988; Payne 1991) or utilise feminist theory in their own analyses (Hugman 1991).

It is clear that feminist ideas have influenced the CCETSW in its development of the DipSW, where gender oppression is now one aspect of anti-discriminatory practice which lies at the core of its value base for social work (CCETSW 1991). The CCETSW's adoption of feminist concerns is, however, rather superficial and confused, in that it has placed most effort and resources into promoting its particular version of anti-racism, which is at the top of its agenda, while other anti-discriminatory issues tend to be treated merely as addenda (a tendency that Hudson noted as early as 1985). It was not until 1992, for example, that the CCETSW published its first, and only, training guide on gender issues (Phillipson 1992), and it has yet to produce any guidance on lesbian and gay issues. This creation of a 'hierarchy of oppression', although by no means unique to the CCETSW, is to be lamented. Feminists now insist on the necessity to understand the overlap and interconnectedness of oppressions; hence the current preoccupation in feminist theory with ideas about 'difference' (Lorde 1984; Ramazanoglu 1989) and the deconstruction of the concept 'woman' (Stanley and Wise 1993). While feminists have been busy deconstructing monolithic categories, as Graham (1992) notes, the CCETSW seems to have begun constructing them.

One measure of the influence of radical or 'subversive' ideas is the extent to which they produce a 'backlash'. Of course the existence of a backlash depends upon how important a set of ideas is seen to have become – how threatening they are: if something is not important, then there is no need to rail against it. The feminist movement, for example, has become used in recent years to a sustained and systematic attack on its most basic principles and perspectives both from 'inside' (Paglia 1992) and outside (Faludi 1991) its ranks, for, in a supposedly 'post-feminist' world, feminist theory and praxis is considered redundant at best and counter-productive at worst. In social work, the backlash against feminist ideas has been spasmodic, with occasional angry outbursts from irate men about particular issues (e.g. *Community Care* 1987), or more usually a patronising and grudging acceptance of the importance of feminism to social work (e.g. Cooper 1993).[1] There is currently a more direct backlash against radical ideas in social work which is couched in the rhetoric of 'political correctness' – a catch-all and derisory term used to discredit all positive action against oppression. What is clear about the debate so far, however, is that it constitutes a backlash against the CCETSW's version of anti-racism in particular, with little reference to other elements of the anti-discrimination agenda (Pinker 1993; Harwin 1993), a reflection of the very high profile given to anti-racism but not to other anti-oppressive issues by the CCETSW.

THE FEMINIST CRITIQUE

Despite its uncertain impact (or perhaps because of it, as I shall argue later), the development of feminist theorising in social work has continued, although to date it has been uneven. That is, while it has made a powerful and far-ranging critique of social work practice it has produced a less well-developed idea of what a positive feminist practice might look like. The feminist critique has changed its emphasis from seeing social work as a state institution that maintains the status quo by keeping women 'in their place' in families (Wilson 1977), to seeing anti-oppressive (including feminist) social work as a potentially empowering force in the lives of both women service users (Ward and Mullender 1991; Dominelli 1992) and women workers (Grimwood and Popplestone 1993). The feminist critique has been particularly powerful in pointing up the institutionalised sexism of modern social work and in convincingly arguing that:

> social work, the reputedly female profession, is led by men. They have planned its policies, determined its academic curriculum, directed its practices, and decided where and for whom its monies are to be spent.
>
> (Norman and Mancuso 1980: 4)

In challenging this situation, feminists have called for radical changes in the current gender structure of social work organisations, where women dominate numerically but men dominate hierarchically (Hanmer and Statham 1988; SSI 1991; Grimwood and Popplestone 1993), as well as in the style and content of social work education and training (Carter *et al.* 1992). In addition, feminist theory developed both outside and inside the social work arena has helped to redefine social problems such as domestic violence and child abuse, and encouraged some writers to challenge the predominant style of knowledge-production in social work, arguing for a practitioner-based research (Wise 1985; Everitt *et al.* 1992) and research which takes seriously the experiences of service users (Hudson 1992).

While the feminist critique has developed and matured, theorising about what positive feminist practice might look like has progressed very little. Some writers have avoided the use of the notion of feminist social work practice, preferring instead to speak of 'woman-centred' practice (Hanmer and Statham 1988), while others see feminism as a perspective which is identified with 'critical education and analysis, rather than with the development of technical skills and competencies' (Carter *et al.* 1992: 126). In this latter approach, feminism is a way of seeing and of understanding in social work which informs practice rather than offering a set of methods which can be labelled 'feminist'. Here, practice is informed by a feminist ethic rather than a set of ethics in the form of guidelines or rules derived from a feminist perspective.

In addition to the eradication of sexism and the use of feminism as an overarching critical perspective, some writers have advocated a feminist social work practice with particular goals and techniques

(Dominelli and McLeod 1989; Dominelli 1992). Typically, the goal is seen as 'empowerment' of the service user and the way of achieving this is seen as the development of egalitarian relationships between worker and service user or the promotion of consciousness-raising and self-help among users through the use of group work.

FEMINIST SOCIAL WORK AS EMPOWERMENT

Empowerment is a term that has come recently into frequent use in social work but is often invoked without being explained (Adams 1990; Ward and Mullender 1991). It appears that empowerment is more than just its common-sense understanding of 'enabling', but instead involves 'a commitment to challenging and combating injustice and oppression, which shows itself in action and in words' (Ward and Mullender 1991: 22). The underlying philosophy of empowerment involves the commitment to encourage oppressed people to understand how structural oppression in its various forms impacts upon them as individuals and to enable them thereby to take back some control in their lives. The preferred means of achieving this is through collective self-help action where people with similar socially structured problems can share experience and learn that their individual problems have a shared social basis.

Empowerment in social work, then, clearly derives from models of self-help, whether this be facilitated or autonomous (Adams 1990). Moreover, the 'best' kind of empowerment is (in self-help terms) that which is mutually empowering between social workers and self-helpers, 'in which each witnessed, and possibly contributed actively towards, the empowerment of the other' (Adams 1990: 122). For those who write specifically of feminist and anti-racist empowerment in social work, self-help also figures large (Ward and Mullender 1991; Dominelli and McLeod 1989; Dominelli 1992), as does the notion of mutual or egalitarian relationships between workers and service users (Dominelli and McLeod 1989; Dominelli 1992). Dominelli neatly summarises an empowering feminist social work thus:

> feminist social work is about creating non-exploitative egalitarian relationships aimed at promoting individual well-being through collective means available to all at the point of need. Thus, feminist social work aims to respond to the individual's

emotional, intellectual and material needs in a context that links individual experience with socially-created structures.

(Dominelli 1992: 88)

This model of feminist social work is fairly representative of writing in this area and contains a number of commonly shared principles. First, services should be available on a universal basis for women in need, and not just for women in their roles as carers. Second, service users and workers are generally assumed to be women and to share some aspects of patriarchal oppression. Third, because of this 'shared oppression', it is argued that there exists the potential for egalitarian work between women workers and women service users. Finally, the result of this equal relationship should be empowerment of the service user.

A case study

There are problems with each of these assumptions, which I should like to deal with by reference to a case study (an approach used to great effect in Rhodes 1986). The case is an example from my own practical experience and is as follows:[2]

> Mrs X was a young, white, working-class woman with two small children who had recently been deserted by her violent husband. She had no friends, no close family, no money, no job, and was desperately unhappy to have lost her husband. She had recently taken to dealing with her loneliness and despair at his loss by going out and getting drunk with a boyfriend and then forgetting to come home. Sometimes she made babysitting arrangements, often not, and the children, 4 and 5, were left completely alone for very long periods overnight. After several warnings, plus offers of practical help (money, suitable babysitters) I took a Place of Safety (Child Protection) Order and removed the children, having found them left for over twenty-four hours in a house without a scrap of food with a terrified and distraught 13-year-old babysitter who had expected Mrs X back the night before.

What is empowering feminist social work in this context? At the time, I tried to understand this woman's situation using the insights of feminist knowledge about the realities of women's lives. This woman, I reasoned, was indeed the victim of sexism. The men in her life abused her and ignored their own and her responsibility towards her children. Her marriage had separated her from friendships with other women, as it so often does for women with violent partners, and from her mother, who had not approved of her husband. Her self-esteem had been tied into her relationship with her husband and, without him, she felt she had to be attached to another man to be 'somebody' as well as to have the financial support to be able to engage with the 'public' world. With a young child at home and no childcare facilities, finding a job to gain money and make new friends was out of the question, not least because her only training and qualifications were for wifedom and motherhood.

Having understood her situation in feminist terms, an empowering solution in the sense of empowerment used above would focus on encouraging or enabling her to understand that her individual problems were socially constructed and shared by others. Thus she might gain insight, strength and self-esteem from the self-help support of other women in the same position as herself (something that I could not offer, having not been through the same experiences, although I might have been able to facilitate the work). Such work might help her to get over her 'failed' marriage and her dependence on unsuitable men and alcohol, and to regain some control over her life. There were, however, pressing difficulties with this approach to her 'problems'.

First, there was the difficulty of whether my definition of the problem was shared. In fact, her definition of the problem was totally different from mine – I thought the men in her life were a problem; she wanted her violent husband back so that she could be a housewife again and they could be a 'happy family'. Which of us was right, and is 'empowerment' here the equivalent of me treating her as 'falsely conscious' and in need of re-education? To put this succinctly, what if I think a woman is oppressed and she does not? What does empowerment mean here – the imposition of my set of values over hers? I could have started with her definition of the situation and tried to work with the husband (if willing) to encourage him to change his sexist view of the world and behave better, but there were problems of resource limitations with such an approach. This was one of many similar cases I was working with at the time – I had only so much time available and only so many resources to call upon, whereas the empowerment approach requires a very long-term strategy.

Second, and of course by far the more important point, there is the fact that the most crucial part of the definition of the problem is missing here. That is, this woman was not the most vulnerable person in this situation: her children were. My first duty was to them and their protection. Although I eschew the notion of a hierarchy of oppression, I think that it is still necessary to work with the idea of a hierarchy of vulnerability (Goodin 1985) in the real world of social work, where choices have to be made and priorities have to be set about where resources are to be spent and conflicting needs adjudicated. The point being made here is that, contrary to the feminist empowerment model, women are not always the target 'client'[3] in a given situation, although they may be the carers of someone more vulnerable. Moreover, the needs of the more vulnerable person – be it a child, elderly relative and so on – may very often conflict with the needs of the woman. It has been suggested that such a conflict is not inevitable if a systems approach to analysing problems is adopted, and that the needs of both the woman and her children can be addressed in working with an example like the one above (McNay 1992). However, here I come back to the realities of the limited time and resources available in addressing such problems, either because of the pressing need to take control of a situation where someone is at risk, or because of the problem of inadequate resources.

My argument, then, is that if we look at real examples of social work practice in a statutory setting, where we are dealing with 'clients' rather than 'service users' (see note 3), enormous problems begin to emerge with the ethic of feminist empowerment. Social services are not provided on a universal basis (although we might argue that they should be), but are instead targeted on people who are felt to be particularly vulnerable. Women are not categorised as such a vulnerable group (and, it could be argued, nor should they be), whereas those who frequently rely on women as carers *are* so designated and social services are mandated to act on their behalf. Often, then, 'the client' in a situation is not a woman, but her dependants, and she becomes a client only by virtue of the need to protect them. Second, the notion of empowering, egalitarian relationships being developed between worker and client becomes problematic once the controlling aspects of social work are recognised. Whatever aspects of oppression might have been shared between myself and this woman (and they were very few indeed), the central feature of our 'relationship' was that it was an artificially created, power-imbalanced imposition upon her.

The absence of power

What I am suggesting here is that what is missing from the ethic of empowerment in such feminist ideas about social work (and in other forms of anti-discriminatory practice) is, paradoxically, any analysis of the very real power divisions that exist in social worker and client relationships in statutory settings. It is not surprising that this is so, however, for three reasons.

First, most theorising about feminist social work and its potential for empowerment in fact is based on feminist alternatives to social work which have been specifically and deliberately constructed outside of mainstream social work, such as Rape Crisis Centres, Women's Refuges, Incest Survivors' Groups and so on and, as Dominelli notes, 'the advance of feminist social work into statutory social work has yet to be formally charted' (Dominelli 1992: 99). The notion of empowerment contained within such feminist organisations builds upon the experiences of modern social movements which have organised through self-help and developed theory and programmes for change, as well as prompting massive personal change for those involved: the civil rights movement, the women's movement, the lesbian and gay movement and the disability movement. Finding that the 'problem with no name' actually does have names (such as racism, sexism, heterosexism or disableism) is empowering because of the huge ontological shifts which it generates for individuals, giving them the tools (that is, the concepts for analysis) with which to build alternatives.

Equally important in this is the *process* by which this happens. It is through solving one's own problems that empowerment occurs, and in developing such groups and organisations, women, along with other oppressed groups, therefore decided to 'look after their own', eschewing the need for paternalistic 'experts' to deal with their problems. It is pertinent to ask, in the light of this, whether the experiences of these alternative services are in any way directly transferable to an analysis of feminism in mainstream statutory social work, when a crucial element in the empowering properties of such services is that they involve *self-help*, which is an essential element of empowerment. Empowerment is not something to be *given* to people, they must *take* it for themselves (Gomm 1993).

Second, because the empowerment model of feminist social work relies so heavily on these non-statutory services, the problem of power and control is elided. Despite an often overly-romantic picture of these feminist alternatives which glosses over difficulties and power battles that occur within them, it is nevertheless the case that these services have been conceived, organised and run around feminist ethical principles derived from the analysis of women's oppression. This clearly is not the case in the services provided in statutory work. Most of my statutory social work experience involved me in having power over clients in one of two ways: either I could do something to them against their will which they could not do to me, or I had something they wanted or needed and I could decide whether to give it to them or not. That is real power, and the only way to deal with it in a non-oppressive way is to make it absolutely impossible to abuse: and that means being 100 per cent open about the fact that it exists, that it can be used and that it is often legitimate to use it, and deriving an ethical framework within which to do so. In the case above this meant being clear that I was not visiting as a friend, nor as an equal, but as someone with powers that I was prepared to use if necessary, not because she was a 'bad mother', but because her children were in danger.

Third, while part of the problem I have identified stems from inappropriate extrapolation from one area to another, another problem is the abstract language within which these debates have been conducted. That is, very few writings about feminist social work are grounded in the realities of everyday practice, which can help us to test out the usefulness of such universalised concepts as empowerment. This is extraordinary, given the commitment of feminism to theorising from experience, or, at the very least, testing out theory against experience. And yet whenever I discuss these issues with practitioners, the response to my critique is always the same: an audible sigh of relief. There are very many feminist practitioners in the field who have become guilty about not being able to live up to this Utopian vision of the empowering model of feminist social work, because the theory simply does not match the reality of their working lives. The gap between academic theory and social work practice is a perennial one, but it is lamentable that these feminist theories of social work have fallen into the same trap. This is what I mean when I suggest that the empowerment model of feminist social work may be de-skilling and disempowering feminist and pro-feminist social workers: it sets them up to fail.

The reason why feminist theorising of statutory social work is, as yet, so unsophisticated is not a mystery: the circumstances simply do not exist in which such theory can grow and develop. Vast amounts of energy are still having to be spent in keeping gender on the mainstream social work agenda and ensuring that feminist theory is taken seriously. In spending so much time on the basics it is extremely hard to move the anti-discrimination agenda to a more sophisticated level. To do this would require a lengthy debate, but with whom? If we debate among those with like-minds (that is, those who acknowledge the validity of anti-oppression analysis), feminists are accused of separatism and are ignored by the mainstream. Alternatively, feminists may find that they are speaking a different language after all, for, as Graham (1992) has noted, mainstream feminist social theory is infinitely more sophisticated than current anti-discrimination debates in social work.[4]

Meanwhile, if feminists try to engage with the mainstream on these issues (Dominelli 1990), they are met with the sexist arrogance of male academics who are totally ignorant of the last 30 years of feminist theory (Webb 1990). The debilitating effect of constantly reiterating basic premises is something that feminists are used to, but it is deeply galling that in a women's profession such as social work it should be necessary. Yet we should not be surprised, since the power structure of social work remains the same now as it was when feminists first began their critique: men are in charge – of the money, of the organisations, and of the parameters of legitimate theoretical debate. Sexism is not a mistake nor an accident. It exists because it serves the interests of men, and the white, heterosexual, able-bodied men in charge of social work appear no more inclined to give up their privileges here than elsewhere. As Hanmer and Statham noted some time ago (1988), we shall only know about the potential of social work to be anti-oppressive when it gets its own house in order. And it is this that has to happen if we are to progress in our development of anti-discriminatory practice.

TOWARDS FEMINIST ANTI-DISCRIMINATORY PRACTICE

The feminist critique of the male stranglehold on social work must continue at every level, until there is sexual equality in every sphere of social work and until feminist knowledge and analysis are accepted as a prerequisite for theorising social work. But at the same time as feminists continue to drag men into the second half of the twentieth century, we must have our eyes firmly fixed on the future to ensure that the anti-discrimination debate progresses, and is informed by feminist ethics. There are ways in which these ends can be forwarded, all of which involve producing clearer and more sophisticated analyses.

First, it is essential to stop equating unlike entities and to begin to make a clear distinction between feminist social work and anti-discriminatory or non-sexist practice. Feminist social work is a particular form of practice which grew out of the political and social movement of 'second wave' feminism in the 1970s and 1980s. It is unique in its origins, its politics and its goals. Feminist social work cannot, and should not, be transported into a statutory framework which is essentially antithetical to those politics and goals but should, instead, be encouraged to flourish and grow separately. I suggest, then, that we retain the description of feminist social work for those alternative services for women that can truly claim the epithet 'feminist'.

Second, the prime concern should be, therefore, with the development of the more liberal approach of anti-discriminatory social work, which is informed by feminist analysis, alongside the analyses of other subjugated groups. But it must be clear what anti-discrimination means in this context: should social work be a force for the liberation of oppressed minorities, or should it instead aim to perform its essentially paternalistic functions of protecting vulnerable people without adding to their vulnerability? As suggested above, in my view the quest for liberation sits uneasily within the framework of state-provided services, and is instead the province of political activists within the social movements already referred to. The aim of not creating, supporting or adding to (rather than trying to eliminate) discrimination and oppression, however, clearly is within the legitimate remit of statutory social work. It needs to be decided if the absence of discrimination in social work practice (a legitimate and not insubstantial achievement) would be sufficient, or whether something more proactive is required (such as some version of 'empowerment').

Third, the terms of these debates must be made clearer. Social work never has been, and never will be, a monolithic and unitary phenomenon and academics must stop trying to erect meta-narratives for analysing it. If an analysis applies to work with 'service users' but not statutory work with 'clients', then this needs to be said. Similarly, the value of meta-ethics in social work, based on generalised and abstract principles of 'rights' and 'justice', needs to be questioned in the light of alternative approaches, in particular that provided by situated or context-specific ethics (Cole and Coultrap-McQuin 1992; Larrabee 1993). In order to reach a greater understanding of what ethical judgements might look like in an applied setting, however, the abstract terms in which feminism and social work are frequently debated must give way to discussion of contextually located, everyday examples of social work practice. It is only when such discussion occurs that we are confronted with the ethical complexities and dilemmas of practice, as I have attempted to demonstrate with the example above.

Finally, the analysis of non-consensual, statutory social work is long overdue and must begin in earnest: it is time to 'formally chart' the reality and potential of feminism for this work.[5] If all men left social work tomorrow, and if all the women left in it were feminists, the problems of how to work in an ethical way in coercive work – with women, with men and with children – would remain. Whatever feminist-influenced ethic of anti-discrimination emerges must be able to inform this kind of work, *especially* where it is with unlovely people who are difficult to respect and whose needs conflict with others who are more vulnerable. This kind of work *is* about the use of power and control and it *does* deal with conflicting needs where some people's rights have to be prioritised over others: and it is in dealing with power in these situations that a feminist analysis is urgently needed.

NOTES

1 Both of these examples are responses to feminist theorising about child sexual abuse which has made a marked impact in social work and also caught a lot of men 'on the raw' (see Hudson 1992).
2 I have used a longer version of this example before (Wise 1985). I use it here again because I am hoping that someone will engage in debate with me about it. For me, taking away a woman's children epitomises the dilemmas for feminists in social work.
3 I found in writing about this case that I slipped intuitively back into use of the word 'client', reflecting the era in which I was in practice. I realised, however, that there may be some conceptual merit in retaining its use and from here on I use 'service user' when I am speaking of recipients of social work intervention voluntarily entered into, and 'client' when referring to those who have social work imposed upon them because the state has a mandated responsibility to protect.
4 An interesting example of this can be found in the debate between Pringle (1992) and Carter (1993), where the former uses essentialised

notions of male sexuality to problematise the involvement of men in social work.

5 I overstate this somewhat, since there are examples (Wise 1985; Langan and Day 1992), but very few which use grounded examples.

BIBLIOGRAPHY

Adams, R. (1990) *Self-Help, Social Work and Empowerment*, London: Macmillan.

Bricker-Jenkins, M. and Hooyman, N. (eds) (1986) *Not for Women Only: Social Work Practice for a Feminist Future*, Maryland: National Association of Social Work.

Brook, E. and Davis, A. (eds) (1985) *Women, the Family and Social Work*, London: Tavistock.

Burden, D. S. and Gottlieb, N. (1987) *The Woman Client*, London: Tavistock.

Carter, P. (1993) 'The problem of men: a reply to Keith Pringle', *Critical Social Policy* **38**: 100–6.

Carter, P., Everitt, A. and Hudson, A. (1992) 'Malestream training? Women, feminism and social work education', in M. Langan and L. Day (eds) *Women, Oppression and Social Work: Issues in Anti-discriminatory Practice*, London: Routledge.

CCETSW (1991) *Rules and Requirements for the Diploma in Social Work (Paper 30)*, London: CCETSW.

Cole, E. B. and Coultrap-McQuin, S. (eds) (1992) *Explorations in Feminist Ethics: Theory and Practice*, Bloomington: Indiana University Press.

Community Care (1987) 'Letters', 26 November: 10–11.

Cooper, D. (1993) *Child Abuse Revisited*, Milton Keynes: Open University Press.

Dominelli, L. (1990) 'What's in a name? A comment on "Puritans & Paradigms"', *Social Work and Social Sciences Review* **2** (3): 231–5.

—— (1992) 'More than a method: feminist social work', in K. Campbell (ed.) *Critical Feminism: Argument in the Disciplines*, Milton Keynes: Open University Press.

Dominelli, L. and McLeod, E. (1989) *Feminist Social Work*, London: Macmillan.

Everitt, A., Hardiker, P., Littlewood, J. and Mullender, A. (1992) *Applied Research for Better Practice*, London: Macmillan.

Faludi, S. (1991) *Backlash*, London: Chatto & Windus.

Gomm, R. (1993) 'Issues of power in health and welfare', in J. Walmsley, J. Reynolds, P. Shakespeare and R. Woolfe (eds) *Health, Welfare and Practice: Reflecting on Roles and Relationships*, London: Open University/Sage Publications.

Goodin, R. (1985) *Protecting the Vulnerable: a Reanalysis of Our Social Responsibilities*, Chicago: University of Chicago Press.

Graham, H. (1992) 'Feminism and social work education', *Issues in Social Work Education* **11** (2): 48–64.

Grimwood, C. and Popplestone, R. (1993) *Women, Management and Care*, London: Macmillan.

Hallett, C. (ed.) (1989) *Women and Social Services Departments*, London: Harvester Wheatsheaf.

Hanmer, J. and Statham, D. (1988) *Women and Social Work: Towards a Woman-centred Practice*, London: Macmillan.

Harwin, J. (1993) 'Safe havens from dogma pedlars', *The Times Higher Education Supplement*, 1 October: 18.

Howe, D. (1987) *An Introduction to Social Work Theory*, Aldershot: Wildwood House.

Hudson, A. (1985) 'Feminism and social work: resistance or dialogue?', *British Journal of Social Work* 15: 635–55.

—— (1989) 'Changing perspectives: feminism, gender and social work', in M. Langan and R. Lee (eds) *Radical Social Work Today*, London: Unwin Hyman.

—— (1992) 'The child abuse "industry" and gender relations in social work', in M. Langan and L. Day (eds) *Women, Oppression and Social Work: Issues in Anti-discriminatory Practice*, London: Routledge.

Hugman, R. (1991) *Power in Caring Professions*, London: Macmillan.

Langan, M. and Day, L. (eds) (1992) *Women, Oppression and Social Work: Issues in Anti-discriminatory Practice*, London: Routledge.

Larrabee, M. J. (ed.) (1993) *An Ethic of Care: Feminist and Interdisciplinary Perspectives*, New York: Routledge.

Lorde, A. (1984) *Sister Outsider*, New York: Crossing Press.

McNay, M. (1992) 'Social work and power relations: towards a framework for an integrated practice', in M. Langan and L. Day (eds) *Women, Oppression and Social Work: Issues in Anti-Discriminatory Practice*, London: Routledge.

Marchant, H. and Wearing, B. (eds) (1986) *Gender Reclaimed: Women in Social Work*, Sydney: Hale & Iremonger.

Norman, E. and Mancuso, A. (eds) (1980) *Women's Issues and Social Work Practice*, Illinois: Peacock Publishers.

Page, R. (1992) 'Empowerment, oppression and beyond: a coherent strategy? A reply to Ward and Mullender', *Critical Social Policy* 35: 89–92.

Paglia, C. (1992) *Sex, Art and American Culture*, New York: Vintage Books.

Payne, M. (1991) *Modern Social Work Theory: a Critical Introduction*, London: Macmillan.

Phillipson, J. (1992) *Practising Equality: Women, Men and Social Work*, London: CCETSW.

Pinker, R. (1993) 'A lethal kind of looniness', *The Times Higher Education Supplement*, 10 September: 19.

Pringle, K. (1992) 'Child sexual abuse perpetrated by welfare personnel and the problem of men', *Critical Social Policy* 36: 4–19.

Ramazanoglu, C. (1989) *Feminism and the Contradictions of Oppression*, London: Routledge & Kegan Paul.

Rhodes, M. (1986) *Ethical Dilemmas in Social Work Practice*, London: Routledge & Kegan Paul.

Rojek, C., Peacock, G. and Collins, S. (1988) *Social Work and Received Ideas*, London: Routledge.

SSI (Social Services Inspectorate) (1991) *Women in Social Services: a Neglected Resource*, London: HMSO.

Stanley, L. and Wise, S. (1993) *Breaking Out Again: Feminist Ontology and Epistemology*, London: Routledge.

Van den Berg, N. and Cooper, L. B. (eds) (1986) *Feminist Visions for Social Work*, Maryland: National Association of Social Work.

Ward, D. and Mullender, A. (1991) 'Empowerment and oppression: an indissoluble pairing for contemporary social work', *Critical Social Policy* 32: 21–30.

Webb, D. (1990) 'A stranger in the academy: a reply to Lena Dominelli', *Social Work and Social Sciences Review* 2 (3): 236–41.

Wilson, E. (1977) *Women and the Welfare State*, London: Tavistock.

Wise, S. (1985) *Becoming a Feminist Social Worker, Studies in Sexual Politics No. 6*, University of Manchester. (An edited version of this monograph was reprinted in L. Stanley (ed.) (1990) *Feminist Praxis: Research, Theory and Epistemology in Feminist Sociology*, London: Routledge.)

—— (1988) *Doing Feminist Social Work: An Annotated Bibliography and an Introductory Essay*, Studies in Sexual Politics No. 21, Manchester: University of Manchester.

Chapter 7

Managerialism and the ethics of management

Maurice Vanstone

INTRODUCTION

Although in this chapter I intend to focus critically on management approaches within the public services, what follows is not an anti-management polemic nor is it intended to be a deconstruction of the concept of hierarchy. Moreover, I start from an acceptance that public service organisations are characterised by hierarchical frameworks which in the foreseeable future are unlikely to change. This is not to imply that hierarchies are necessarily the only effective way to organise the delivery of services; there is, indeed, a place for the espousal of different organisational models. Hugman (1991), for instance, has argued effectively that hierarchy is not a 'natural' organisational form but is the result of the 'struggle between state control and occupational autonomy' which occurred during the professionalisation and organisational unification of social work. My concerns, therefore, are first with how hierarchies function, and how the people on every level interact, exercise responsibility, make decisions, use power, learn and develop and participate in the fulfilling of policy and practice; and second, with what informs the thoughts and actions of those with managerial responsibility. In elaborating those concerns I shall aim to unpack what I see as the pivotal problems of modern public service management; to offer a distinction between management and managerialism; to explore the implications of power and leadership for managers, and to describe an ethically informed management model which is ensconced in problem solving and learning. Finally, I should explain that although my arguments are directed at public service management generally, many of the illustrations are drawn from my experience in the Probation Service.

The growth and increasing complexity of public service organisations have been piecemeal, and characterised by decisions made at the micro rather than the macro level of policy and strategy. The process has been largely responsive rather than proactive, driven by increasing demands on scarce resources, more complex tasks, and pressures from greater exposure to outside scrutiny. Each child abuse inquiry and each moral panic has heightened management dilemmas about how to control and hold people to account, and how to avoid the next public relations disaster while simultaneously attempting to ensure a quality service.

My point is not that those in management positions are indifferent to the need for good practice, but that in a hostile climate (and the 1980s and early 1990s have been characterised by policies inimical to the concept of service) defensive reaction is more likely than creative problem solving. At the same time the administrative, managerial layer thickens, and the distance between managers and practitioners increases, making effective communication increasingly difficult; meanwhile, increasingly rule-bound practitioners dream of a mythical golden age of autonomy and high-quality practice, and besieged managers learn to mistrust and survive. A pejorative generalisation, no doubt, but there is evidence of a lessening of cooperativeness and shared commitment to the goals of organisations (Humphrey and Pease 1992; May 1991). These goals are invariably to do with the increasing of effectiveness, and the quality of the services (Coker 1988; Leigh 1986); so why are they not enthusiastically embraced by a grateful workforce?

External pressures, as I suggested above, provide an explanation for increased pressures; privatisation (or the threat of it), and the introduction of a market philosophy into the public sector, heighten a sense of vulnerability, but they do not explain the fragmentation of cooperation. The answer lies in the midst of a number of distinct, but interrelated problems, the first of which has been the adoption of an outmoded and inappropriate management model. Organisational effectiveness is increasingly linked in the management literature to problem solving, involvement of all employees, and teamwork (Adair 1988); but perversely, public service developments have been characterised by a 'hard-nosed' management culture (Lewis 1991) which encourages the kind of manager described by Coulshed (1990: 4):

> the ruthless, single-minded manager who is wily about office politics, who can get the better of subordinates and superiors

and who thinks that most problems can be solved by rational-technical tools and mechanical use of flow charts, practice manuals, decision-making models.

The second problem has been precipitated by a tendency to operate as if a social work agency is an economic organisation, thus leading to direct conflict with its social work purpose (May 1991). Accountancy is, of course, of increasing importance in an environment of constrained resources chasing competing needs; however, the growing distance between managers and the core tasks of social work agencies has led to those resourcing decisions being made on the basis of managerial and economic expediency rather than on client need. In describing how management consultants worked with probation services to introduce the Financial Management Initiative, Humphrey illustrates how a combination of, on the one hand, expectations that social workers be cost rather than welfare effective, and, on the other, the allure of accounting techniques, dissolved in the face of the complex reality of the probation service (Humphrey 1991).

The third problem is the difficulty of sustaining an organisation which is supportive of innovation and improvement when its burgeoning bureaucratic structure increases the remoteness of management. We know that committed leadership is an important prerequisite of effective practice (Macdonald *et al.* 1992; McIvor 1990), but in turn effective leadership is dependent on good communication.

The fourth factor is the manipulation of information technology exclusively for managerial purposes. An effective service organisation is dependent on evaluation, and we know that practitioners are often at best indifferent to research activity which they perceive as 'academic' and threatening (Smith 1987). However, any progress towards the creation of cultures of curiosity has been seriously retarded by the short history of information systems in social work agencies. The probation service is a case in point. During the past ten years (longer for some) information systems have been set up in order to facilitate management by objectives. Invariably, these systems have been located in headquarters, and structured so that management can be provided with information about the work of practitioners. Inexorably, performance indicators, inputs and outputs have become the currency of managerial activity. Unsurprisingly staff have seen all this as irrelevant to their concerns, and more to do with criticism and attack (Humphrey and Pease 1992). As a consequence, an opportunity to promote interest in evaluation, and encourage practitioners to explore whether or not their efforts are achieving the intended results, has been missed.

The study undertaken by Humphrey and Pease is particularly interesting because it focuses on a metropolitan probation service which has many of the characteristics of larger social services departments. The researchers acknowledge that the public sector generally has come under increasing external pressure to demonstrate efficiency and effectiveness, and argue that there is limited evidence of any success in establishing appropriate measures of service quality. Part of the problem lies with the difficulty in defining effectiveness and quality, discourses about which can be markedly different even in the same organisation. However, Humphrey and Pease also attribute the failure to the inadequacy of 'the simple underlying model of organisational behaviour' used in the implementation of performance indicators in the face of growing diversity of organisational life. In order, therefore, to inform a debate about the practicalities of measuring performance, they interviewed in depth thirty-five people, drawn from all probation officer grades, and including justices' clerks, magistrates and senior treasury and information officers. Their findings are particularly helpful in clarifying why attitudes to information and evaluation within organisations are so disparate. Their conclusions underline the point that the implementation of information systems does not, of itself, ensure an increase of efficiency in the organisation; account also needs to be taken of the nature and history of the organisational culture, the style of management, and the attitudes and morale of other workers in the hierarchy. These factors will determine whether the gathering, monitoring and use of information increase the constraints on staff, or free them to respond creatively to the challenges posed. The responses from middle managers and practitioners reported in the survey suggest a widening gap not only between the concerns of managers and practitioners, but also between their day-to-day activities. Middle managers, or team leaders as they were often called, are becoming preoccupied with administrative tasks to the exclusion of a staff development focus, while practitioners report a sense of the irrelevance of gatekeeping processes and targets which they see as owned by headquarters staff. The critical problem is not to do with information systems themselves, but with insufficient attention being given to those aspects of management practice which contribute to the evolution of a culture which promotes positive attitudes towards evaluating the outcome of practice effort. I shall return to the intricacies of how to achieve that later in this chapter.

The fifth factor has been the limited success of equal opportunities policy. Whilst over 67 per cent of probation students commencing training in 1991, and nearly 50 per cent of main grade officers, are women, there are still only eight (15 per cent) female chief probation officers (Home Office 1991). Moreover, out of a hundred or so directors of social services departments, only about 10 per cent are women: and there are significantly fewer people from ethnic minorities represented at managerial level than at lower levels in the hierarchy (Coulshed 1990; Peters 1993). I am not attempting to minimise the efforts of managers in the public sector to develop equal opportunities policies and training; indeed, there are examples of praiseworthy attempts to seek amelioration of problems faced by minority groups (Divine 1989). However, the fact is that too few women, and even fewer black men and women, occupy positions of power and influence in public sector organisations, and until they do those organisations are unlikely to convert policy to practice in a way which takes account of the complex problems faced by people from minority groups. This is equally applicable to organisations which have well-developed equal opportunities policies. In a limited but nevertheless interesting study of two Scottish local authorities, self-administered questionnaires were used with a sample of five staff groupings which included both a practitioner and manager perspective (Cadman and Chakrabarti 1991). Unsurprisingly perhaps, in the authority with the poorer policy the staff displayed less awareness of, and interest in, black people's problems. However, the study of both authorities revealed that the level of skills and knowledge within the organisation inhibited their ability to provide a quality service to black people. This, in part, is explained by the lack of a black perspective which would have heightened the chances of an effective response to what otherwise remained elusive problems. An example given by the researchers is that of agencies failing to take account of the fact that many black settlers have had a much more limited opportunity than the indigenous population to accumulate information about services and entitlements. The problem, however, is not simply one of a lack of perspective; our concerns must also focus on the nature of that perspective, and how compatible it is with accepted social work values. It is clearly problematic when women who attain management positions feel pressured to adopt macho-management styles, or express enthusiasm for them (Hayes 1989; Saiger 1992).

The final problem lies in the decreasing relevance of an industrial model of management to the core purposes of welfare agencies (McWilliams 1992; May 1991). Earlier in the chapter I referred to the problems of communication in organisations with increased layers of administration and management, but that is not my concern here; rather it is to do with the kind of perspective encouraged by an inappropriate model. A concern with performance indicators premised primarily on quantitative analysis neutralises the kind of concerns which are stimulated by daily exposure to the environments of poor, troubled people. They can then easily be transformed from those who need help to those who need to be controlled, manipulated and subjected to surveillance. The process is obviously more intricate that that; I am attempting to generalise about trends rather than examine specific instances. The issue of who is the 'client' is infinitely more complicated than it was in the heady days of the treatment model; the 'child' as opposed to the 'family' or the 'court' or 'victim', as opposed to the probationer – or even the 'public'. Furthermore, there are powerful arguments against managers' being embroiled in practice, not the least of which is the need for managers to take on responsibility in its fullest sense for policies of anti-discrimination. I am not arguing then, that managers should be practitioners, although there are viable arguments that team leaders should; it is the focus of their attention which is important.

A distinction between instrumental and expressive objectives is useful for the purposes of my argument. Instrumental objectives are concerned with achievements which can be measured quantitatively, whereas expressive objectives are 'concerned solely with quality, and they do not specify behaviour in advance' (McWilliams 1989). An example of an instrumental objective might be to reduce the number of black children going into care; an expressive objective might be effectively to represent a black child's interests in a case conference. Both types of objectives should be the concern of practitioners and managers, but the emphasis is likely to be different. Another way of describing the problem of management remoteness is to suggest that managers have become almost exclusively concerned with instrumental objectives. A shift of focus, therefore, towards expressive objectives is likely to increase the degree to which managers are actually, as well as seen to be, in touch with the experience and concerns of practitioners. But a solution on these lines would necessarily be dependent on changes in power relationships, leadership and values: and I shall come to those later.

Having delineated some of the key obstacles to effective management, and before proposing constructive changes, it is necessary to draw a distinction between management and managerialism. Because both words are often used as shorthand for the same thing, the drawing of a distinction is in danger of appearing contrived. In my view, however, management and managerialism are clearly distinguishable, and public services will be enhanced both by the eschewing of managerialism and the use of an appropriate management model. Within the context of my definition, it is possible for a public service agency to have an absence of managerialism but an inappropriate model of management, or an appropriate model of management tainted by managerialism. In essence management is a set of methods, skills, knowledge and values which can help the achievement of an organisation's and individual's objectives; whereas managerialism is an ideology about control. Management which is congruent with an organisation's values and purpose fulfils the following functions:

- promoting the effectiveness of the activities of the organisation;
- empowering its staff and freeing them to exercise their responsibilities in a creative way;
- evaluating and encouraging the evaluation of performance at all levels of the organisation;
- providing feedback based on that evaluation;
- promoting effective and necessary communication;
- involving all staff in common and shared goals; and
- fostering an organisational culture premised on inclusion.

Managerialism in contrast, is characterised by:

- manipulative and covert activity;
- disempowerment and alienation of staff, particularly the most vulnerable;
- direction and coercion rather than influence and persuasion;
- defensiveness and denial of legitimate criticism;
- dysfunction and creation of a climate of subversion; and
- exclusion of staff from decision making and goal setting.

In order to highlight the distinction I have deliberately used ideal and extreme forms. The reality is that movement either way between the two will have the result of increasing or diminishing organisational effectiveness; in other words, more managerialism equals less organisational health.

The challenge to the public services is therefore to eliminate managerialism, and to construct a management model which fits the function and purposes of the ideal of service to people. While this need is accepted by some commentators, sometimes there is a failure to confront the implications of that acceptance. For example, in a recent edited book containing a number of contributions on management in the probation service, one of the writers acknowledges the need to develop a style of management relevant to the service, but then goes on to argue that in the short term this will mean taking on the concepts and language of industrial commercial management (Statham 1992). It is this acceptance of the market philosophy in relation to managing services to people who are in need of help which lies at the heart of the problems of effectively delivering that help in an environment which is increasingly hostile to the vulnerable. For this reason, I believe, the model required needs to be constructed on a re-evaluated ethical foundation.

A useful starting point for the argument is Bill Jordan's analysis of social work's central dilemmas (1990). He begins by succinctly summarising the key pressure on social work as the new orthodoxy which requires social workers to recognise 'the clash of interests between the moral majority and the deviant minority, and act clearly and decisively on behalf of the former against the latter' (Jordan 1990: 12). He believes that the social work profession has been heavily influenced but not carried away by that pressure, because its value base has enabled it to retain a commitment to the weak and vulnerable. Nevertheless, he believes the value base to be threatened, and, therefore, emphasises the need to clarify an ethically-informed aproach to practice. My point is that without a concomitant concern with ethically informed management practice, the vulnerability of the value base will continue to increase. Jordan's explanation about why ethical issues arise in social work practice can be reshaped slightly to accommodate a perspective on management. Accordingly, ethical issues arise for managers because, first, practitioners' decisions have implications for others; and, second, managers share a responsibility with practitioners to ensure that the activities of the organisation accord with the public interest in the promotion of certain standards and the prevention or reduction of wrongs such as child abuse and crime. In other words, the focus of management is on the tension between the professional decision-making of individual social workers and the fulfilling of organisational responsibilities. It therefore has to be concerned with the formal life of the organisation, which is characterised by hierarchy, administration, rules, guidelines and accountability, and with its informal life, which is characterised by cooperation, democratic decision-making processes, support and flexible responses. An ethically based management perspective on this task will inform us about how the organisation will go about achieving effectiveness, and also about what that effectiveness will be like.

In order to understand what that perspective might be, it is helpful to look outside the confines of social work towards the provision of medical services (in suggesting that I do not mean to imply that social work is 'treatment', but that the ethics of health care might provide us with fertile ground for elaborating an ethical management model). In an interesting exposition of the ethical issues for health service managers, Kurt Darr (1987) argues that not only should organisations formulate a clear philosophy, but that each individual manager should develop a personal ethic. He then helpfully delineates four basic principles which provide a context for health service management – autonomy, beneficence, non-maleficence, and justice. In describing them I shall attempt to explore their relevance for public service management generally.

The principle of autonomy requires us to act towards people on the basis that they are free to choose and pursue a course of action; this requires them to be rational and uncoerced and thereby entitled to respect. Managers, therefore, have to treat all members of the organisation, patients, and any others with whom the organisation is involved, in a manner which is consistent with the principle of autonomy.

Beneficence means simply acting with charity and kindness, and can be broken down further into providing benefits and balancing benefits and harms. It is seen as a positive duty to act in the best interests of actual patients; there is a lesser duty to apply the principle to potential patients.

Non-maleficence, the third principle, is based on the moral rule of avoiding harm, and should prompt managers to avoid the taking of risks unless it can be justified by the potential results. It is accepted that the principle cannot be an absolute one because it may be necessary to cause harm in order to avoid greater harm; the example given is of a surgical operation.

The fourth principle is justice, which, it is argued, is particularly important as far as resource allocation is concerned, but also important in relation to how employees are treated. In exploring what is meant by justice (and by implication, fairness) Darr cites the Aristotelian concept that 'equals are treated equally; unequals, unequally'. He describes how the process of the deployment of greater resources on those with greatest need is an expression of the concept in the health service.

He points out that the four principles, depending on the circumstances or situation, may carry different weights or take a different order of precedence; the determinant of this will be the particular ethical problem or issue. While there may be differences in individual personal philosophies, Darr argues that the principles provide a framework for the operations of management as a whole in its relationships within the organisation.

There will, of course, be differences in the kind of ethical situations faced by health service and other public service managers. However, the principles can form the basis of management practice across the different disciplines in so far as they provide a touchstone for the resolution of organisational problems. The degree to which management practice is informed by those principles will be demonstrated by how managers look after all staff; how they use power; the leadership style adopted; and the problem-solving model adopted.

SUPPORT FOR STAFF

In a recent examination of the issue of evaluating quality of service and quality of life in the human services, Stephen Osborne argues that for a service to people to satisfy the test of quality it 'must be born fit for its purpose and excellent in experience (or disposition)' (Osborne 1992). If we accept this argument it follows that the members of the organisation, and, in particular (because they are delivering the service), the practitioners, need to be in good shape, and this will be determined to a large extent by the structures in place for supporting staff in their day-to-day working lives. That those lives are stressed goes almost without saying; however, research on the stresses experienced by social workers provides insight into the extent and nature of that stress, and outlines possible courses of action for its amelioration (Jones *et al.* 1991). Too much work, threats of and actual violence, sexual harassment and the physical environment of the workplace were cited as sources of stress by the respondents to a questionnaire. Additionally, the way in which changes were introduced was seen as unhelpful, and significantly policy and procedures were thought to be unclear by almost a half of the respondents. Perhaps a more graphic illustration of the level of pressure is provided by the fact that almost one third (31 per cent) felt that during the previous two years they had come near to breakdown. Juxtapose these findings to the fact that there was still a high level of job satisfaction expressed, and the importance of management's contribution to the survival of the implied commitment to the job is put into sharp relief. The researchers suggest a number of courses of action which might impact positively on stress levels. These include organisational changes involving the physical environment and quality and level of equipment; improved methods of workload monitoring and review; quality supervision linked to development plans; confidential staff counselling services; support for victims of assault or threats; and stress management training. All, however, are remedial in so far as they are a response to the consequences of poor management practice. In saying that I do not mean to suggest that stress can be eliminated, but management thinking and behaviour which is driven by respect for persons, beneficence, non-maleficence and justice is less likely to produce the kind of environment experienced by the subjects of this research. Moreover, it is likely to lead to a respect for industrial relations machinery designed to negotiate pay and conditions promoting health and safety, settling disputes, managing fair disciplinary procedures, and combating discrimination. It will also heighten the possibility that a critical component of looking after staff – staff development – is based on a strategy informed by the intricacies and dynamic nature of the processes of providing helpful services (McWilliams 1980).

THE USE OF POWER

Perhaps the single most powerful indicator of the abuse of power within social work organisations is the under-representation of black people in all grades of staff, and of black people and women in management grades. Ethically informed management practice of the kind being suggested in this chapter is axiomatically anti-discriminatory, and its permeation into all aspects of the life of an organisation is likely to stimulate a strategy aimed at eliminating all forms of oppression and discrimination (Kett *et al.* 1992; Dominelli 1988; Peters 1993). This imperative is given greater urgency by Bandana Ahmed's powerful elucidation of the importance of a collective power base within organisations which is built on information and knowledge about 'local communities and their socio-economic positions and resources, local authority structures and procedures, associations and trade unions and race related institutions and organisations' (Ahmed 1990: 59).

However, the kind of management model which is sensitive to anti-discrimination has little chance of survival unless there is a clear ethical context for the use of power. French and Raven (1959) have provided us with a well used but nevertheless enduringly useful definition of the sources of power: reward power, based on the capacity to reward and remove bad consequences; coercive power, drawn from the capacity to punish; legitimate power, based on official roles within the organisation; referent power, conferred because of admiration and respect; and expert power, drawn from the possession of relevant skills and knowledge. Application of the principles espoused by Darr eliminates reward and coercive power as considerations for managers. If people are to be treated as autonomous beings, they in turn are likely to respond to the appropriate use of power by managers whom they respect for their skills, knowledge and behaviour. Coercive and reward power generates mere compliance; internalisation of policy is only likely to occur when processes of discussion, persuasion and negotiation take place, and when the behaviour an individual is being asked or required to adopt is congruent with her or his value system, useful for problem solving, and congenial to his or her needs (Forsyth 1990). Accordingly, distinguishing the appropriate use of power, and contributing to a situation in which it is distributed throughout the organisation, is a vital ingredient of management (managerialism, as defined above, is often associated with reward and coercive power). The test as to whether managers achieve that or not is the degree to which the needs are met of those staff who for reasons of ethnic origin, sex, disability, sexual preference or position in the hierarchy are more vulnerable to misuse of power.

LEADERSHIP STYLE

How power is used and shared implies a certain style of leadership consistent with Darr's principles. A useful elaboration of that style can be drawn from the distributed actions theory as described by Johnson and Johnson (1991), and situational leadership theory as outlined by Forsyth (1990). The former describes an approach to leadership which disregards status; encourages the location of the leadership function to be determined by needs and situation; is concerned with fostering a culture which encourages curiosity about effectiveness and a desire for improvement of practice; works at inspiring a collective view of what is to be achieved; organises and encourages staff so that they work together with a sense of being valued and having power; and models openness, appropriate risk-taking and cooperation. The latter theory is premised on the notion that groups derive most benefit from leadership which matches the needs of the group members; those needs are defined by levels of experience in dealing with particular situations or problems. Leadership involvement will be greater or lower, or task oriented or relationship oriented, depending on need. Within this theoretical framework flexibility is the key to effective leadership. A leadership style which incorporates the core of both theories is likely to promote cooperation and commitment from staff, but they in turn have a shared responsibility for the organisational culture within which people work. If, despite working in an environment conducive to effective performance, individuals do not exercise that responsibility, management responses might involve disciplinary action. The point is that even when such responses are necessary they should be taken with the same ethical considerations in mind.

A PROBLEM-SOLVING MODEL

The commitment to solving ethical problems which, I have argued, should underpin management practice, will in itself stimulate an ethical approach to solving problems; the two are interdependent, and essential for an organisation to be dynamic and self-critical. The final and central piece of the ethical jigsaw is the problem-solving model itself. Above all, a manager's business is how an organisation's problems are resolved. What follows is a ten-stage model which draws on the work of Raynor (1988) and Forsyth (1990).

1 *Orientation*: understanding of value base and ethical issues, and clarification of policy.
2 *Defining the problem*: finding out what is happening now; identifying the ethical issues.
3 *Discussion*: working and consulting with all the appropriate people within the organisation.
4 *Gathering information*: identifying and evaluating alternatives.
5 *Decision making*: choosing the solution(s), framing provisional change objectives, and provisional practice change.
6 *Checking out* the congruence of those decisions with value base.
7 *Implementation* of the decisions.
8 *Monitoring* adherence to the decisions, practice and outcomes.
9 *Evaluating* the achievement or otherwise of the objectives.
10 *Feedback* and learning.

CONCLUSION

Much contemporary writing on management ignores the ethical dimension to management concerns and responsibilities. In arguing for an approach to management which is informed by a clear value base, and characterised by ethical problem solving as well as a concern to resolve ethical problems, I have taken the view that hierarchical structures are not in themselves impediments to such an approach. Instead, I have argued that the ideology of managerialism, which has permeated public service organisations during the 1980s, has obscured their central purposes of helping those in need and contributing to the reduction of community problems. A proper concern with the ethics of management provides the best chance of re-establishing the primacy of those purposes.

BIBLIOGRAPHY

Adair, J. (1988) *Effective Leadership*, London: Pan.
Ahmad, B. (1990) *Black Perspectives in Social Work*, Birmingham: Venture Press.
Cadman, M. and Chakrabarti, M. (1991) 'Social work in a multiracial society: a survey of practice in two Scottish local authorities', in *One Small Step Towards Racial Justice*, London: CCETSW.
Coker, J. (1988) *Probation Objectives: A Management View*, Norwich: University of East Anglia.
Coulshed, V. (1990) *Management in Social Work*, London: Macmillan.

Darr, K. (1987) *Ethics in Health Services Management*, New York: Praeger.

Divine, D. (1989) *Towards Real Communication*. Unpublished research report to the West Midlands Probation Service.

Dominelli, L. (1988) *Anti-Racist Social Work*, Basingstoke: Macmillan.

Forsyth, D. R. (1990) *Group Dynamics*, California: Brooks/Cole.

French, J. R. P. and Raven, B. (1959) 'The bases of social power', in D. Cartwright (ed.), *Studies in Social Power*, Ann Arbor: Institute for Social Research.

Hayes, M. (1989) 'Promotion and management: What choice for women?', *Probation Journal* 36 (1): 12–17.

Home Office (1991) *A Digest of Information on the Criminal Justice System*, London: Home Office Research and Statistics Department.

Hugman, R. (1991) 'Organisation and professionalism: the social work agenda in the 1990s', *British Journal of Social Work* 21: 199–216.

Humphrey, C. (1991) 'Calling on the experts: the Financial Management Initiative (FMI), private sector management consultants and the probation service', *Howard Journal of Criminal Justice* 30 (1): 1–18.

Humphrey, C. and Pease, K. (1992) 'Effectiveness measurement in the probation service: a view from the troops', *Howard Journal of Criminal Justice* 31 (1): 31–52.

Johnson, D. W. and Johnson, F. P. (1991) *Joining Together: Group Theory and Group Skills*, Englewood Cliffs, NJ: Prentice-Hall.

Jones, F., Fletcher, B. and Ibbetson, K. (1991) 'Stressors and strains amongst social workers: demands, supports, constraints and psychological health', *British Journal of Social Work* 21: 443–69.

Jordan, B. (1990) *Social Work in an Unjust Society*, Hemel Hempstead: Harvester Wheatsheaf.

Kett, J., Collett, S., Barron, C., Hill, I. and Metheren, D. (1992) *Managing and Developing Anti-Racist Practice within Probation: A Resource Pack for Action*, Liverpool: Merseyside Probation Service Resource and Information Unit.

Leigh, A. (1986) 'Nine steps to excellence', *Community Care*, 18 September: 22–3.

Lewis, P. (1991) 'Learning from industry: macho management or collaborative culture?' *Probation Journal* 38 (2): 81–5.

Macdonald, G. and Sheldon, B. with Gillespie, J. (1992) 'Contemporary studies of the effectiveness of social work', *British Journal of Social Work* 22: 615–43.

McIvor, G. (1990) *Sanctions for Serious or Persistent Offenders: A Review of the Literature*, Stirling: Social Work Research Centre, University of Stirling.

McWilliams, W. (1980) 'Management models and the bases of management structures'. Unpublished mimeograph.

—— (1989) 'An expressive model for evaluating probation practice', *Probation Journal* 36: 58–64.

—— (1992) 'The rise and development of management thought', in R. Statham and P. Whitehead (eds) *Managing the Probation Service: Issues for the 1990s*, Harlow: Longman.

May, T. (1991) *Probation: Politics, Policy and Practice*, Milton Keynes: Open University Press.

Osborne, S. P. (1992) 'The quality dimension: evaluating quality of service and quality of life in human services', *British Journal of Social Work* **22**: 437–45.

Peters, G. (1993) 'On the slippery slope', *Community Care*, 20 May: 14–15.

Raynor, P. (1988) 'Measuring effectiveness in a principled service', Paper presented to NPRIE Conference, Sheffield University.

—— (1990) 'Measuring effectiveness in a principled probation service', in *Assessing the Effectiveness of Probation Practice: Proceedings of the 1988 Probation Research and Information Exchange*, Sheffield: University of Sheffield.

Saiger, L. (1992) 'Probation management structures and partnerships in America: lessons for England', in R. Statham and P. Whitehead (eds) *Managing the Probation Service: Issues for the 1990s*, Harlow: Longman.

Smith, D. (1987) 'The limits of positivism in social work research', *British Journal of Social Work* **17**: 401–16.

Statham, R. (1992) 'Managing the future', in R. Statham and P. Whitehead (eds) *Managing the Probation Service: Issues for the 1990s*, Harlow: Longman.

Willson, M. (1986) 'The changing environment of the professional worker', *Probation Journal* **33** (2): 54–7.

Chapter 8

Enforced altruism in community care

Ann Davis and Kathryn Ellis

INTRODUCTION

Most people needing additional support in managing their lives find
what they want by using their own resources or drawing on those of
friends and family. Social work with adults has, therefore, always
involved practitioners working within a 'mixed economy' of care
provision and the evidence suggests that they only become involved
as a last resort. Community care policies recently introduced into
the personal social services have sought to change the form but
certainly not the balance of this established pattern of response.
Indeed some commentators predict a further retreat of social workers from direct contact with vulnerable adults (Baldock 1993;
Hallett 1991). The role of local authority social service departments
is being shifted from that of service 'provider' to 'enabler', placing
the emphasis within adult – or community care – services on social
workers devising individualised 'packages' of services from a range
of 'suppliers' such as private households, voluntary and private
sector organisations.

The territory of community care in which social workers now find
themselves is one which is being negotiated through new legislation,
government promotion of traditional family values and responsibilities and a stated commitment from CCETSW to anti-racist and anti-
discriminatory social work practice. It is a territory in which service
users and social workers are finding their encounters shaped by
contradiction, compromise and resource constraint. Some commentators have suggested that the foundation has now been established
for 'a two-tier welfare system in which the private and voluntary
sectors look after anybody who can raise the required funds, while
the local authority deals with a residuum of the poorest and most

difficult' (Langan 1990: 69; see also Lawson 1993; Schorr 1992). Within the newly emerging structures social workers are finding themselves being offered new posts as care managers or specialist senior community care practitioners. Establishing an understanding of what constitutes ethical practice in such a climate is difficult work. The difficulty of building an ethical basis for community care practice is not just a matter of identifying an ethical practice orientation in a restructuring service. It also stems from the challenges and changes which are facing social work as an occupation. The debates which surfaced in the 1970s and early 1980s around establishing a Code of Ethics which a profession of social work should aspire to (Watson 1985), are ill-fitted to the present era. The erosion of a commitment to establishing a strong, generic profession, and the sustained critique of social workers' failure to manage individuals and families at risk in increasingly impoverished and divided communities, has left social workers feeling unprotected in a hostile climate (Cochrane and Clarke 1993). In this climate many social workers are struggling to make sense of attempts by their employing organisations to reformulate their task to fit the 'welfare business' and 'quality' agendas of the 1990s.

Community care policy and legislation were being fashioned in the 1980s as social work qualifying training underwent a major change. The introduction of a new professional qualification – the Diploma in Social Work – brought with it a declared commitment to anti-racist and anti-discriminatory practice. The accrediting body, CCETSW, described social work as an 'accountable professional activity' which 'promotes social welfare and responds to wider social needs promoting equal opportunities for every age, gender, sexual preference, class, disability, race, culture and creed' (CCETSW 1991: 8). Professional education and training for social work became a matter of 'achieving competence in practice' and such competence is described as requiring 'the understanding and integration of the values of social work' (*ibid.*: 15). In specifying the values of social work which are to be regarded as essential to achieving competence, CCETSW has placed a requirement on practitioners in training which looks very much like a substitute for a professional code of ethics.

This chapter will consider the political, professional and personal contexts in which social workers are developing community care practice. It will look at the ethical dilemmas which arise from the policy and organisational imperatives with which social workers are being confronted. It will then go on to consider the dilemmas which arise from the way in which the labour of caring is undertaken in the domestic contexts which are the primary sites in which social workers are expected to deliver community care. In examining what is happening in both of these practice territories we will draw on material from recent studies of community care, including a study of practice in this area undertaken by the authors in two local authorities in the early 1990s (Ellis 1993).

THE POLITICAL AND PROFESSIONAL CONTEXT OF COMMUNITY CARE POLICIES AND PRACTICE

The response of the state to the welfare of adults has always been one of promoting a mixed economy of care (Walker 1982; Moroney 1976). The emphasis underlying a succession of ill-defined community care policies in the post-war period has been on supporting arrangements already in place in households, families and neighbourhoods (Bulmer 1987). The conditions under which the state has been prepared to supplement these arrangements have been restrictive and have been offered with an explicit concern that they do not undermine the primacy of the individual's or families' responsibility for their own welfare (Moroney 1976; Finch 1989).

The current constellation of community care policies is the product of the response of successive Conservative administrations to economic decline, increasing inequality, and demographic change in the UK. The result has been to restrict public expenditure and restructure the role of the statutory sector in a mixed economy of welfare (Johnson 1990; Hills 1990; Taylor-Gooby 1991; Walker 1993). Since the mid-1980s a changed emphasis in Conservative policy has been identified, which is of particular relevance to social work staff in social services departments. Taylor-Gooby and Lawson point to a shift from simply reducing to restructuring state welfare services using techniques imported from the private sector. At the same time, a continuing commitment to spending cuts and privatisation has exercised a particular influence on the way the principal features of 'new managerialism' – decentralisation, marketisation, choice and consumerism – have been operationalised (Taylor-Gooby and Lawson 1993).

Decentralisation to the lowest possible level of management is a strong theme of community care reforms. Central government has devolved responsibility for setting priorities, defining need and establishing policies on key operational areas to local authority members and senior officers. Within social services authorities, administration and operations are further decentralised through internal markets and the contracting out of services to the non-statutory sector (DoH 1990; SSI 1991a, 1991b; Audit Commission 1992a, 1992b).

Paradoxically, decentralisation has been accompanied by a greater centralisation of powers. Progress towards desired objectives is monitored by central government through the community care plans prepared annually by local authorities. Policy guidance from the centre is reinforced by the work of the Audit Commission and Social Services Inspectorate (SSI) in promoting and monitoring the restructuring of local community care services. Within authorities, outcome measures hold managers to account for performance and spending, devolved budgeting turns spenders into resource managers. Crucially, though, given tight controls over local government spending in the 1980s and 1990s, local authorities have been given the responsibility for managing services without the funds calculated to be necessary to meet demographic changes in need (Hills 1990; Glennerster 1992). Commentators suggest that managerialism has depoliticised the community care debate by redefining choices about priorities as technical issues (Trevillian 1989; Taylor-Gooby and Lawson 1993). Spending cuts have been disguised by making cost-efficiency the prime policy objective. Saving money has become an end in itself rather than a means to deliver more effective services.

Social workers and service users have seen these community care reforms legitimised, in part, by claims that they are about delivering more responsive services and greater consumer choice. Care management and assessment have been promoted as the 'cornerstone' of good quality services. It has been argued that bringing service users closer to purchasing decisions will facilitate consumer empowerment and individualised, flexible responses to need (DoH 1990; SSI 1991a, 1991b; Audit Commission, 1992a, 1992b).

In delivering on this agenda social workers as specialist practitioners and care managers must simultaneously take account of both service users and organisational needs. Social Services Inspectorate guidelines remind care managers that, while users' and carers' views should be central, their assessments must nevertheless be 'rooted in an appreciation of the realities of service provision' (SSI 1991b: 14). Given the real and increasing resource constraints under which local authorities are operating it is likely that the criteria local authorities apply to determine 'value for money' and 'efficiency' will be at odds with a commitment to respond sensitively and flexibly to individuals in need. In the face of this very real dilemma SSI guidance exhorts budget holders managing their accountability to service users and employing agency to 'sustain with integrity a measure of independence from both parties while safeguarding the interests of both' (SSI 1991a: 111).

This balancing act is to be performed in the face of another resource context which government publications fail to address. As Schorr comments in his appraisal of the recent direction of personal social services and social work in Britain, 'the clients of the personal social services are mainly poor people and the poor do not have social or family resources to spare. On the contrary, what they are giving now is given with great difficulty' (Schorr 1992: 25). User empowerment and choice is therefore constrained further by the inability of most 'consumers' to exit from the social welfare market (Walker 1993: 221). 'Money after all is part of the currency of empowerment in everyday life' (Stevenson and Parsloe 1993: 28). As a result the social worker is precariously placed with a brief to manage the substantial imbalance of power between a state agency and its users.

While the values prescribed by the accrediting social work body (and most local authority employers) are those of equal opportunity and anti-discrimination, these rest uneasily with agendas promoting the efficient and rational management of resources as the primary objective of community care practice. In the absence of rights to independent representation outlined in the unimplemented sections of the Disabled Persons (Services, Consultation and Representation) Act 1986, service users' interests may become difficult to pursue. On what basis, then, do social workers make decisions about the exercise of their power in influencing outcomes for people who are service users?

COMMUNITY CARE: ETHICAL DILEMMAS IN PRACTICE

The social work values which CCETSW is promoting through qualifying education and training are one source on which practitioners can draw in addressing ethical dilemmas posed for practice. In 1991 CCETSW stated that for the award of Diploma in Social Work it required those in training to demonstrate their competence through the understanding and integration of the values of social work. This set of values can essentially be expressed as a commitment to social justice and social welfare, to enhancing the quality of life of individuals, families and groups within communities, and to a repudiation of all forms of negative discrimination.

(CCETSW 1991: 15)

Practitioners applying these values to community care practice are likely to generate a wide range of interpretations of key phrases such as 'social justice', 'social welfare' and 'negative discrimination'. Requirements couched in these terms fail to address the complex relationships which exist between personal, professional and political values and the task of social work (BPQP 1991). Indeed the manner and language in which the 1991 CCETSW Paper 30 outlined the content of, and relationship between, the core values, knowledge and skills required by a competent practitioner resonate with the centralised managerialism of the community care policy arena already described. In Timms' words:

Social work is now to be considered as a collection of assessable competencies from which social work emerges fundamentally as a matter of management: the selves of social workers and clients are to be managed as are time, objectives, limited contracts and resources[. . .] the new Diploma represents the triumph of function and of an instrumental orientation.

(Timms 1991: 213)

In clarifying the way in which anti-discriminatory practice is understood and developed, and its relationship to personal, professional and political values, practitioners need to resist accommodating to such instrumentalism. As Stevenson and Parsloe comment in their account of the climate in which user involvement and empowerment are being developed in the context of community care, 'Social work is based upon moral imperatives, it cannot be a collection of competencies, although, of course, social workers must be competent. . . . Anti-oppressive work and empowerment cannot adequately be described in terms of competency' (Stevenson and Parsloe 1993: 50).

Working with the notion of anti-oppressive practice has the potential of providing practitioners with a primary orientation in which explicitly to address the role they play in mediating between state agencies and groups who have little power within society. This is an agenda which is increasingly critical to community care practice in an era of diminishing state resources.

Our study undertaken in 1990–91 on the involvement of users and carers in needs assessments by social services workers suggested there was little evidence from observations, verbal and written accounts, of social work practice reflecting a commitment to anti-oppressive values. Most social work practitioners described their distinctive approach to assessment in terms of their personal qualities and practice experience rather than a set of values to which they subscribed as social workers. In only one instance did a social worker, who was working with the deaf community, express a belief that openness with service users in respect of negotiating assessment objectives was a positive and empowering step to take. It was more usual for workers to focus on the difficulties they faced in communicating and sharing information with service users. Practitioners' explanations of these difficulties located them firmly in the characteristics (or pathologies) of users who were perceived to lack the skills required to work with social workers on an equal basis. This account of users' deficits was typically rooted in a medical model of disability.

> Both occupational therapists (OTs) and social workers tended to see impairment in terms of loss and bereavement. People becoming disabled were believed to go through a grieving process for which the practitioner required special skills. Further training in the 'psychology of disability' or loss and bereavement were cited by groups of social workers and OTs respectively as desirable for work with people with disabilities. These two professional groups regarded particular provinces as their own; psychological dysfunction was best tackled by the social worker, physical dysfunction by the OT.
>
> (Ellis 1993: 12)

The consequences of this perspective for practice could mean the setting aside of users' own definitions of their needs and priorities for help, as in this example:

> Sight loss had radically altered the life-style of an older woman living alone. Having led a very active social life, she had never previously felt lonely but now lacked confidence to go out alone. Depressed and fearful of losing further sight she had lost a considerable amount of weight, which meant her clothes no

longer fitted. Once proud of her smart and youthful appearance she now avoided visiting friends, thus reinforcing her loneliness.

The social worker believed the case constituted a hierarchy of losses in which the traumatic loss of a parent was the most fundamental and unresolved issue. The practitioner theorised that, although loss of sight had become the focus for other losses, it was actually the least significant.

Although the user felt she lacked the confidence for mobility training, the rehabilitation officer identified lack of social contact as the main issue, planning to enable her to get out and about independently. Believing her more capable than she claimed, however, the social worker doubted the efficacy of such training, describing the user as 'emotionally housebound'.

The older woman was appreciative of all the efforts the workers were making on her behalf. However, all she really wanted was somebody to take her out every now and then, particularly shopping.

(*ibid.*: 12)

If it is the case that approaches such as these currently characterise the mainstream of social work community care practice, it will be interesting to trace whether the requirements of the new qualification in social work have a transforming influence in this sphere. Stevenson and Parsloe (1993: 15) have suggested there is 'a mine-field of ethical issues and dilemmas' facing social workers who are working with notions of empowerment and user involvement. Concerns about the vulnerability and competence of service users, their need for protection and issues of risk are all matters where social workers need to take full account not just of the situation they are working with but the way in which they choose to exercise their power in relation to that situation.

In our study risk management was, on occasion, a source of friction between practitioners and users. The tension between care and control, providing protection and promoting autonomy, under-lay several of the judgements made by social workers. For example, a group of young disabled men living in accommodation supported by the local authority felt that mixing in 'bad company', skipping appointments, missing out on benefits because they failed to complete forms, letting the housework go, eating junk food, were part of their chosen life-style in which they were restricted by the over-protective attitude of their social worker. By contrast, the social worker defined her actions in terms of protecting users from any negative consequences of their behaviour as well as ensuring the most effective and efficient use of local authority resources.

Practitioners were generally concerned about their role in allocating the scarce resources of the department which employed them. We found, at times, that practitioners dealt with these concerns by expressing moral judgements about the people who were seeking help from social services. People who appeared knowledgeable about their entitlements could find themselves labelled by practitioners as 'demanding'. People who tried to exercise choice or challenge workers' judgements could be described as 'fussy' or 'manipulative' (Ellis 1993).

As Smith and Harris (1972) pointed out over 20 years ago, a 'moral ideology' is the most effective means by which social workers responsible for both assessing need and determining eligibility for services can ration scarce resources. Our study suggests that the practice of most practitioners is more likely to be informed by moral judgements than by a set of attitudes and practices reflecting a commitment to working in an open, sharing and anti-oppressive way with service users. This form of 'moralising', buttressed by a medical model of disability and a concern with rationing scarce resources, is inconsistent with the tenets of anti-discriminatory practice. On the occasions that we identified a different type of practice, it was significant that the workers concerned shared an approach to practice which encompassed far more than their social services brief. Social workers supporting the deaf community in both local authorities identified their task as tackling wider structural and attitudinal barriers by raising awareness of disabling policies and practices locally. In their work with individuals they assisted users in overcoming low confidence and limited expectations through information, advocacy and support in accessing a range of resources jointly identified as necessary to increase individuals' choice in, and control over, their lives.

'ENFORCED ALTRUISM'

Gendered patterns of caring

The government acknowledges the primary role of informal carers in the mixed economy of welfare from which resources for community care are drawn – 'most support for vulnerable people is provided by families, friends and neighbours' (DoH 1990: 28). Although estimates vary (Arber *et al.* 1988; Green 1988; Parker 1989), studies have consistently indicated it is women who predominate in providing informal care for adults of all ages (Baldwin and Twigg 1991). The current debates on community care, and the policies and social work practices emerging in local authorities, have a particular impact on the gendered world of caring, relating to the roles and the responsibilities which individuals assume as family members.

Since 1979 governments have explicitly placed issues about the division of responsibilities between the individual, the family and the state on social policy and social work agendas. As part of an ideological commitment to reinforce citizen independence, families have been encouraged to take care of their members and change the perceived relationship of dependency between individual and state and family and state. Concern has been expressed by politicians about the family's failure to take responsibility not only for children but for adults needing support and care. Decreasing dependency on state services has meant a call for increased dependence by individuals on their immediate family as well as members of their extended family. The role of the state is increasingly to ensure that families fulfil their obligations to support their members – substitute services available to individuals in crisis have become more limited. Social workers, working with individuals, families and communities who lack resources, have found themselves being called on to support this vision of the resourceful family.

As research has shown (Ungerson 1987; Qureshi and Walker, 1989; Finch and Mason 1993), what families can and do offer their members is negotiated as part of a complex interaction of duty, obligation and responsibility where choices are constrained by economic, social and cultural factors. Within this context 'rights, duties and obligations work differently for women and men in practice' (Finch 1989: 143). The evidence is that women are faced with more pressures to deliver care and more conflicts about who from the range of needy family members to provide care for (Lewis and Meredith 1988). In Schorr's view 'Informal care within the family is not a simple matter of altruism' (Schorr 1992: 9).

In distinguishing 'caring for' and 'caring about', feminist writers on informal caring have identified its duality. The physical tasks of tending are intertwined with the emotional content of the caring relationship. Because the provision of care is so intimately tied up with female identity, women feel a strong sense of obligation to take on the caring role. At the same time

> The sense of love or responsibility that may be involved in giving care is mixed with a feeling that past favours are being returned or current or future favours will be rendered. It is mixed also with the expectation that, in a market economy, payment is due for some kinds of services and a conviction that the roles of state and family are distinguishable. While some things are expected from the family other things are expected from the state.
>
> (Schorr 1992: 9–10)

To describe the care provided by relatives and friends as 'free', as did a recent Audit Commission report (Audit Commission 1992a: 3), is to ignore not only the physical and emotional costs of caring, but also the material disadvantages women experience as a result of the low social and economic value attached to paid and unpaid caring work and their unequal status in the labour market (Leat 1988).

Land and Rose (1985) use the term 'compulsory altruism' to capture this conjunction of powerful cultural assumptions underlying the role of informal carers and the state's reliance on their cheap labour. The desired relationship between statutory providers and carers is deemed to be one of 'mutual support' and 'shared responsibility' (DoH 1990: 28). Yet guidance on eligibility criteria for community care services suggests that, in reality, only those who evidence 'high burdens' will qualify for help (SSI 1991b: 53). Recent studies of existing practice indicate local authority services are targeted on people without carers (Arber et al. 1988; Qureshi and Walker 1989; Parker 1990). The 1994 Carers' National Association survey of carers' experiences of the first year of the full implementation of the National Health Service and Community Care Act revealed that four out of five carers surveyed found that implementation had made no difference to them. Three-quarters of the carers reported that the person they cared for had not been assessed by social services and only 8 per cent of carers said they had received new or additional support during the year (CNA 1994).

The costs of the 'enforced altruism' demanded of informal carers are also borne by those receiving care from partners and other relatives (Locker 1983; Morris 1989, 1993; Parker 1989). Suggesting that the underlying meaning of 'caring for' is custodial, Morris argues that the physical tasks of caring should be separated from the relationship, or the 'caring about'. Because informal caring

situations can entail a loss of reciprocity in close personal relationships, the autonomy of the person receiving the care is restricted; at
worst they are vulnerable to abuse. Older and disabled people
should, she maintains, be able to choose and direct their own
personal care, provided from outside the confines of close personal
relationships.

The language of community care policy reinforces the identity of
older and disabled people as 'vulnerable', 'sick and dependent' and
in need of care, at the same time obscuring the extent to which they
are active participants in the life of the household and wider community. The medicalisation of need inherent in organisational and
professional definitions underlines societal assumptions that a physical inability to perform certain tasks means an overall inability on
the part of older and disabled people to take control of their lives.
The idea that service users act as their own care managers attracts
very lukewarm official endorsement (DoH 1990: 25; SSI 1991b:
21–2).

If reducing public expenditure is accepted as the underlying
agenda for community care reforms, then this apparently odd juxta-
position between a positive valuation of independence and choice on
the one hand and a reinforcement of care and dependency on the
other becomes more intelligible. In official documentation, promoting independence is negatively interpreted as non-interference in
people's lives. 'Formal intervention should be kept to the minimum
necessary in the interests of all concerned' (SSI 1991b: 62). But just
whose interests are served? A policy of managing physical dependency 'in the family' is fundamentally different from the ideals of
the independent living movement which stress that the right to
autonomy of disabled people can only be secured by having choice
in and control over personal assistance (statement drawn up at
Strasbourg Independent Living Experts seminar, quoted in Bornat
et al. 1993: 269–71; see also Barnes 1991; Morris 1993).

Autonomy is not just about physical functioning; it is also about
the opportunity for social participation (Doyal and Gough 1991).
Yet the primary site of social care is a person's own home. Although
SSI guidance recommends full assessments to take account of
people's interpersonal, health, social and financial needs, not only
are such assessments to be rationed but a far wider definition of
community care would be required to make a reality of the support
implied. Ironically, targeting those most at risk of entering residential care is unlikely to prevent a wider group of older and disabled

people being 'institutionalised' by the low level of support in the community (Morris 1993).

Conservative individualism reinforces a tendency in community care policy and practice to miss out the social and interpersonal context of people's lives. The exigencies of informal caring routines and the centring of services on physical functioning often prevent older and disabled people from sustaining their customary role within the household. Yet to maintain reciprocity, the management of dependence has to be continually negotiated and renegotiated both within caring relationships and between participants and their informal network and statutory agencies (Blaxter 1976; Locker 1983; Parker 1989; Qureshi and Walker 1989; Ellis 1993; Morris 1993). Gender, age, class, 'race', sexuality have all been shown to influence the outcome of negotiations within caring relationships. Although there is a dearth of work on the meaning of care for working-class households, or within gay and lesbian or Black and minority ethnic communities, there is sufficient evidence to suggest that the heterogeneity of caring situations is at odds with the rationalised techniques for controlling human and material resources which underpin community care reforms (Mirza 1991).

The extent to which the implementation of reforms can minimise dependency for both carer and person cared for, and offer each increased choice and control over their lives, will help determine the continuing existence of 'enforced altruism'. The part that social workers are playing in bolstering or challenging this pattern of caring raises a number of ethical dilemmas in practice.

Ethical dilemmas in practice

The ethical dilemmas facing social workers in their work with situations of 'enforced altruism' arise from at least two sources. The first is through working with the complex, and possibly incompatible, needs of users and carers, and the second is the way in which social workers are faced by demands to reduce the complex needs identified in caring relationships to resource-led needs criteria.

In our study the way in which service users negotiated with members of their households and neighbours was critical to their feelings of independence and well-being. A recurrent theme of interviews with users was the constant battle they faced in preventing others from taking control of areas of their life in which they could still exercise autonomy. Women becoming disabled, in particular, strove after independence in order to reclaim their accustomed role as care-givers. Yet, as in the case of an over-stretched carer who had to refuse his partner's wish to help with housework as 'just something else to organise', the exigencies of caring routines could reduce scope for independence. At the same time several couples were reluctant to involve members of their extended network in caring tasks for fear of disrupting carefully planned routines (Ellis 1993: 26–7).

We found that social workers stood out as a group in their awareness of the part played by family interactions and dynamics in caring. In comparison with other workers, who tended to view informal carers instrumentally as a means of maintaining the inde-pendence of the user, social workers displayed a greater awareness of the differing needs and responses to changed circumstances of all those concerned in caring situations (Ellis 1993: 31).

In working sensitively with informal caring situations, social work practice has to look explicitly at the way in which interde-pendence is experienced by those concerned. For people involved in informal caring situations who wish that relationship to continue, social work practice needs to focus on supporting participants to negotiate their interdependence as equitably as possible, helping them to obtain the level and type of resources which best support that arrangement. However, evidence from our study suggested that a lack of time and other resources can compromise workers' abili-ties to engage in the kind of work required to prevent caring situations breaking down.

Social workers have traditionally been responsible for accom-modating the complexity and individuality of people's living situa-tions within the confines of bureaucratic decision making. The greater formalisation of practice poses a threat to such flexibility. SSI guidance points to the tension between capturing the indivi-duality of need and the use of standardised recording devices in care management and assessment (SSI 1991a: 47, 1991b: 56). However, conflating the recording of need with the management of budgets – in assessment pro-formas and care plans – may turn out to be a more significant source of distortion.

In our study, social workers displayed some resistance to the standardisation of needs recording which they saw as undermining their ability to respond sensitively and flexibly to unique situa-tions. Moreover, they believed the unskilled task of information-gathering had to be distinguished from expert interpretation of that information. Yet expert interpretation meant, at times, screening out the priorities of users and carers. For example, one social worker refused to pursue a couple's request for additional domiciliary support while the carer was recovering from an operation on the grounds that the user was 'over-focused on practical issues'. The user's angry response to this decision was attributed by the worker to unresolved psychological problems around sight loss (Ellis 1993: 30).

Given the weak rights of users, user empowerment depends on open practice. The duality of assessment is presented as sequential in Social Services Inspectorate guidance – need is assessed before eligibility is determined. The assumptions on which this approach is based have resonances with those underlying the Seebohm Report on which unified social services departments were founded in the early 1970s. Need was seen to have tangible properties and was amenable to measurement and assessment. However, phenomeno-logical research undertaken in the early days of the reformed services suggests that the concept of need is inseparable from the activities and attitudes of assessors (Rees 1978; Smith 1980). Our study indicates that the exigencies of rationing, not least front-line practitioners' time, continue to compromise the objectivity, creativity and breadth of the assessment approach assumed by most recent reforms. The research also suggests that the restrictive practices of 'street-level bureaucrats' (Lipsky 1980) are still relevant to practice in the 1990s. To survive difficult encounters practitioners exercise their discretion in irrational, covert and punitive ways, blocking information about resources, making stereotyped responses and basing decisions on moral judgements about the deservingness and undeservingness of those seeking help (Ellis 1993; see also Satyamurti 1981).

Practitioners can choose to use their discretion positively in the interests of the user or negatively in their own interests or those of their department. Stevenson and Parsloe suggest the choices made depend on the orientation of individual practitioners (Stevenson and Parsloe 1993: 10), a view supported by our research. Pursuing users' and carers' interests within severe resource constraints demands a personal commitment on the part of practitioners to advocate on behalf of people in need. Individuals can find themselves as a result of this approach feeling 'out of step' with colleagues and the wider organisation. With a Social Services Inspectorate directive recom-mending that unmet need identified during assessment should not be disclosed to users for fear of legal action against authorities, ethical dilemmas in this area are likely to be heightened.

Anti-oppressive practice suggests that social workers have a part to play in challenging the underlying values and interests of policies for which they have a responsibility to implement. Yet the version of citizenship underlying community care policy, which stresses an obligation to fend for oneself rather than a right to support when in need, appears inconsistent with such an emphasis on equity and social justice.

Performance measures devised primarily to constrain expenditure and reinforce top-down control cannot empower users, carers or workers; final prioritisation will continue to be determined by departments. Furthermore, an undertaking to feed unmet need into service development means only that, at some unspecified date, the individual concerned may or may not benefit under conditions largely beyond her or his control. To further equity and democracy, managerialist techniques of control have to be countered by the politics of representation and participation in which practitioners work not only with individual service users but also with groups and user-led organisations.

Because the formalisation of policy and practice is as much about excluding as giving people access, the potential of anti-oppressive practice is to exert a counterbalancing force, instilling in the less powerful a sense of their entitlement to help, and providing the knowledge and support with which to exercise their rights (Rees, 1991). Information-giving may mean more than simply iterating service criteria or agency procedures; adequacy may mean more than satisfying performance measures; and ensuring that people's interests are represented may mean more than using departmental complaints procedures. Given the extent of inequality in other areas of people's lives, practitioners' expectations may often be modest. Yet 'choice about small issues represents small victories' (Stevenson and Parsloe 1993: 8).

In the emerging territory of community care such victories are likely to be hard won, and there is little evidence as yet of collective dialogue and strategising to support individual practitioners who choose to challenge and advocate. Social workers in community care need to extend their understanding of the political, professional and personal influences which are shaping their practice. They need to take account of the experiences of service users as well as the impact of wider social, economic and cultural forces on caring situations. These developments are essential if social workers are to open up their community care practice to ethical considerations and give primacy to the interests of a vulnerable and increasingly dispossessed group of users and carers.

BIBLIOGRAPHY

Arber, S., Gilbert, N. and Evandrou, M. (1988) 'Gender, household composition and receipt of domiciliary services by elderly disabled people', *Journal of Social Policy* **17** (2): 153–75.

Audit Commission (1992a) *Community Care: Managing the Cascade of Change*, London: HMSO.

—— (1992b) *The Community Revolution: Personal Social Services and Community Care*, London. HMSO.

Baldock, J. (1993) 'Old age', in R. Dallos and E. McLaughlin (eds) *Social Problems and the Family*, London: Sage.

Baldwin, S. and Twigg, J. (1991) 'Women and community care – reflections on a debate', in M. Maclean and D. Groves (eds) *Women's Issues in Social Policy*, London: Routledge.

Barnes, C. (1991) *Disabled People in Britain and Discrimination, A Case for Anti-Discrimination Legislation*, London: Hurst / University of Calgary.

Blaxter, M. (1976) *The Meaning of Disability*, London: Heinemann.

Bornat, J., Pereira, C., Pilgrim, D. and Williams, F. (eds) (1993) *Community Care: A Reader*, Basingstoke: Macmillan.

BPQP (Bradford Post Qualifying Partnership) (1991) 'Antiracism requirements and the Diploma in Social Work', in *One Small Step Towards Racial Justice*, London: CCETSW.

Bulmer, M. (1987) *The Social Basis of Community Care*, London: Unwin Hyman.

CCETSW (1991) *DipSW: Rules and Requirements for the Diploma in Social Work (Paper 30)* (2nd edn), London: CCETSW.

CNA (Carers' National Association) (1994) *Community Care – Just a Fairy Tale?* London: Focus.

Cochrane, A. and Clarke, J. (eds) (1993) *Comparing Welfare States: Britain in International Context*, London: Sage.

DoH (Department of Health) (1989) *Caring for People, Community Care in the Next Decade and Beyond* (Cmd. 849), London: HMSO.

—— (1990) *Community Care in the Next Decade and Beyond*, London: HMSO.

Doyal, L. and Gough, I. (1991) *A Theory of Human Need*, Basingstoke: Macmillan.

Ellis, K. (1993) *Squaring the Circle: User and Carer Participation in Needs Assessment*, Community Care/Joseph Rowntree Foundation.

Finch, J. (1989) *Family Obligations and Social Change*, Cambridge: Polity Press.

Finch, J. and Mason, J. (1993) *Negotiating Family Responsibilities*, London: Routledge.

Glennerster, H. (1992) *Paying for Welfare: The 1990s*, London: Harvester Wheatsheaf.

Green, H. (1988) *Informal Carers: A Study*. London: OPCS/HMSO.

Hallett, C. (1991) 'The Children Act and community care: comparisons and contrasts', *Policy and Politics* **19** (4).

Hills, J. (1990) *The State of Welfare*, Oxford: Clarendon Press.

Johnson, N. (1990) *Reconstructing the Welfare State*, London: Harvester Wheatsheaf.

Land, H. and Rose, H. (1985) 'Compulsory altruism for some or an altruistic society for all', in P. Bean, J. Ferris and D. Whynes (eds) *In Defence of Welfare*, London: Tavistock.

Langan, M. (1990) 'Community care in the 1990s', *Critical Social Policy* **29**: 58–70.

Langan, M. and Day, L. (eds) (1992) *Women, Oppression and Social Work: Issues in Anti-discriminatory Practice*, London: Routledge.

Lawson, R. (1993) 'The new technology of management in the personal social services', in P. Taylor-Gooby and R. Lawson (eds) *Markets and Managers: New Issues in the Delivery of Welfare*, Milton Keynes: Open University Press.

Leat, D. (1988) 'Using social security payments to encourage non-kin caring', in S. Baldwin, G. Parker and R. Walker (eds) *Social Security and Community Care*, Aldershot: Avebury.

Lewis, J. and Meredith, B. (1988) *Daughters Who Care: Daughters Caring for Mothers at Home*, London: Routledge & Kegan Paul.

Lipsky, M. (1980) *Street-Level Bureaucracy*, New York: Russell Sage.

Locker, D. (1983) *Disability and Disadvantage: The Consequences of Chronic Illness*, London: Tavistock.

Mirza, K. (1991) 'Community care for the Black community: waiting for guidance', in *One Small Step Towards Racial Justice*, London: CCETSW.

Moroney, R. (1976) *The Family and the State: Considerations for Social Policy*, London: Longman.

Morris, J. (ed.) (1989) *Able Lives*, London: The Women's Press.

—— (1993) *Community Care or Independent Living?*, Community Care/ Joseph Rowntree Foundation.

Parker, G. (1989) *With This Body: Caring and Disability in Marriage*, Milton Keynes: Open University Press.

—— (1990) *With Due Care and Attention: A Review of the Literature on Informal Care* (2nd edn), London: Family Policy Studies Centre.

Qureshi, H. and Walker, A. (1989) *The Caring Relationship: Elderly People and their Families*, London: Macmillan.

Rees, S. (1978) *Social Work Face to Face*, London: Edward Arnold.

—— (1991) *Achieving Power, Practice and Policy in Social Welfare*, Sydney: Allen & Unwin.

Satyamurti, C. (1981) *Occupational Survival*, Oxford: Basil Blackwell.

Schorr, A. (1992) *The Personal Social Services: An Outside View*, Community Care/Joseph Rowntree Foundation.

Smith, G. (1980) *Social Need: Policy, Practice and Research*, London: Routledge & Kegan Paul.

Smith, G. and Harris, R. (1972) 'Ideologies of need and the organisation of social work departments', *British Journal of Social Work* **2** (1): 27–44.

SSI (Social Services Inspectorate) (1991a) *Care Management and Assessment: Managers' Guide*, London: HMSO.

—— (1991b) *Care Management and Assessment: Practitioners' Guide*, London: HMSO.

Stevenson, O. and Parsloe, P. (1993) *Community Care and Empowerment*, London: Community Care/Joseph Rowntree Foundation.

Taylor-Gooby, P. (1991) *Social Change, Social Welfare and Social Science*, London: Harvester Wheatsheaf.

Taylor-Gooby, P. and Lawson, R. (eds) (1993) *Markets and Managers: New Issues in the Delivery of Welfare*, Milton Keynes: Open University Press.

Timms, N. (1991) 'A new diploma for social work, or Dunkirk as total victory' in P. Carter, T. Jeffs and M. K. Smith (eds) *Social Work and Social Welfare Year Book 3*, Milton Keynes: Open University Press.

Trevillian, S. (1989) 'Griffiths and Wagner: which future for community care?', *Critical Social Policy* **24**: 65–73.

Twigg, J. (1989) 'Models of carers: how do social care agencies conceptualise their relationships with informal carers?', *Journal of Social Policy* **18** (1): 53–66.

Ungerson, C. (1987) *Policy is Personal: Sex, Gender and Informal Care*, London: Tavistock.

Walker, A. (ed.) (1982) *Community Care: The Family, the State and Social Policy*, Oxford: Blackwell and Robertson.

—— (1993) 'Community care policy: from consensus to conflict', in J. Bornat, C. Pereira, D. Pilgrim and F. Williams (eds) *Community Care: A Reader*, Basingstoke: Macmillan.

Watson, D. (ed.) (1985) *A Code of Ethics for Social Work: The Second Step*, London: Routledge & Kegan Paul.

Wilding, P. (1982) *Professional Power and Social Welfare*, London: Routledge & Kegan Paul.

Chapter 9

Can social work empower?

Julie Browne

INTRODUCTION

A new mood prevails over institutions such as the National Health Service, public education, the criminal justice system and social services. This has not been solely influenced by government moves such as the introduction of the Citizen's Charters, ostensibly in the direction of consumer rights, but has also been a product of consumer and pressure groups who are concerned with the representation of clients and accountability to them. Groups such as these offer a challenge both to the right of powerful institutions to define problems and solutions, and to the traditional hierarchical structures of these institutions wherein the client, patient, student or victim has the least input in determining policy directions. This chapter uses a specific area, social work and child sexual abuse, to examine whether individuals can be empowered while being subordinate to a hierarchical organisation. Ethical issues such as those involved in child sexual abuse cannot be discussed without consideration of the relative position of workers, clients and organisations involved in service provision. Child sexual abuse provides a useful illustration of these issues as it cuts across worker–client lines and challenges organisational responses to uncomfortable and difficult social problems.

During doctoral research on the approaches taken to the problem of child sexual abuse by different interest groups, the author compared those taken by welfare professionals to those adopted by survivors' organisations. These are organisations run for and by survivors which offer helping services and often carry out pressure group activities. The research indicated that not only were the activities and ideology distinctly different but there were also many structural and organisational differences between the professionals and the survivors. If the experiences of sexual abuse hold true for other areas, then it is argued in this chapter that, in order to empower, a new way of thinking needs to be adopted on the role of professionals in social work.

WHAT IS EMPOWERMENT?

Although ideas of empowerment, and their focus on consultation, user control and information are currently being used in the areas of race, disability and learning difficulties, this does not indicate a new trend in thinking. The school of radical social work flourished fifteen to twenty years ago, but has declined under the present government. Langan and Lee (1989) describe how the concept of empowerment evolved out of the radical social work movement.

> Radical social work sought to generate a wider awareness of the power that social workers had by virtue of their access to information and resources that were not readily available to service users. 'Empowerment' was the process of transferring this power into the hands of the people who were systematically denied it within the framework of the welfare state.
>
> (Langan and Lee 1989: 9)

'To empower' is defined by the *Oxford English Dictionary* as 'to impart power, to enable', and by *Roget's Thesaurus* as 'to endow and strengthen'. If we talk about empowering users of social services, therefore, we are talking about enabling them in some way. Enabling is defined by Roget as facilitating, unobstructing and unrestraining, and by the *OED* as 'supplying with means, opportunities or the like'. If we ask the question 'Can social work empower?' in cases of child sexual abuse, we are presumably asking whether it is possible to enable child victims to end their abuse by providing them with opportunities and strengthening them.

There is no obvious reason why the concept of empowerment should not be applied to all areas of social work, and its application in the field of child sexual abuse raises some issues in a particularly sharp form. Whereas social workers do not typically share their clients' experiences in cases of homelessness, old age and disability, there is an obvious overlap in childhood sexual abuse. As there is a rise in both awareness and training about child sexual abuse within and across professions it becomes more and more apparent that large numbers of social workers and other professionals who come into contact with abused children have themselves been abused. First, it is statistically unlikely that this would not be the case. A prevalence study carried out in the UK by Baker and Duncan (1985) found that 12 per cent of all females interviewed and 8 per cent of all males reported having been sexually abused before the age of 16, and the authors estimated that there are over 4.5 million adults in Great Britain who were sexually abused as children. The most recent survey on prevalence, carried out by Kelly *et al.* (1991), found that 27 per cent of women and 11 per cent of men had suffered some form of sexual abuse involving contact. These figures are likely to be an underestimate due to (1) a reluctance to disclose past abuse, even as an adult, (2) the fact that children may have been victimised by more than one offender and (3) an inability in adults to remember being abused. There is evidence that a young age or the trauma of the abuse may cause the experiences to be 'blocked out'. Home Office studies (1988) on convictions for child abuse show that children may be most at risk of sexual assault when aged between 5 and 9. Hobbs and Wynne (1987) note a high incidence of buggery in very young children. If sexual assault occurs when the victim is young it is unlikely that he or she will remember it.

Second, it is likely that survivors of sexual abuse are over-represented among social workers, as childhood experiences may be a motivating factor for entry into social work and the other 'caring' professions. During the course of research carried out by the author, evidence was collected that many social workers, teachers and other health professionals frequently suffer emotional stress during training sessions on sexual abuse as memories of their own abuse become too painful, and that training or casework can trigger off memories for the first time.

There is a considerable reluctance within these professions, however, to acknowledge the possibility that social workers and other professionals have either specific needs or skills as a result of their childhood sexual abuse. This has led Summit to comment:

> We are all players in a strange charade in which everyone assumes the role of the untouched. Perpetrators circulate in unknown numbers, making policy and influencing opinion, while a horde of survivors shrinks from one another as if each were the enemy.
>
> (Summit 1988: 45)

A failure to address this issue not only results in increased stress suffered by child abuse survivors working within the caring professions, but also has implications for their ability to ameliorate the effects of child sexual abuse or attempt its prevention. This chapter will examine some of the explanations for this failure within social work and ask if social work is able to empower either its own workers or its users.

SOCIAL WORK AND CHILD SEXUAL ABUSE

A considerable body of evidence and commentary exists which argues that the current methods of dealing with child sexual abuse, which are heavily biased towards criminal investigation and prosecution of the offender, are not empowering to the child in the sense that they neither offer child victims real opportunities to end the abuse nor serve to strengthen their position.

It is an undisputed fact that the majority of child victims never disclose their abuse, with the consequence that only a small proportion come to the attention of the social services. Using prevalence studies such as those mentioned above and government statistics (OPCS 1989), it is possible to estimate that there are at least 200,000 new cases of sexual abuse every year. Childline has reported up to 10,000 attempted calls a day, yet children rarely give their names or addresses. Spink and Tutt (1989: 314–15) question the adequacy of telephone helplines.

> There is a great reluctance on the part of many of these callers to reveal their full identity. Children are nearly always aware of the more extreme consequences of disclosure, both the reactions inside and outside the family. . . . Whilst these children undoubtedly appear to be receiving therapeutic help through the telephone counselling, how to find ways to encourage them or their families to come forward and seek help in preventing the recurrence of the abuse must be the single most significant question facing our services to children today.

The NSPCC report that in 1989/90 only 4.5 per cent of referrals came from children themselves (NSPCC 1990); this is despite having a Child Protection Helpline with publicity directed at children. The facts speak for themselves: children are reluctant to avail themselves of the 'opportunities' current social work intervention presents. While there may be more media attention to child sexual abuse and more open discussion about the subject, there has been little which might encourage children to believe that the options presented by disclosure have either increased or improved. The media attention paid to Cleveland, to Orkney and to the Frank Beck cases of abuse in care would do little to encourage a child to overcome the fear that being a victim of abuse engenders. When we look at the options of (a) criminal prosecution of the perpetrator (b) civil proceedings possibly leading to local authority care and fostering and/or (c) some form of therapy, we may begin to understand why they are not necessarily viewed favourably by child victims of sexual abuse.

At present only cases in which there is good medical evidence, an admission of guilt, a strong statement by the child or strong corroborative evidence are likely to result in a successful conviction. As there is physical evidence in only 5–15 per cent of cases (estimated by Faller 1989 and Schultz 1979), as the rules against hearsay limit admissible corroborative evidence, and as it is hardly in the accused's interests to admit guilt, convictions are hard to obtain. Even where there is a strong statement by a child, the Crown Prosecution Service is often reluctant to proceed with the prosecution if it is strongly considered that the child may retract his or her accusation under family pressure, or may break down under cross-examination. Social workers interviewed by Campbell commented:

> Our training tells us we should not interview children, even as witnesses, without their parents being present. But you can't expect a girl to be forthcoming in front of her parents if the abuse is intra-family – how can she say what's happened, knowing it will shatter the family? I can't think of anything more difficult. That's why you get a high rate of retraction. Retraction is part of the overall thing. When a child realises the enormity of it, she often retracts.
>
> (Campbell 1988: 107)

The child needs to have good verbal skills, but many sexually abused children are too young or too distressed to provide the required testimony. Both Faller (1989) and Krieger and Robbins (1985) note that children may be further damaged by the requirements of the legal process and court testimony. Ordway (1983: 69) comments:

After suffering the probes of investigators, prosecutors and others, the victim faces the ordeal of testifying in court where she may be accused of seductive behaviour, lying or wanting to hurt her family or father. Because of the combination of the incest taboo, the victim's youth and the victim's close relationship with the accused, the present pretrial interview process and testifying in court may cause the child severe emotional distress, confusion and feelings of guilt.

The trauma of disclosure, of court testimony and the subsequent break up of the family, not surprisingly, leads many children to regret making the disclosure. Peace and McMaster (1989) comment that it is as if the current criminal procedure 'had been determined by a team of child molesters'. Given recent revelations about organised abuse, perhaps this is not far from the truth. Just how traumatic a court appearance can be is illustrated by Kelly's (1992) observations of the experiences of abused, disabled children in court. One child had severe hearing difficulties and another was doubly incontinent:

> The defence counsel had laughed at the child's difficulty in hearing and said, 'Can't hear or is it that you don't want to answer?' One of the other children was humiliated by the defence counsel saying, 'Who would want a smelly, shitty boy on their lap, no one hugs smelly, shitty boys like you'. The child was giving evidence on video-link and became so upset he was 'switched off' so that he was no longer visible to the court.
>
> (Kelly 1992: 189)

The boys' carers reported that subsequent to the case they suffered from nightmares and a fear of male figures in positions of authority. For another account of the abusive nature of criminal justice proceedings see Dunhill (1989). The author recounts the experiences of Helen, who suffered abuse by her father and a group of other men for many years. The insensitive and traumatic treatment she suffered through the police and court system led Helen to comment: 'They just treat you as if you're the one who has done something wrong. There's no way if you've been to them once, you'll ever want to go to them again.'

Although suggestions have been made on how to improve the position of children appearing as witnesses in criminal prosecution, including the removal of wigs and gowns by court personnel, video-links, allowing the introduction of video-taped evidence, the use of child advocates (Reifen 1984; Morgan and Zedner 1992), allowing hearsay evidence (Peace and McMaster 1989) and the preparation of children for court appearances, it is still debatable how far these changes would minimise the trauma suffered by the child. Despite the fact that the Criminal Justice Act (1991) gives a judge discretion on whether to allow cross-examination via video-links, the defence still maintains the right to cross-examine the child and to attempt to destroy and discredit his or her testimony. O'Hara (1989) reports that in the US and Canada, where pre-recorded video evidence has been used for some time, videos are increasingly being used by defence counsel to challenge a child's evidence. This is done by identifying apparent discrepancies between the video evidence and the child's evidence in court; another strategy is to allege the use of 'leading' questions by the adults conducting the video-taped interview.

It seems likely that for a significant number of children, staying in the home and being abused is preferable to the range of options social work has to offer. Another alternative, running away from the abusive situation, also seems to some to be preferable to social services intervention. Kelly (1988) reports that all but two of the 15 incest survivors she interviewed had considered running away but realised that there was nowhere they could go, or that they were too young to survive on their own. Many children, both male and female, leave anyway and end up homeless and/or involved in prostitution, child pornography and drugs (Silbert and Pines 1981; Briere and Runtz 1987). Nearly 100,000 children run away from home every year, and in a study reported by Newman (1989), 18 per cent of children admitted to a 'safe house' voluntarily disclosed sexual abuse. Further sexual abuse while in care, by carers, other children and foster parents, is not unknown.

While social workers may feel that it is their statutory obligations and lack of resources that prevent them from addressing some aspects of the problems inherent in child sexual abuse, others are more within their power to change. Feminists and others (Armstrong 1978; Russell 1984; Sheppard 1982; Rush 1980; Kelly 1988) have argued that the steps being taken to deal with child sexual abuse are piecemeal and inadequate because they are being proposed and adopted without sufficient consideration of the social context in which child sexual abuse occurs. Because of this failure it can be argued that social work is not merely impotent in any meaningful attempt to tackle sexual abuse, but that by adopting a pathologising, stigmatising approach to the problem, it actually promulgates it. In one view:

> Psychiatrists, sociologists, psychologists and social workers have become the new administrators of the power structure. In the measure that they soothe conflicts, break down resistance, and 'solve' the problems created by situational realities, they perpetuate the global violence by convincing the individuals to accommodate the oppressive conditions.
>
> (Mebane-Francescato and Jones 1974: 104)

There is only limited availability of therapy due to a lack of resources, facilities and trained personnel, and even when available it may not be provided to a child who will have to testify in court (which may be years in the future), for fear of 'tainting' their evidence. Despite being heavily criticised by feminists (e.g. Nelson 1987; Rush 1980), family therapy still holds considerable sway in this country and may be the only type of therapy offered. Family therapy not only requires both parents to admit joint responsibility for the incest, but it is also usually based on the assumption that the successful outcome of the programme is to reunite families. Berliner, on the other hand, believes that:

> Most kids after incest don't in fact feel closeness or affection towards the father, so they are put in a psychological bind which is reinforced by most mental health professionals who believe that all children want to stay with their families and that is better for them.
>
> (Quoted in Fairclough 1983: 30)

Although social work as a profession can hardly be blamed for the use and misuse of children in society and its lack of awareness of children's needs and feelings, it is possible to lay blame at its door for a significant failure to address the needs of its own workers. In many ways the treatment of social workers who are survivors replicates that of sexually abused children. The question has to be asked: How can any organisation which manifests this type of behaviour ever hope to empower others? An awareness of this issue and an attempt to empower its own workers could encourage a redefinition by social workers of the problem of child sexual abuse – and therefore of its solutions.

SOCIAL WORKERS AS SURVIVORS

Despite the fact that the incidence of child sexual abuse is known to cut across all barriers of class, race, gender and disability, there still seems a reluctance to accept that survivors also form a substantial proportion of the caring professionals. Many of the workers who deal with child sexual abuse cases, including teachers, doctors, nurses, social workers, probation officers, psychologists and the police, have been sexually abused themselves. Yet at a recent conference the organiser stressed that the conference was aimed at *professionals*. One delegate felt the need to stand up and stress that it wasn't that simple, as many of those attending would also be survivors. Where sexual abuse survivors have disclosed their past abuse to colleagues and management there has not just been a lack of support but also more direct repercussions. Margaret Kennedy of the National Deaf Children's Society and BASPCAN (the British Association for the Study and Prevention of Child Abuse and Neglect) commented on cases she has known. 'Some disclosures have had dire consequences – being taken off cases, being moved and generally having their professionalism questioned' (Kennedy 1992). Yet workers who are forced to deny their own abuse face a conflict between their exhortations to their clients to disclose abuse and their own feelings of having to keep a shameful secret (Doyle 1991). They are painfully aware, while trying to reassure children that they can put the abusive incidents behind them and recover, that the reality is that many of their colleagues still view childhood sexual abuse as conferring a degree of pathology and/or tend to regard a survivor with a prurient sexual curiosity (Kennedy 1993).

There seems to be a variety of explanations as to why social work has failed its own workers. The first is that social workers are notoriously under-resourced and over-stressed, with burn-out in child protection work being common. They may feel that the additional 'burden' of colleagues suffering personal difficulties cannot be countenanced. A second explanation is an uneasiness with sexual abuse despite working with it; as one ex-therapist commented to me, 'in many ways it is easier to say you've got AIDS than you were sexually abused'. One ex-social worker told me: 'A social work office is the worst place to have personal problems. Despite our caring, supportive image you were encouraged to remain detached, to "not get involved" with clients or their problems. Pretty soon you became detached and uncaring about each others' problems and then your own families' and friends' problems.' The third explanation concerns the need to keep a rigid distinction between 'professional' and 'user'. The respondent above explained: 'You weren't allowed to discuss your own personal life because then the barriers between them and us broke down, and that couldn't happen because we were the "professionals" and they were the needy ones.' So it seems as though barriers are erected in order to avoid the necessity of facing the lack of distinction between clients and workers. A fourth explanation is, paradoxically, that survivors of sexual abuse who have 'dealt with' their own abuse *are* recognised to have certain skills, and extra sensitivity in dealing with cases of sexual abuse (Briere 1990). One project, where the childhood sexual abuse of the workers involved was openly acknowledged, reports: 'many of the most effective social workers, foster carers and other professionals in the field of sexual abuse are also survivors themselves' (Pringle 1990: 93).

One worker who was abused comments that when she began working in child protection she felt comfortable with dealing with child sexual abuse victims, whereas other workers felt horror or disgust. An awareness that this difference exists may threaten those who do not have these skills.

Stanton (1990: 125) notes that:

> closed, controlling, hierarchical staff relations undermine attempts to work openly, equally and in ways that respect the rights of people who use the agency. Individuals and small groups struggle to make improvements despite what goes on in an office or department.

What workers need, Stanton argues, is more effective communication and work environments where people can feel confident that they can be open and honest about their views, doubts and feelings. Whatever the reason, or combination of reasons, for a failure to recognise the true impact of child sexual abuse, it is essential that efforts are made to resist the tendency to pathologise, and to distance the problem of child sexual abuse from the widespread experience it really is. What is needed is a readiness to recognise that clients and social workers, survivors and non-survivors, are all human. Each member of each group is going to have problems at some time. Pathologising these problems may also mean de-humanising. Once the label of 'dysfunctional family', or 'non-protective mother', has been attached, 'clients' may cease to have human rights. Angela

Rivera (1989), a counsellor with ISOSAC (In Support of Sexually Abused Children), a voluntary organisation, quotes from a conversation she had with a social worker. When she talked about avoiding a 'them and us' attitude when working with mothers, the social worker commented, 'Yes, we must bring ourselves down to their level.' Once this approach has become the norm anyone who experiences difficulties becomes tarred with the same brush. Actual requirements for support, however, may be tremendously varied: they may relate to social, psychological, emotional, family, legal or personal matters. It is undoubtedly the case that social workers do need support in these areas, just like anyone else. Doyle (1991) writes of how one social work colleague felt pushed to the edge of suicide after having taken part in a child sexual abuse training session. Social workers, just like their clients, must be able to obtain information, support, counselling and, if they feel it necessary, therapy, whether mainstream psychotherapeutic or alternative. If these are not available, and if in addition there is a punitive, stigmatising atmosphere, well-qualified and well-motivated staff are going to consider leaving the field of child protection or social work altogether.

What ought to be done, therefore, to make social work more empowering for its workers and its clients?

EMPOWERING SOCIAL WORK

To survivors of child sexual abuse, empowerment means having a real choice of different courses of action. At present, as Wyre (1991) comments:

> We don't seem to be able to get round that the system models the very abusing system that the child is in. The abuser is using the child for his own purposes, his interest isn't in the welfare or the care of the child, and of course the moment the child tells, basically, we are going to use the child to get evidence against a person, and therefore anything that might hinder that or any therapeutic approach which might help the child, is then deemed influencing and affecting the child as a witness.

Some commentators (e.g. Findlay 1988; Neate 1991) have argued that non-statutory solutions such as the Confidential Doctor service offered in Holland and Belgium provide a service to the child which does work at the child's pace, and, due to the rarity of criminal proceedings, evidence which will stand up in court is hardly ever needed. Other choices range from a child having the right to choose between a male or female social worker or therapist to having a choice of safe living accommodation. Newman (1989) describes a safe house for runaways, which clearly indicates the need for this type of accommodation. She writes:

> It is perhaps in the area of child sexual abuse that the need for a confidential place of safety for young people to go has proved to be of paramount importance because before the opening of the project young runaways were frequently returned home to their abusers. Another positive advantage of having a safe house where young people can stay for a period of time is that it allows time for trust to be built up before a disclosure is made. Several young people disclosed sexual abuse only on their second or third admission to CLTP after a long period of time. Workers were providing the right climate of safety, belief and understanding for the young people to disclose. It may have also been that some young people had not previously disclosed sexual abuse simply because no one had broached the subject or asked them if they had been abused.
>
> (Newman 1989: 133)

Fairtlough (1983) describes a refuge set up in Holland which was set up as a complementary service to those offered by social services:

> Working in collaboration with the social services the refuge offers space for girls to review their lives and make plans for the future. The workers believe that the specific needs of girls in residential care are not recognised and they point to the case of a girl who came to the refuge after being raped in a children's home. Not surprisingly the refuge rapidly became full. Sheltered housing schemes for older girls and the recruitment of female foster parents willing to care for the younger ones are being developed to overcome this problem.
>
> (Fairtlough 1983: 27)

Others see empowerment in term of knowledge, and therefore have an emphasis on providing children with information about sex, about abuse and about where they can go for guidance and support should they need it. Rape Crisis and survivors' groups have provided leaflets for school children, entitled, for example, 'Your Body Your Rights', and have run awareness days on sexual abuse, as well as 'No means No' campaigns. Kelly (1988) recounts how, as children, the women in her study felt that their limited knowledge of anatomy and sexuality meant that they had no words to describe what had happened. All the incidents were, at the time, confusing and in many cases frightening. None of the adults who were told about the sexual abuse subsequently provided the girls with correct information about what had happened to them.

> At the time the abuse began, most of the incest survivors interviewed did not know the names of the sexual organs. This, coupled with the verbal strategies the abusive men used to rationalise their actions and/or prevent disclosure, gave them very few ways to make sense of what was happening to them. This, in turn, meant that they were less likely to tell anyone else.
>
> (Kelly 1988: 142)

As Dominelli (1989: 300) comments:

> innocence is used to deny children access to certain types of information. Lack of information increases a child's powerlessness because knowledge is itself a form of power. As a child's access to information is largely controlled by adults including its parents, parental power can also be increased via this route.

Another area which is felt to be important is contact with other survivors. Survivor organisations often run newsletters and magazines with names such as 'Fighting Back' and 'Speaking Out'. They recognise that the knowledge that there are other survivors 'out there' is empowering in itself. During research carried out by the author it was found that many adult survivors, having attended survivors' groups, felt the need to 'do something' about child sexual abuse. This often involved becoming active within survivors' groups and becoming volunteer counsellors, trainers and administrators. Survivors' groups generally carry out activities which raise awareness of the nature of child sexual abuse and their right to speak about it. Motivated, articulate and increasingly visible, they represent a strong model of empowerment which contrasts sharply with the practices found within social work. Perhaps, therefore, it is with the survivors' movement that social work needs to forge links if it is to attempt to be truly empowering. The survivors' organisations interviewed in the author's research are committed to providing services which are, as one respondent commented, 'very much what we would have wanted as kids'. Interviews with survivors carried out by the author revealed that the three most important components of help they would have liked as children were:

1 Readily accessible information and avenues of help.
2 Reliable, trustworthy adults who would have believed them and then helped.
3 Real alternatives as to the steps they could have taken: for some this would have been therapy, for others, safe accommodation.

Survivors' organisations are aware of the needs of survivors because many of them operate in a non-hierarchical way, and engage in consultation with their members on all policy issues. In addition, they perform a constant user-evaluation of the services they offer and encourage feedback and discussion. A further commitment is made to under-represented groups. When monitoring of users reveals an absence of ethnic minorities, survivors with disabilities, and gay or older survivors, attempts are made to reach these groups and, if necessary, to make special provision for them. They particularly note the need for black and Asian workers to be available to support the needs of survivors from these groups.

While social workers may claim to be under-resourced, survivors' groups often have no resources and frequently operate from home and with volunteer help. Yet many social workers are unaware of the work of the survivors' movement and of other voluntary programmes such as Newpin and Parents Anonymous. Rarely, if ever, are they discussed in social work training. Despite the widespread endorsement of both the success and cost-effectiveness of programmes of this kind (see Cohn 1979; Daro 1988; McIvor 1990), which offer an alternative or complementary solution to statutory intervention and assistance, funds and recognition for the work of these groups are slow in arriving. Among the survivors' groups interviewed in the author's research none had formal channels of communication with social services, and they generally dismissed the possibility, because, as one commented, 'they have a different way of looking at the problem from us'.

So what is to be done? The Women's Support Project (WSP) recommend the setting up of workers' support groups. The WSP believes that these support groups can answer the needs for clear and practical information as well as team building, both in and between professions and in the community. They recommend that these groups should be open to workers and to interested individuals from a wide range of backgrounds, including volunteers, nursery school teachers, social workers, foster mothers, teachers, mothers, community education workers (or youth workers in England and Wales), Women's Aid workers and health visitors. Without exception, they comment, the groups have proved to be invaluable sources of information, support and shared experience. It is in this kind of context that workers who are survivors can be given permission to talk about sexual abuse. Sgroi (1982) describes how hearing someone else describe the dynamics and mechanics of child abuse 'in front of God and everybody' both validates the sexually abusive experience and at the same time releases the victim from the burden of keeping the guilty secret forever.

Second, links with survivors' groups can show social work how to help their workers. Support from colleagues, counselling if necessary, and open and frank discussion about personal difficulties and child sexual abuse cases are necessary. One model of this type of working is described by Pringle (1990). A willingness to acknowledge the existence of local groups, and to recommend them to, for example, mothers of abused children, as well as some allocation of resources, would also help. It is acknowledged, however, that there is likely to be considerable reluctance to take this step. Doyle (1991) reports that many social workers feel that they cannot go to Incest Survivor Groups as they might find that they are being helped by their own clients. This, they feel, would be an unacceptable role reversal. Unfortunately, it is difficult to see how social work can empower without exactly this type of role reversal.

Advocates of empowerment (e.g. Thompson 1993) note a professional tendency among social workers to emphasise both the weakness and dependence of their clients and their own strength and competence. Survivors would probably concur with Freidson (1972), quoted by Silbey and Sarat (1989), who argues that 'expertise is more and more in danger of being used as a mask for privilege and power than, as it claims, as a mode of enhancing the public interest'. It is this kind of 'them and us' mentality which has to be broken down before progress can be made in addressing the problem of child sexual abuse. As Pringle (1990: 93) comments:

Any approach which embraces a simple dichotomy between professionals, who have skills, and victims who have problems to be worked upon is doomed to failure. Our practice confirms what is increasingly clear from the literature, that the people best able to help victims of sexual abuse discover power within themselves are often other victims and survivors of sexual abuse. Future provision of services must include more acceptance of professionals and survivors of each others' contribution. The irony is that there is undoubtedly a large overlap between the two.

Fritz (1986), Director of Parents Anonymous in California, comments that despite research evaluations which have shown it to be the most effective treatment resource, the organisation still runs into much professional resistance. She attributes this partly to the fear that the organisation, which charges no fee and relies exclusively on volunteer professionals, is taking away a client pool which could and should potentially 'belong' to them. Voluntary workers at Parents Anonymous work in a way which does not pathologise those attending its groups and breaks down the distinction, so prevalent in the professions, of 'them' and 'us':

> they ask none of the usual questions and usually relate to the parent on a level of equality that is not the norm in clinical settings. Sponsors in Parents Anonymous divulge information about themselves as people; they talk about their own lives and share both the good and bad about themselves.
>
> (Fritz 1986: 122)

Because child sexual abuse cannot be defined as a crime being committed by a tiny proportion of mad or bad 'people', but as a societal ill, it has to be addressed within the community, by taking the kind of action being taken by the survivors' movement already. Summit (1990: 13) argues that professionals

> ought to be leaders in a crusade for normalizing the experience of sexual abuse in terms of getting equal *rights* for survivors even as we lead in pathologizing it in terms of understanding the special *needs* of some survivors.

A commitment also has to be made to types of research into, and evaluation of, social work practices which involve both children and adult survivors of child sexual abuse. Involvement with the survivors' groups or individual survivors should not be undertaken in an exploitative way but should have as its goal 'interdependence', as described by Phillipson (1989).

Stanton (1990) writes that trying to empower people who use services, without at the same time developing a collaborative and empowering culture among agency staff, is inconsistent – even bad faith. Social work has the option of rejecting its role of pathologising both perpetrator and victim and taking its place in the community as an accessible and potentially empowering resource. The survivors' movement, and other non-stigmatising, non-statutory groups such as Newpin and Parents Anonymous, it is argued in this chapter, give a powerful illustration of how this could be done. A good starting point and training ground for social work would be with its own workers.

BIBLIOGRAPHY

Armstrong, L. (1978) *Kiss Daddy Goodnight*, New York: Hawthorn Books.

Baker, A. and Duncan, S. P. (1985) 'Child sexual abuse: a study of prevalence in Great Britain', *Child Abuse and Neglect* 9: 457–67.

Briere, J. (1990) Paper presented at the Conference on *Professionals and Volunteers with a History of Abuse*, Alabama: National Children's Advocacy Center.

Briere, J. and Runtz, M. (1987) 'Post sexual abuse trauma. Data and implications for clinical practice', *Journal of Interpersonal Violence* 2 (4): 367–79.

Campbell, B. (1988) *Unofficial Secrets*, London: Virago.

Cohn, A. (1979) 'Effective treatment of child abuse and neglect', *Social Work* 24: 513–19.

Daro, D. (1988) *Confronting Child Abuse. Research for Effective Programme Design*, New York: Macmillan.

Dominelli, L. (1989) 'Betrayal of trust: a feminist analysis of power relationships in incest abuse and its relevance for social work practice', *British Journal of Social Work* 19: 291–307.

Doyle, C. (1991) 'Caring for the workers', *Child Abuse Review* (Winter 91/92): 25.

Dunhill, C. (1989) 'Helen's story: child sexual abuse and the law', in C. Dunhill (ed.) *The Boys in Blue: Women's Challenge to the Police*, London: Virago.

Fairclough, A. (1983) *Responsibility for Incest*, Norwich: University of East Anglia.

Faller, K. C. (1989) *Child Sexual Abuse: An Interdisciplinary Manual for Diagnosis, Case Management and Treatment*, London: Macmillan.

Findlay, C. (1988) 'Child abuse: the Dutch response', *Practice* 4: 374–81.

Freidson, E. (1972) *The Profession of Medicine*, New York: Dodd, Mead.

Fritz, M. (1986) 'Parents Anonymous: helping clients to accept professional services. A personal opinion', *Child Abuse and Neglect* 10: 121–3.

Hobbs, C. J. and Wynne, J. M. (1987) 'Child sexual abuse – an increasing rate of diagnosis', *Lancet* (10 October): 837–41.

Home Office (1988) *Statistical Bulletin 42. Criminal Proceedings for Offences Involving Violence Against Children*, London: Home Office.

Kelly, L. (1988) *Surviving Sexual Violence*, Cambridge: Polity Press.

———— (1992) 'Can't hear or won't hear? – The evidential experience of children with disabilities', *Child Abuse Review* **1** (3): 188–90.

Kelly, L., Regan, L. and Burton, S. (1991) *An Exploratory Study of the Prevalence of Sexual Abuse in a Sample of 16–21-Year Olds*, London: Child Abuse Studies Unit, Polytechnic of North London.

Kennedy, M. (1992) Personal communication.

———— (1993) Personal communication.

Krieger, M. J. and Robbins, J. (1985) 'The adolescent incest victim and the judicial system', *American Journal of Orthopsychiatry* **55**: 419–25.

Langan, M. and Lee, P. (1989) 'Whatever happened to radical social work?' in M. Langan and P. Lee (eds) *Radical Social Work Today*, London: Routledge.

McIvor, G. (1990) *Sanctions for Serious or Persistent Offenders: A Review of the Literature*, Stirling: University of Stirling Social Work Research Centre.

Mebane-Francescato, D. and Jones, S. (1974) 'Radical psychiatry in Italy', in Radical Therapist/Rough Times Collective (eds) *The Radical Therapist*, Harmondsworth: Penguin.

Morgan, J. and Zedner, L. (1992) *Child Victims: Crime, Impact and Criminal Justice*, Oxford: Oxford University Press.

Neate, P. (1991) 'Child abuse in Europe: 2. Belgium', *Community Care* **10** (10): 15–17.

Nelson, S. (1987) *Incest: Fact and Myth*, Edinburgh: Stramullion Cooperative.

Newman, C. (1989) *Young Runaways: Findings from Britain's First Safe House*, London: The Children's Society.

NSPCC (1990) *Protecting Children into the Nineties: Annual Report 1990*, London: NSPCC.

———— (1991) *Child Protection in the Community* (Conference Report) London: NSPCC.

O'Hara, M. (1989) 'The role of courts in cases involving the sexual abuse of children', Paper presented at the *Sex Offenders and the Law Conference*, Howard League for Penal Reform, New College, Oxford, September.

(OPCS) Office of Population Censuses and Surveys (1989) *Mortality Statistics Area Series DH5 No 13*, London: HMSO.

Ordway, D. (1983) 'Reforming judicial procedures for handling parent–child incest', *Child Welfare* **63**: 68–75.

Peace, G. and McMaster, M. (1989) *Child Sexual Abuse. Professional and Personal Perspectives*, Cheshire: Boys and Girls Welfare Society.

Phillipson, C. (1989) 'Challenging dependency: towards a new social work with older people', in M. Langan and P. Lee (eds) *Radical Social Work Today*, London: Routledge.

Pringle, K. (1990) *Family Placement Project – Managing to Survive: Developing a Resource for Sexually Abused Young People*, Newcastle: Barnardos, North East.

Reifen, D. (1984) 'Legal protection of children in sexual assault cases', in A. Carni and H. Zimrin (eds) *Child Abuse*, Berlin: Springer.

Rivera, A. (1989) 'Working with mothers of sexually abused children', (Talk given at Child Abuse Studies Unit, Polytechnic of North London, 18 May. Reported in *Incest & Child Sexual Assault* No. 12, June 1989).

Rush, F. (1980) *The Best Kept Secret*, New Jersey: Prentice-Hall.

Russell, D. (1984) *Sexual Exploitation: Rape, Child Sexual Abuse and Workplace Harassment*, Beverly Hills, Calif.: Sage.

Schultz, L. (ed.) (1979) *The Sexual Victimology of Youth*, Springfield, Ill.: Charles C. Thomas.

Sgroi, S. (1982) *Handbook of Clinical Intervention in Child Sexual Abuse*, Springfield Mass.: Lexington Books.

Sheppard, M. (1982) *Perceptions of Child Abuse. A Critique of Individualism*, Norwich: University of East Anglia.

Silbert, M. and Pines, A. (1981) 'Sexual child abuse as an antecedent to prostitution', *Child Abuse and Neglect* 5: 407–11.

Silbey, S. and Sarat, A. (1989) 'Reconstituting the sociology of law', in J. F. Gubrium and D. Silverman (eds) *The Politics of Field Research: Sociology Beyond Enlightenment*, London: Sage.

Spink, C. and Tutt, N. (1989) 'Child sexual abuse', *Practice* (Autumn/ Winter), 3/4: 310–31.

Stanton, A. (1990) 'Empowerment of staff: a prerequisite for the empowerment of users?', in P. Carter, T. Jeffs and M. Smith (eds) *Social Work and Social Welfare Year Book 2*, Milton Keynes: Open University Press.

Summit, R. C. (1988) 'Hidden victims, hidden pain, societal avoidance of child sexual abuse', in G. E. Wyatt and G. J. Powell (eds) *Lasting Effects of Child Sexual Abuse*, Newbury Park, Calif.: Sage.

——— (1990) Paper presented at the Conference on *Professionals and Volunteers with a History of Abuse*, Alabama: National Children's Advocacy Center.

Thompson, N. (1993) *Anti-Discriminatory Practice*, Basingstoke: Macmillan.

Women's Support Project (undated) *Child Sexual Abuse – The Importance of Workers' Support Groups*, Glasgow: Women's Support Centre.

Wyre, R. (1991) Personal communication.

Chapter 10

Towards a new view of probation values

Mike Nellis

INTRODUCTION

A Chief Probation Officer has observed, quite rightly, that 'the probation service has always been fiercely proud of its values and has fought to protect them in an often hostile "law and order" climate'. 'Curiously', he goes on, 'there is no probation service statement of values . . .' (Mathieson 1992: 146). This absence has meant that in its more proud and protective moments the service has repeatedly fallen back on 'the social work ideal', for which the phrase 'advise, assist and befriend' was once a kind of moral shorthand. From 1988 onwards, in particular, the service stridently proclaimed this ideal, drawn from a *generic*[1] understanding of 'social work', to ward off the threat of the government's 'punishment in the community' strategy (Home Office 1988; 1990a; 1990b; 1991; see also Allan 1990), which was to culminate (initially) in the Criminal Justice Act (CJA) 1991, the imposition of National Standards in eight areas of probation practice, and a Three Year Plan (Home Office 1992b).[2] In their subsequent belief that 'punishment in the community' was perhaps no more than a 'public relations shorthand for controlling offenders, diverting them from further crime and enabling them to become responsible citizens' (Mathieson 1992: 147), the majority of probation managers seem to have concluded that generic values could, and indeed should, be reaffirmed within the new policy framework.

This chapter will take a different view,[3] not least because by the end of 1993 much of the policy framework established by the CJA 1991 had been sacrificed to political expediency. In the 27-point plan to combat crime announced at the October 1993 Conservative Party conference, in the dismissive government reaction to key recommendations by the Royal Commission on Criminal Justice, and in proposals to centralise control of the police and to restore a 'prison works' philosophy, the outline of something altogether more repressive could be discerned. Within this new framework, genericism, as a body of technical and ethical knowledge, is even less well equipped to give the probation service a sense of identity and direction that it had been in respect of the CJA 1991. In my view, this is largely because of its persistent failure to engage with criminological debate (Nellis 1993a), for the general political context in which the service operates, the nature of the many changes to which it is subject, and also the opportunities which exist for progressive practice, have been far more comprehensively mapped by criminologists than (with honourable exceptions) by social work theorists. But until the limitations of genericism are understood, the promise of criminology will not be appreciated, and it is with those limitations that I shall begin.

THE LIMITS OF GENERICISM

Quite apart from the fact that it played supremely well into the hands of Home Office critics who believed that it 'is not always clear what a social work base does and does not mean' (Faulkner 1989: 1), the service's retreat into its social work identity as a means of resisting government-imposed 'controlism' (Raynor 1985) ignored the limited contribution which generic social work had made, historically, to innovation in probation practice, or to the 'successful revolution' (Jones 1993) in juvenile justice which had occurred in the 1980s. The service simply took for granted that genericism was where its future lay, despite the CCETSW's neglect of major penal issues and key criminological debates throughout the whole of its history (Nellis 1993a).

Generic values were not, however, as dependable as the service might have hoped. Traditionally such values had consisted of 'lists of principles about how the social worker ought to treat the individual client', ultimately deriving from the Kantian notion of 'respect for persons' (Banks 1990: 93) and characterised by McWilliams (1987) as 'personalism'.[4] By the late 1980s these values were being criticised from a variety of positions, all of which converged on the point that, even where they were not undermined by bureaucratic pressures, such values concentrated too much on guiding work with individuals or families, neglecting the structural factors which created or shaped 'personal' problems in the first place.

The liberal version of this argument emphasised the tension between client- or family-centredness and the common good (Clarke and Asquith 1985; Horne 1987) so as to provide a sounder basis for the social worker's exercise of both authority and advocacy skills. The Marxist and feminist versions (Walker and Beaumont 1981; Senior 1989; Dominelli and McLeod 1989) emphasised the inequality of class, and latterly race and gender relations, in order to identify the vested interests which probation really served, and to map out the limited spaces in which 'defensive action' (Hugman 1980) on behalf of clients was feasible. A more nebulous, post-structuralist critique questioned the 'humanist' assumptions which underpinned the very idea of 'respect for persons' (Rojek *et al.* 1988; Biehal and Sainsbury 1991), accusing them of failing to address 'power relations' in either structural or interpersonal set-tings.[5] It was partly – only partly – from a combination of Marxism and the anti-humanist critique, as reformulated by the CCETSW, the National Institute of Social Work (NISW) and the National Association of Probation Officers (NAPO), that a new value-base, focused on the concepts of anti-oppressive and anti-discriminatory practice, emerged in he late 1980s.

This shift in the value-base certainly introduced new and neglected elements *into* genericism, notably race, but left the boundaries of genericism intact and as inhospitable as ever to criminological debate. In addition, the compatibility of the new and old value bases was not explored (Jordan 1992) and the new was adopted rather uncritically – in part because of the manifest failings of the old. According to Clarke and Asquith (1985: 85) the lists of principles (e.g. BASW's Code of Ethics) and catchphrases (e.g. advise, assist and befriend) to which the once rich and critical 'humanist' tradition had been reduced (by genericism), 'suffer from a deep-seated ambiguity or perhaps lack of clarity as to what kind of statement they are trying to make'. Banks (1990: 100) was even more scathing of BASW, noting that 'many social workers (even if they are aware of the Code's existence) claim to find it of little use'. The same could as easily be said of probation officers, and it is therefore surprising to find a Chief Probation Officer remarking quite recently that it is 'often accepted' that the BASW Code 'appropriately encapsulates the essence of probation work' (Mathieson 1992: 146).

This statement, like much social work writing, confuses 'humanist' values with genericism, which, despite its pretensions to the contrary, has never had a monopoly on them. It is, as Mathieson, and more recently, Rutherford (1993) (who prefers the term 'liberal and humanitarian' to 'humanist')[6] suggest, of the utmost importance to defend such values, but in respect of the probation service it is important to formulate them in a way which specifically guides progressive action in the criminal justice arena. This genericism has never done, despite opportunities.[7] In any case, Mathieson's readiness to settle for the abstractions of the BASW Code hardly does justice to the range and complexity of academic and political debate that has in fact occurred on the subject of probation values (incomplete though it has been). It omits, for example, the attempt to convince probation officers that the framework in which they work has always involved administering pain (defined broadly to encompass restricting liberty (Christie 1982), and the argument that even before desert theory had penetrated into the writing of court reports and the implementation of the probation order itself there had been little point in laying claim to a *pure, caring* 'social work' identity (Harris 1989). Wasik and von Hirsch (1988), for example, explored the ethics of non-custodial action in terms of 'just deserts', and, following this, Bottoms (1989a: 92) suggested that within an 'essentially offence-based framework the probation service's role would then be effectively to manage within the community, using social work and other skills, those offenders who had been awarded certain intermediate sanctions by the courts'.

Not all writers have been prepared to concede the inevitability of desert theory or its compatibility with social work values (Hudson 1987). Some have insisted on a firm distinction between control and punishment, endorsing the former but not the latter (Shaw and Haines 1989). Blagg and Smith (1988) and Raynor (1988) articulated growing doubts about the 'nothing works' thesis, and as it came to be accepted that a closer reading of the available evidence suggested that some interventions worked with some offenders in some circumstances, the value of rehabilitation (defined less as 'cure' and more as 'restoration to full citizenship') was reaffirmed (McWilliams and Pease 1990; McLaren and Spencer 1992). Much of this interest is now focused on the 'reasoning and rehabilitation' programme (Ross *et al.* 1988; Weaver and Bensted 1992; Lucas *et al.* 1992), although the extent to which it meets 'humanist' criteria and avoids cognitive manipulation is open to argument (Neary

1992). The attempt to evolve a 'something works' philosophy (Pitts 1992) has merit, but those undertaking it should recognise that rehabilitation alone is insufficient as a value-base for probation, not only because the service undertakes a range of worthwhile activities which are not essentially or primarily rehabilitative (e.g. bail support), but also because the placing of offenders' needs and interests *above*, as opposed to *alongside*, the rights of victims and the requirements of public safety lacks moral justification and, in the 1990s, political credibility.

The breadth and complexity of the professional and academic debate that took place in the late 1980s in fact had little impact on the official bodies responsible for training (and, historically, for defining values). When the CCETSW had the opportunity to outline the values which trained probation officers should possess, it produced only the following:

> demonstrate knowledge and understanding of ethical issues and dilemmas, including the potential for conflict between organisational, professional and individual values;

> recognize the need for and seek to promote policies and demonstrate practices which are non-discriminatory and anti-oppressive;

> manage the tension between the court, the offender, the probation service, the family and the wider community.
> (CCETSW 1991, Annex 2: 3)

Such are the limits of the generic vision. Whatever the merits of the first two (and neither are beyond criticism), the third, at least in the context of prevailing criminal justice policy, has a stale and dated feel to it. Although it agrees with the view that probation is about holding the balance between court and offender (Davies 1989) it fails to engage with any kind of concern (government, professional or radical) to reduce crime and to reduce the use of custody, as if such ambitions were somehow outside social work, as indeed, within a generic framework, they always have been.

The most that genericism has contributed to probation values has been a debate on the respective merits of welfare and control, and while this debate remains important – see Silverman (1993) for a recent reworking of it – it no longer has pride of place. It is none the less possible to argue that those issues which have displaced it in recent values debate – desert theory, rehabilitation and anti-discriminatory practice – still fail to exhaust all that could be said about specifically probation values. Even within a 'humanist' (liberal and humanitarian) framework, reflection on what these values might be does not lead inexorably back to genericism, nor to the view that the only way to preserve a 'social work' (i.e. respectful, caring and decent) ethos is by making rehabilitation, once again, into the cornerstone of probation practice. The liberal and humanitarian tradition need not be departed from, for it contains within it both a necessary deep regard for individuals (Ignatieff 1984) and – because liberals are 'people who are more afraid of being cruel than anything else' (Rorty 1989: 192) – an imperative to resist injustice and oppression. But the managerial culture which is steadily tightening its grip on the service does not square easily with this tradition, and before outlining new values it is necessary to comment further on the constraints which managerialism imposes on ethical debate and action.

THE RISE OF BENEVOLENT CORPORATISM

McWilliams (1987) recognised immediately that the growth of corporate management within the probation service represented as strong a challenge to the nature of probation practice – defined in terms of 'personalism' – as the toughening-up of community penalties. Numerous accounts exist of how managerialism developed (Peters 1985; Pratt 1989; Statham and Whitehead 1992; Rutherford 1993) and do not bear detailed repetition, although we should note that only in Chomsky (1989), Galbraith (1992) and Christie (1993) is it properly connected to the growth and centralisation of state-corporate power, rather than simply presented as a means of achieving greater efficiency, economy and effectiveness. Essentially the service has been compelled to adopt a rather idealised version of private sector management techniques (Stewart 1992), which are arguably more authoritarian than those now used in industry itself (Lewis 1991). The effect has been the creation of a regulatory culture in the probation service which imprisons practitioners, and indeed managers themselves, in a hierarchy of policies, guidelines and monitoring arrangements which rob lower level staff of the last remnants of discretion, turning them – more than they have ever been before – into 'competent functionaries' (Howe 1991a).

Much effort has been expended by probation managers and also by those whom Chomsky (1989: 46) calls 'technocratic and policy-oriented intellectuals' to portray this not only as a necessary development, but also as a progressive one. A variety of discourses (e.g. about enterprise, consumerism,[8] etc.) have combined to create an image of *benevolent corporatism* as a superior and legitimate successor to the semi-independent bureau-professionalism (Parry and Parry 1979) which prevailed before, a structure in which 'the basic values of the Service will hold good and not be lost' (Statham 1992: 74). Roger Shaw (1992) has argued rather idealistically that within such a corporate framework each member of staff will be valued as an 'intellectual resource', while Fellowes (1992) boldly suggests that the loss of personal discretion, coupled with the feeling of security attendant on following a clear policy, will actually constitute a form of staff empowerment, although staff themselves seem not to experience it this way (Watson 1993). Only Saiger (1992), among recent writers, honestly admits that managerialism, with its essential emphasis on hierarchy and on encouraging and enforcing obedience to policy and procedure, is at heart coercive, but she fails to see that strategies of authorisation (orders from the top), routinisation (standardised techniques of working) and sur- veillance (monitoring) lead inexorably to the depersonalisation of those on the receiving end (see Millgram 1974; Bauman 1989), whether basic grade officers or offenders to whom the regulatory ethos is inevitably passed on.

   In deriding the qualities of autonomy, self-determination and discretion (which are arguably the prerequisites of genuineness, warmth and empathy), managerialism is clearly incompatible with the traditional approach to 'social work' values and with the liberal and humanitarian assumptions which underpinned it. There is a much greater degree of 'fit', however, between managerialism and the ostensibly radical anti-discriminatory/equal opportunity dis- course which emerged at the same time as manager/employer interests increased their influence within the CCETSW (Howe 1991a).[9] No discourse has in fact done more to legitimise a manage- rial culture on the probation service than that of anti-discriminatory practice, and, as McWilliams (1987) anticipated, a close affinity has now developed between the radical and managerialist positions. There are steep ironies here, for while claiming always to recognise and resist the 'risk of incorporation' (Senior 1989: 316) and to be 'in and against the state', radicals seem not to have noticed how effortlessly government officials have, however disingenuously, used the crisis of discrimination against black people in the criminal justice system to augment their own case for greater oversight and regulation of practice (Faulkner 1989; Flescher 1992).

For all its oppositional pretensions, and its confrontational ethos, much contemporary radical thinking in social work and probation falls well within 'the extremes of permissible dissent from government policy' (Chomsky 1989: 65). By time-worn means it has helped to widen and strengthen the regulatory net within welfare organisations by suggesting, for example, in respect of anti-racism, that 'management needs to be encouraged to develop effective policies that check on individual practice' (Senior 1989: 314) and by supporting the case for National Standards on the grounds that 'we cannot demand tough sanctions . . . over racist practice if we do not accept the need for standards over other aspects of our daily practice' (Senior 1990: 31). Pressure for the dispersal of finely calibrated forms of regulation throughout the probation service has come, in the name of anti-discriminatory practice, as much from NAPO as from government; initiatives from below mesh more seamlessly with initiatives from above than might at first appear to be the case. The surveillance of speech (euphemistically called 'monitoring') which NAPO (undated) has introduced at its conferences and in its branches has made its own insidious contribution to the culture of fear and obedience (Watson 1993) which government agencies and probation managers, using more overtly 'cost-effective' arguments for regulation, might not have been able to create on their own.

These comments draw on the concerns of some black critics that when the struggle for racial justice becomes too enmeshed in 'local state structures' (i.e. managerialism), it begins to exhibit 'dictatorial' tendencies and 'conceptual trading' with those who oppose them (Gilroy 1992: 49 and 60). There is a manifest need to challenge racism within the criminal justice system and also to construct convivial visions of multicultural futures, but it should not be too readily assumed that the CCETSW/NAPO version of anti-discriminatory practice best exemplifies progressive democratic politics. Current policies on anti-discrimination and equal opportunities, which create the 'necessary illusion' (Chomsky 1989) of openness, debate and respect of difference within corporate culture (while remaining firmly within its very narrow parameters), may have nothing at all to do with the democratic advancement of women or ethnic minorities. Given Cohen's (1985: 155) reminder that 'everything we know about the way social control ideologies originate and function . . . warns us about the delusion of ever expecting a synchronisation of words and deeds', the possibility ought at least to be considered that in both social work and probation such policies mask a process by which black and Asian people are being sidelined into 'de-professionalised' occupations of declining significance and prestige, diminishing resources and/ or heightened control functions.

Even if it could be argued that anti-discriminatory and equal opportunity strategies are successfully tackling racism and sexism within the criminal justice system, their failure to offer guidance on progressive forms of penality means that in themselves they are no more adequate as a value-base for probation practice than the BASW Code of Ethics had been. They were developed within a generic framework, and have inherited the same resistance to criminological insights. The more fundamental concept of 'anti-oppressiveness', however, can be revised to produce new ways of thinking about probation values. So long as the concept of oppression is used carefully to characterise excesses of state-corporate power and serious restrictions on daily living, and not as the 'common denominator of a wide variety of social processes' (Cohen 1989: 348), 'anti-oppressiveness' is a serviceable basis for the development of further arguments.

Even in the context of genericism, anti-oppressiveness has not been adequately theorised, and until such work is done its intellectual foundations will remain precarious.[10] It is not my intention here to ground anti-oppressiveness in broader traditions of political philosophy, but to suggest that if a number of developments within both mainstream and critical criminology were incorporated within it powerful new values for the probation service could begin to emerge. For the mainstream, Bottoms (1987: 263), for example, sees criminology as being 'at the centre of contemporary debates about the basis of legal and social order at the end of the twentieth century'; so, too, is the probation service. According to de Haan (1990: 18), critical criminologists have 'taken a radical political stance against law enforcement and unequal social structures, thereby making an effort to be explicit about their own normative assumptions and reflective about their own value commitments' – much as generic 'social workers', albeit in a non-criminological context, have also been encouraged to do.

Thus, drawing on ideas from criminology, the rest of this paper will suggest that a new probation value-base could be constructed around the three elements of anti-custodialism, restorative justice and community safety. Thomas Mathiesen's (1990) recent writing on abolitionism, which particularly informs the first of these, also contains accounts of the second and third elements, albeit using his own distinctive terminology. It is because the second and third elements exist as policy debates in their own right that a three-fold division has been followed here, but it is my intention, like Mathiesen's, that they be seen as a coherent and integrated set of values.

Value 1: Anti-custodialism

Despite Hugman's (1980: 151) demand that 'diversion from custody must be a priority aim', Senior's (1989: 298) recognition of wide-spread probation 'support for decarceration', and the observable fact that there are 'no probation officers who like to see their clients being sent into custody' (Millard 1991), an explicit anti-custodial stance has never been incorporated in statements of 'social work' values. In the 1980s juvenile justice workers (largely based in Social Services Departments and voluntary organisations) did develop anti-custodialism as part of their working philosophy (Children's Society 1988; Rutherford 1989) and some drew specifically on the aboli-tionist literature then available (Holt 1985; Pitts 1988), but their message was heard only faintly in the probation service, and in the CCETSW not at all.

The term *abolitionism* can be off-putting because of its ostensibly utopian connotations, but in fact all attempts to theorise it allow for the restraint of the few for whom incarceration is the only option (PREAP 1976; de Haan 1990), and there is some overlap (and dialogue) between the abolitionist position and that of the more moderately named 'reductionists' (Rutherford 1984; see Carlen 1990: 118–19 for an abolitionist engagement with this position). Neither group feels confident that its goals will be achieved in the near future, given present political trends, but the abolitionists seek, first, to sustain and extend a particular analysis of imprisonment's political functions, and, second, to insist upon the symbolic impor-tance of ceaseless argument against the normality and necessity of prison, and against the inexorability of its expansion, whether in public or private forms (Mathiesen 1990; Christie 1993).

It is in the analysis of the socio-political functions of imprison-ment (see Aptheker (1971) for an early black contribution to this), and in its mapping out of the conditions, strategies and tactics necessary to achieve a minimal use of custody, that abolitionism connects to the concept of anti-oppressive practice, although difficult questions remain about the range and levels of intrusiveness acceptable in any 'alternative' measures. The functions Mathiesen (1974; 1990) describes as expurgatory (removal of surplus populations), power-draining (neutralisation of political resistance), diverting (shifting attention from the crimes of the powerful, legal or otherwise), symbolic (fabricating boundaries between good and evil) and action-signifying (enabling pro-prison governments to say 'something is being done' about crime levels) all relate directly to oppression and to the ways in which its operation is disguised and mystified.

The strategies of resistance outlined in Mathiesen's (1990) later work involve counter-functional work, counter-denial work, victim work and offender work. Counter-functional work consists of making visible, by argument, imagery and research, the oppressive functions which the prison serves, questioning the value of segregating offenders and the false reassurance that something is being done by building more prisons and by increased custodial sentencing. The need for counter-denial work (a very Chomskyian term!) arises because governments invariably deny the harm that prison does, and consistently seek new justifications for its use – whether it is conceived in rehabilitative, preventive or deterrent terms. Several penal reform organisations and a handful of academics and journalists already do this, but if anti-custodialism is to become a defining attribute of democratic societies, its cultural and political prestige must be greatly enhanced and, like the rule of law, embedded as an ideal in larger organisations working at the centre rather than the margins of the criminal justice system.[11]

Value 2: Restorative justice

The concept of restorative justice is associated with two kinds of project, one concerned with victim–offender mediation, the other with neighbourhood dispute settlement. Over the past decade, the probation service has been involved with both types, recognising, in the case of the former, that meeting a victim can sometimes foster increased personal responsibility in offenders, and in the case of the latter, that the settlement of disputes between neighbours may prevent escalation into criminal activity (Kennedy 1990). The

Home Office intention was to fit such projects into existing philosophies of diversion from prosecution and crime prevention, but the discourse which actually developed around them was also permeated by more radical ideas from a semi-independent mediation movement. This promotes and envisages a move towards informal processes of community justice and away from state-administered systems, which, in some formulations, converges with later developments in abolitionist thinking (Christie 1982; de Haan 1990).

The flux of influences behind restorative justice, and the different points on the political spectrum to which this or that aspect of it appeals, have been mapped elsewhere (Harding 1989; Wright 1991). The more radical versions treat crime as a species of interpersonal conflict, or as a civil tort, discourage the appropriation of such conflicts by state-based professionals, and seek to avoid the compounding of one harm (the crime) by another (the punishment) (de Haan 1990). All but the most conservative versions accept that so long as most of the victim's needs are met, and their rights respected, a broadly rehabilitative, and socially integrative, approach can be pursued with offenders. This draws on existing practice and is compatible with the 'offender work' required by Mathiesen's abolitionist strategy.

Despite probation involvement in the pioneer schemes of mediation and reparation, opinion in the service has been divided as to their viability; such schemes have not become commonplace. The more negative responses have in fact highlighted the rather limited conception of 'social work' values which has prevailed in probation circles, because despite the obvious affinity between the principles of restorative justice and the (supposed) principles of good 'social work' practice – a focus on problem-solving rather than blame-fixing, on the future rather than the past, on empowering participants to find a solution rather than on coercive intervention by the state, on meeting both parties' needs, on the total context of the offence, and on 'right' relationships rather than 'right' rules (Zehr 1990: 211–14) – mediation and reparation were once looked upon by NAPO as being 'outside the Service's mainstream activities' (Gretton 1988: 78). While there is indeed room for argument as to whether such work is better sited with the probation service or in independent agencies outside it (there have been successful examples of both), the service has, in my view, no real choice as to whether it promotes restorative values, for it is only in the context of genuine concern for the needs and experiences of crime victims that concern for offenders (expressed as rehabilitation) will have any political plausibility.

A semi-independent mediation movement, focused on the pressure group Mediation UK and various Christian groups, will continue to exist outside the existing criminal justice system, and its efforts to promote a vision of justice distinctively different from current practices should be watched with interest, and debate encouraged. A fully reparative criminal justice system is unlikely, but the philosophy and practice of restorative justice could, if orchestrated by the probation service, become much more widespread than is currently the case. A number of Chief Probation Officers have recently renewed interest in it (Lacey 1993; Mace 1993); one has spoken openly of the 'challenge of restorative justice' for the service, noting rightly that 'judged alongside the concept of restorative justice, the concept of punishment in the community (the heart of the Criminal Justice Act 1991) seems decidedly narrow' (Mathieson 1992: 156). As with other aspects of progressive practice, however, it is not primarily retribution, but the imperatives of a managerial culture, which stand in the way of serious probation involvement in its further development, for as a former chief officer said:

> In a climate of cost-effectiveness it is not easy to argue for an approach which is long term, necessarily low profile, and concerned to encourage communities to work at their own tensions in a creative, healing way rather than rely on the intervention of the formal law and order system.
>
> (Michael Day, quoted in Gretton 1988: 80)

Value 3: Community safety

Neither anti-custodialism nor restorative justice, even together, form an adequate value-base for probation practice, for as Mathiesen (1990) now recognises, with his suggested strategies of 'vulnerability reduction' and 'anxiety reduction', it would be difficult for any agency to articulate these sentiments if it was not also sensitive to the impact of crime, and the fear of crime, on ordinary people, and to their reasonable desire for a safe and reassuring environment. Using whatever purchasing power they have, the comfortable, affluent and wealthy within 'the culture of contentment' (Galbraith

1992) can become consumers of security, locking, lighting and zoning themselves out of harm's way; but poorer people are more vulnerable, and it is their need for protection and safety which the probation service, if it is to be anti-oppressive, cannot ignore.[12]

Those most at risk of crime tend to be the already disadvantaged members of society – poor women, long-term unemployed young men, and ethnic minorities; for some, their experience of crime compounds, and in some analyses (Campbell 1993) constitutes, their sense of oppression. Feeling underpoliced and underprotected by courts, some individuals, with the encouragement and support of their neighbours, may become vigilantes, a form of community self-help which is perhaps inevitable in present circumstances, but which represents the negative side of the 'active citizenship' once envisaged by the government (McCrystal 1993).

That is not to say that the general arguments for community safety centre only on the needs of the poor and the oppressed, for the existence of fear and insecurity, and the 'fortress mentality' which can result from it, is not a healthy political development. Crime and the fear of crime, particularly in respect of burglary, assault, domestic violence and autotheft, seriously affect the quality of life for many people in both rural and urban areas. Left unchecked this fear invariably fuels demands among poor and affluent alike for the kind of law and order policies (Lea and Young 1993) which make other probation values difficult to promote or sustain. The amount and type of crime is routinely distorted by the mass media, leading people to exaggerate the risk to which they are exposed, to take unnecessary precautions and perhaps to make unnecessary political demands, and this must be tackled as a problem in its own right, over and above attempts to reduce crime itself.

It has been government policy for more than a decade to develop multi-agency responses to crime reduction (Bottoms 1989b; Tilley 1993). This has involved the establishment of many varied coalitions, and the promotion of a variety of social and situational measures, under a variety of names, targeted on particular localities. Although it has not always meshed well with the pressure being put on the service to become an agent of 'punishment in the community', probation involvement in this has been encouraged (Geraghty 1991; Sampson and Smith 1992). However, as in the case of reparation and mediation, this involvement has not been welcomed by all in the service, yet in view of 'social work's' acknowledged role in protecting victims of child abuse (and latterly domestic violence), it is again rather strange that within debate on generic 'social work' values the notion of safety has not been enlarged and expanded to cover crime victimisation generally. If safety had been more clearly understood as a 'social work' value, then sections of the probation service might have been less ambivalent than they have been towards crime prevention strategies, particularly their situational elements (Harris 1992), and more aware of how these strategies could become, and be understood as, anti-oppressive work.

The glossy brochures which herald and explain crime prevention policy to the public rarely acknowledge just how desolate life in high crime localities has become (Foster 1989; Robins 1992; Campbell 1993), and how difficult it is to reduce crime, let alone restore a sense of community, in such places, although there have been successful examples. Much depends on how well statutory agencies work with local people. The probation service's forays into community work have been few and far between (see Broad (1988) for a review) but in the aftermath of a riot within its boundaries one service at least has begun to see that the local credibility of its work depends crucially on taking community safety seriously:

> Because the Probation Service is predominantly associated with its work with offenders and our understanding of their needs, the effects of crime on the community can sometimes seem to be of less concern to us. . . . The Scotswood team reports that 'people are afraid to leave their homes for fear of attack, harassment, burglary, arson and vandalism, and are intimidated by the gangs on the streets, whether they do anything or not'. . . . In an atmosphere such as this we should not be surprised if many local residents are suspicious of the role of our Service and the 'explanations' which we appear to offer for crime.
>
> (Northumbria Probation Service 1992: 9–10)

CONCLUSION

It is sad testimony to the disabling influence of genericism that anti-custodialism, restorative justice and community safety will seem to some to be extraordinarily strange concepts on which to construct a value-base for probation practice, both as concepts in their own right and in terms of the interrelationship between them. Although all three are grounded in existing aspects of probation practice (and are not therefore 'unrealistic'), they have hardly ever figured in previous discussion of 'social work' values, and have never been articulated within either the personalist framework or the anti-oppressive framework which superseded it.

It is therefore time for the probation service to ask what it gains from continuing to think of itself as a 'social work' agency, and whether more might be gained from thinking of itself as a 'community justice' agency or even as a broadly conceived penal reform body. It does not need – and in the past it has not benefited from – the false protection of genericism in order to express or defend progressive values. These exist independently of genericism (Rutherford 1993; Garland 1990) and can be – and are – expressed in settings outside 'social work'. Such old probation values as need to be preserved can be contained in the new framework.

It is, however, one thing to show that new values are necessary, but quite another to set them in place. As practitioners inexorably succumb to managerial authority, persuaded by this or that discourse that it is a good thing, there will be fewer and fewer people within the service who struggle 'to find some practical expression of their political commitment and *personal philosophy* in their daily work as probation officers' (Hugman 1980: 123, emphasis added). Their contract with the service will be a purely calculative, financial one (Walker 1991); personal commitments will gradually be eroded by management demands to implement the prevailing policy. It is because 'the expression of humane values within criminal justice ultimately resides with practitioners' that Rutherford (1993: xii) believes its absence will produce 'apathy and, ultimately, violence' in all the control agencies involved.

Rutherford, however, is something of an exception in believing that practitioners can, in fact, influence policy for the better; in general there is a dearth of optimism in regard to the penal policies we are likely to be pursuing at the turn of the century, and thereafter. Radzinowicz (1991) considers us to be on the cusp of 'conservative' and 'authoritarian' solutions to crime, and several serious novelists (James 1992; Kerr 1992) have recently explored the different forms which such authoritarianism might take. Even Galbraith's (1992: 172) 'one confident prediction' is 'of the likelihood of an increasingly oppressive authority in areas of urban desolation', and if this comes to pass – more than it has already – the government will doubtless expect the probation service to be part of it. Christie

(1993) foresees a relentless toughening up of both community-based and institutionally based measures, and insists grimly that there are 'no built in guarantees against such a development, no democratic imperative against which totalitarian forces will founder once an obsession with efficiency has obliterated all forms of moral thinking'.

There are large political issues here, not merely penal ones, and it is only in the resolution of the latter that an organisation as small as the Probation Service can reasonably be expected to play a part. With the shadow of totalitarianism falling across debates on European penal policy for the first time in sixty years, Rutherford's (1993: 160) 'imperative to undermine [the] prevailing ethos' of manage-rialism in such spheres that the service can influence, and to expose the social forces which lie behind it, assumes a new urgency. The values sketched here, even if 'continually reactivated and vigorously held onto in day-to-day practice' (*ibid.*: 24) may still be insufficient to prevent the worst from coming to the worst; but unless they are adopted in some shape or form, in the spirit of what Anthony Giddens (1990: 154) has called 'utopian realism' – 'alternative futures whose very propagation may help them to be realised' – the probation service will be alarmingly unprepared for the seasons of fury which lie ahead.

NOTES

1   The prevailing conception of genericism is built around the rather dubious notion that certain knowledge, skills and values are common to all forms of 'social work', and that only generic values bestow moral authority. Yet, for all its apparent breadth and elasticity, genericism has been strangely impermeable to the criminological knowledge which might have specifically informed probation practice. Furthermore, the knowledge, skills and values which, at a fairly abstract level, are indeed common to all forms of 'social work' in Britain are also common to occupations that are explicitly not regarded as 'social work', such as youth work, counselling, psychology and psychiatry. They have tradi-tionally derived from a broad liberal tradition which can be articulated independently of genericism, and which could generate a morally authoritative probation value-base quite distinct from other types of 'social work'. Social work, if the term must be used, is best conceived as 'a federation of specialised interests' (Nellis 1993a), not as a unified occupation with a common knowledge or value-base.

2   The Three Year Plan offered an interesting list of 'Responsibilities' and 'Commitments' (akin to 'values', though the word was not mentioned) which, although it generated little debate, was an improvement on an

earlier version (Home Office 1992a), which had rather fatuously included 'persevering' as an example of a probation value. This earlier version set out 'what the probation service is in being for (its *functions*); what it aims to achieve (its *goals*); and what the service stands for (its *values*). As McWilliams (1992a) pointed out, this gave the clear impression that the functions of the service were determined independently of, and prior to, its values.

3   The focus throughout will be on the service's work with offenders, not with Family Court work, which requires separate attention.

4   McWilliams' (1987) division of the probation service into three schools of thought – radicalism, personalism and managerialism – was heuristically useful at the time, but needs updating. What it said of each was broadly true, if rather general. It was always misleading, however, in implying that a truly personalist concern cannot be combined with a radical concern to challenge social injustice, as the theoretical work of, for example, Eric Fromm (1956) and Paulo Freire (1972) indicated some decades ago.

5   Rojek *et al.* (1988) use the concept of 'humanist' to describe the cluster of values that Rutherford calls liberal and humanitarian. One only has to recall Tom Paine to know that this tradition is perfectly capable of challenging unjust power relations. We should note also that it was as a self-proclaimed humanist (but also democratic socialist) that E. P. Thompson (1983) challenged the authoritarianism of structuralist Marxism. A critique of 'anti-discriminatory practice', which has affinities with structuralist thinking, could and should be mounted from the same philosophical base.

6   There is room for argument as to what Rutherford (1993: 18) means by 'liberal and humanitarian values' because their substance as he describes it – 'empathy with suspects, offenders, and the victims of crime, optimism that constructive work can be done with offenders, adherence to the rule of law so as to restrict state powers, and an insistence on open and accountable procedures' – could equally be claimed by democratic socialists. Both, via Dickens and Orwell respectively, have championed the 'decency' which Rutherford wants to see pursued in criminal justice agencies.

7   There have been at least two such opportunities. First, the CCETSW (1978) itself acknowledged the distinctiveness of probation practice, albeit without repudiating genericism, in a report which regrettably had little subsequent impact (see Nellis 1993a). Second, some of the locally drawn up responses to the Statement of National Objectives and Priorities (Home Office 1984) articulated probation-specific values, but this went largely unnoticed at the time (see Lloyd 1986 for examples), even among academic commentators, and certainly by the CCETSW. If a criminologically sophisticated value-base had been kindled at this point the service might have had less need, later in the 1980s, to fall back on the vagaries of its 'social work' identity as a defence against punishment in the community.

8   Recent attempts to use consumerism and the Citizen's Charter as a basis for sharpening up probation values founder, in my view, because they

take for granted the hegemony of managerialism and accept too readily the constraints this imposes on moral debate. *Pace* Kemshall (1993), a concern with quality services and consumer rights is in no way the equivalent of a concern with humanitarian values and social justice. The 'probationer's rights' outlined by Broad and Denney (1992) are conceived within the spirit of the Citizen's Charter, but the failure to grant equal status to 'victim's rights' means that they make only a limited contribution to probation values. More fundamentally, they ignore Ignatieff's (1984: 13) view that 'we are more than rights-bearing creatures and there is more to respect about a person than his rights. The administrative good conscience of our time seems to consist of respecting individual's rights while demeaning them as persons.' In so doing Broad and Denney remain firmly within the managerial perspective they purport to criticise.

9   Such conjunctions are always interesting. Howe (1991b: 161) has noted that 'the conjunction of managerialism and family therapy is a happy one, but hardly accidental'. He goes on: 'There are times when there is a common outlook on material and social life. The ideas and the logic that produced rational management techniques also produced the climate that led to systemic family therapy.' And, it could be added, anti-discriminatory practice. The move, a decade ago, from race awareness training to anti-racist training, characterised by those who approve of it as a consequence of the former's ineffectiveness, can be understood as a move from an educational model to a managerial model of challenging injustice, or from an appreciative to a correctionalist stance (see Nellis 1993b).

10   An attempt to theorise anti-oppressiveness could usefully draw on the literature of civil disobedience and non-violence, as well as rediscovering the work of Paulo Freire (1972), one of the few genuine radicals to have influenced social work, although – significantly – he fell from favour as the radical-managers gained their ascendancy.

11   Making anti-custodialism central to probation values does not mean that probation officers should withdraw from work in prisons or be hostile to people who work there. There is valuable humanitarian work to be done in prisons, but by and large the best efforts of the best people working in them do not redeem them as a social institution.

12   The philosophy of community safety, as opposed to the techniques of crime prevention, is less well developed in criminology than either abolitionism or restorative justice. It is perhaps worth noting that one of the earliest prison abolitionist groups in America was subsequently recast as the Safer Society Programme (Knopp 1991) and that similar values to the ones I have promoted here are central to the American school of 'peacemaking criminology' (Pepinsky and Quinney 1991), albeit not solely for probation services.

BIBLIOGRAPHY

Allan, R. (1990) 'Punishment in the Community', in P. Carter, T. Jeffs and M. Smith (eds) *Social Work and Social Welfare Yearbook 2*, Milton Keynes: Open University Press.

Aptheker, B. (1971) 'Social functions of prisons in the United States', in A. Davis (ed.) *If They Come in the Morning*, London: Orbach and Chambers.

Banks, S. (1990) 'Doubts, dilemmas and duties: ethics and the social worker', in P. Carter, T. Jeffs and M. Smith (eds) *Social Work and Social Welfare Yearbook 2*, Milton Keynes: Open University Press.

Bauman, Z. (1989) *Modernity and the Holocaust*, Cambridge: Polity Press.

Biehal, N. and Sainsbury, E. (1991) 'From values to rights in social work', *British Journal of Social Work* 21: 245–57.

Blagg, H. and Smith, D. (1989) *Crime, Penal Policy and Social Work*, Harlow: Longman.

Bottoms, A. E. (1987) 'Reflections on the criminological enterprise', *Cambridge Law Journal* 46: 240–63.

—— (1989a) 'The concept of intermediate sanctions and its relevance for the probation service', in R. Shaw and K. Haines (eds) *The Criminal Justice System: A Central Role for the Probation Service*, Cambridge: University of Cambridge Institute of Criminology.

—— (1989b) 'Crime prevention facing the 1990s', *Policing and Society* 1 (1): 1–44.

Broad, B. (1991) *Punishment Under Pressure: The Probation Service in the Inner City*, London: Jessica Kingsley.

Broad, B. and Denney, D. (1992) 'Citizenship, rights and the probation service: a question of empowering or oppressing service users?', *Probation Journal* 39: 170–4.

Campbell, B. (1993) *Goliath: Britain's Dangerous Places*, London: Methuen.

Carlen, P. (1990) *Alternatives to Women's Imprisonment*, Milton Keynes: Open University Press.

CCETSW (1991) *Paper 30, Rules and Requirements for the Diploma in Social Work* (2nd edn), London: CCETSW.

Children's Society (1988) *Penal Custody for Juveniles: The Line of Least Resistance*, London: The Children's Society.

Chomsky, N. (1989) *Necessary Illusions: Thought Control in Democratic Societies*, Montreal: CBC Enterprises.

Christie, N. (1982) *Limits to Pain*, London: Martin Robertson.

—— (1993) *Crime Control as Industry*, London: Routledge.

Clarke, C. and Asquith, S. (1985) *Social Work and Social Philosophy: A Guide for Practice*, London: Routledge & Kegan Paul.

Cohen, S. (1985) *Visions of Social Control*, Cambridge: Polity Press.

—— (1989) 'The critical discourse on "social control": notes on the concept as a hammer', *International Journal of the Sociology of Law* 17: 347–57.

Davies, M. (1989) *The Nature of Probation Practice Today: An Empirical*

Analysis of Skills, Knowledge and Qualities used by Probation Officers, London: Home Office.

de Haan, W. (1990) *The Politics of Redress: Crime, Punishment and Penal Abolition*, London: Unwin Hyman.

Dominelli, L. and McLeod, E. (1989) *Feminist Social Work*, Basingstoke: Macmillan.

Faulkner, D. E. R. (1989) 'The future of the probation service: a view from government', in R. Shaw and K. Haines (eds) *The Criminal Justice System: A Central Role for the Probation Service*, Cambridge: University of Cambridge Institute of Criminology.

Fellowes, B. (1992) 'Management and empowerment: the paradox of professional practice', in R. Statham and P. Whitehead (eds) *Managing the Probation Service: Issues for the 1990s*, Harlow: Longman.

Flescher, T. (1992) 'Initial thoughts of the head of probation at the Home Office', *NAPO News* 40: 6–7.

Foster, J. (1989) *Villains?: Crime and Community in the Inner City*, London: Routledge.

Freire, P. (1972) *Cultural Action for Freedom*, Harmondsworth: Penguin.

Fromm, E. (1956) *The Sane Society*, London: Routledge & Kegan Paul.

Galbraith, J. K. (1992) *The Culture of Contentment*, Harmondsworth: Penguin.

Garland, D. (1990) *Punishment and Modern Society*, Oxford: Clarendon Press.

Geraghty, J. (1991) *Probation Practice in Crime Prevention* (Home Office Crime Prevention Unit Paper 24), London: Home Office.

Giddens, A. (1990) *The Consequences of Modernity*, Cambridge: Polity Press.

Gilroy, P. (1992) 'The end of anti-racism', in J. Donald and A. Rattansi (eds) *'Race', Culture and Difference*, London: Sage/Open University.

Gretton, J. (1988) 'Can victim–offender mediation change the face of criminal justice?' in A. Harrison and J. Gretton (eds) *Crime UK: An Economic, Social and Policy Audit*, Newbury: Policy Journals.

Harding, J. (1989) 'Reconciling mediation with criminal justice', in M. Wright, and B. Galaway (eds) *Mediation and Criminal Justice: Victims, Offenders and Community*, London: Sage.

Harris, R. (1989) 'Social work in society or punishment in the community?' in R. Shaw and K. Haines (eds) *The Criminal Justice System: A Central Role for the Probation Service*, Cambridge: University of Cambridge Institute of Criminology.

—— (1992) *Crime, Criminal Justice and the Probation Service*, London: Routledge.

Holt, J. (1985) *No Holiday Camps: Juvenile Justice and the Politics of Law and Order*, Leicester: Association of Juvenile Justice.

Home Office (1984) *Statement of National Objectives and Priorities*, London: Home Office.

—— (1988) *Punishment, Custody and the Community* (Cm 424), London: HMSO.

—— (1990a) *Crime, Justice and Protecting the Public* (Cm 965), London: Home Office.

—— (1990b) *Supervision and Punishment in the Community: A Framework for Action* (Cm 966), London: Home Office.

—— (1991) *Organising Supervision and Punishment in the Community: A Decision Document*, London: Home Office.

—— (1992a) *Statement of Purpose for the Probation Service*, London: Home Office.

—— (1992b) *Three Year Plan for the Probation Service 1993–96*, London: HMSO.

Horne, M. (1987) *Values in Social Work*, Aldershot: Gower.

Howe, D. (1991a) 'Knowledge, power and the shape of social work practice', in M. Davies (ed.) *The Sociology of Social Work*, London: Routledge.

—— (1991b) 'The family and the therapist: towards a sociology of social work method, in M. Davies (ed.) *The Sociology of Social Work*, London: Routledge.

Hudson, B. (1987) *Justice Through Punishment: A Critique of the 'Justice' Model of Corrections*, Basingstoke: Macmillan.

Hugman, B. (1980) 'Radical practice in probation', in M. Brake and R. Bailey (eds) *Radical Social Work and Practice*, London: Edward Arnold.

Ignatieff, M. (1984) *The Needs of Strangers*, London: Chatto & Windus.

James, P. D. (1992) *The Children of Men*, London: Faber.

Jones, D. (1993) 'The successful revolution continues', *Justice of the Peace*, 8 May.

Jordan, B. (1992) 'Competencies and values', *Social Work Education* **10** (10): 5–11.

Kemshall, H. (1993) 'Quality: friend or foe?', *Probation Journal* **40** (3): 122–6.

Kennedy, L. W. (1990) *On the Borders of Crime: Conflict Management and Criminology*, New York: Longman.

Kerr, P. (1992) *A Philosophical Investigation*, London: Chatto & Windus.

Knopp, F. H. (1991) 'Community solutions to sexual violence: feminist/abolitionist perspectives', in H. Pepinsky and R. Quinney (eds) *Criminology as Peacemaking*, Bloomington: Indiana University Press.

Lacey, M. (1993) *Restorative Justice: Note for the ACOP Probation Practice Committee* (personal communication).

Lea, J. and Young, J. (1993) *What is to be Done about Law and Order* (2nd edn), London: Pluto Press.

Lewis, P. (1991) 'Learning from industry: macho management or collaborative culture?' *Probation Journal* **38** (2): 81–5.

Lloyd, C. (1986) *Response to SNOP*, Cambridge: University of Cambridge Institute of Criminology.

Lucas, J., Raynor, P. and Vanstone, M. (1992) *Straight Thinking on Probation, One Year On*, Bridgend: Mid-Glamorgan Probation Service.

McCrystal, C. (1993) 'Heroes and villains', *Independent on Sunday*, 11 July: 2–4.

Mace, A. (1993) 'Foreword' in D. Quill and J. Wynne (eds) *Victim and Offender Mediation Handbook*, London: Save the Children.

McLaren, V. and Spencer, J. (1992) 'Rehabilitation and CJA 1991: a world still to win', *Probation Journal* **39** (2): 70–3.

McWilliams, W. (1987) 'Probation, pragmatism and policy', *Howard Journal* **26** (2): 97–121.

———— (1992a) 'Statement of Purpose for the Probation Service: a criticism, *NAPO News*, April, no. 39.

———— (1992b) 'The rise and development of management thought in the English Probation Service', in R. Statham and P. Whitehead (eds) *Managing the Probation Service: Issues for the 1990s*, Harlow: Longman.

McWilliams, W. and Pease, K. (1990) 'Probation practice and an end to punishment', *Howard Journal* **29**: 14–24.

Mathiesen, T. (1974) *The Politics of Abolition*, London: Martin Robertson.

———— (1990) *Prison on Trial*, London: Sage.

Mathieson, D. (1992) 'The Probation Service', in E. Stockdale and S. Casale (eds) *Criminal Justice Under Stress*, London: Blackstone Press Ltd.

May, T. (1991) *Probation: Politics, Policy and Practice*, Milton Keynes: Open University Press.

Millard, D. (1991) Letter, *Probation Journal* **38** (4): 218.

Milgram, S. (1974) *Obedience to Authority: An Experimental View*, London: Tavistock.

NAPO (undated) *Monitoring: Advice and Guidelines*, London: NAPO.

Neary, M. (1992) 'Some academic freedom', *Probation Journal* **39** (4): 200–2.

Nellis, M. (1993a) 'Criminology, crime prevention and the future of probation training', in K. Bottomley, T. Fowles and R. Reiner (eds) *Criminal Justice: Theory and Practice: British Criminology Conference 1991*, Selected Papers, vol. 2, London: British Society of Criminology/ ISTD.

———— (1993b) Review of Denney, D. (1992) *Racism and Anti-Racism in Probation*, *British Journal of Criminology* **33** (4).

Northumbria Probation Service (1992) *The Dog That Finally Barked: The Tyneside Disturbances of 1991 – A Probation Perspective*, Newcastle: Northumbria Probation Service.

Parry, N. and Parry, J. (1979) 'Social work professionalism and the state', in N. Parry, M. Rustin and C. Satyamurti (eds) *Social Work, Welfare and the State*, London: Edward Arnold.

Pepinsky, H. and Quinney, R. (1991) *Criminology as Peacemaking*, Bloomington: Indiana University Press.

Peters, A. (1985) 'Main currents in criminal law theory', in J. van Dijk *et al.* (eds) *Criminal Law in Action*; Arnhem: Gouda Quint.

Pitts, J. (1988) *The Politics of Juvenile Crime*, London: Sage.

———— (1992) 'The end of an era', *Howard Journal* **31** (2): 133–49.

Pratt, J. (1989) 'Corporatism: the third model of juvenile justice, *British Journal of Criminology* **29** (3): 236–54.

PREAP (1976) *Instead of Prison: A Handbook for Abolitionists*, Syracuse, New York: Prison Research Education Action Project.

Radzinowicz, L. (1991) 'Penal regressions', *Cambridge Law Journal* **50** (3): 422–44.

Raynor, P. (1985) *Social Work, Justice and Control*, Oxford: Basil Blackwell.

———— (1988) *Probation as an Alternative to Custody*, Aldershot: Gower.

Robins, D. (1992) *Tarnished Vision*, Oxford: Oxford University Press.

Rojek, C., Peacock, G. and Collins, S. (1988) *Social Work and Received Ideas*, London: Routledge.

Rorty, R. (1989) *Contingency, Irony and Solidarity*, Cambridge: Cambridge University Press.

Ross, R., Fabiano, E. A. and Ewles, C. D. (1988) 'Reasoning and rehabilitation', *International Journal of Offender Therapy and Comparative Criminology* 32: 29–35.

Rutherford, A. (1984) *Prisons and the Process of Justice*, Oxford: Oxford University Press.

———— (1989) 'The mood and temper of penal policy: curious happenings in England and Wales in the 1980s', *Youth and Policy* 27: 27–31.

———— (1993) *Criminal Justice and the Pursuit of Decency*, Oxford: Oxford University Press.

Saiger, L. (1992) 'Probation management structures and partnerships in America: lessons for England', in R. Statham and P. Whitehead (eds) *Managing the Probation Service: Issues for the 1990s*, Harlow: Longman.

Sampson, A. and Smith D. (1992) 'Probation and community crime prevention', *Howard Journal* 31 (2): 105–19.

Senior, P. (1989) 'Radical probation: surviving in a hostile climate', in M. Langan and P. Lee (eds) *Radical Social Work Today*, London: Unwin Hyman.

———— (1990) 'Standardisation: assessing the consequences for probation practice', in D. Woodhill and P. Senior (eds) *Criminal Justice in the 1990s: What Future(s) for the Probation Service?*, Sheffield: PAVIC Publications, Sheffield City Polytechnic.

Shaw, R. (1992) 'Corporate management in probation', in R. Statham and P. Whitehead (eds) *Managing the Probation Service: Issues for the 1990s*, Harlow: Longman.

Shaw, R. and Haines, K. (eds) (1989) *The Criminal Justice System: A Central Role for the Probation Service*, Cambridge: University of Cambridge Institute of Criminology.

Shaw, S. (1992) 'Prisons', in E. Stockdale and S. Casale (eds) *Criminal Justice Under Stress*, London: Blackstone Press Ltd.

Silverman, M. (1993) 'Ethical issues in the field of probation', *International Journal of Offender Therapy and Comparative Criminology* 32 (1): 85–94.

Statham, R. (1992) 'The strategic dimensions', in R. Statham and P. Whitehead (eds) *Managing the Probation Service: Issues for the 1990s*, Harlow: Longman.

Statham, R. and Whitehead, P. (eds) (1992) *Managing the Probation Service: Issues for the 1990s*, Harlow: Longman.

Stewart, J. (1992) 'Guidelines for public services management: lessons not to be learned from the private sector', in P. Carter, T. Jeffs and M. Smith (eds) *Changing Social Work and Welfare*, Milton Keynes: Open University Press.

Thompson, E. P. (1983) *The Poverty of Theory*, London: Merlin Press.

Tilley, N. (1993) 'Crime prevention and the safer cities story', *Howard Journal* **32** (1): 40–57.

Walker, H. and Beaumont, B. (1981) *Probation Work: Critical Theory and Socialist Practice*, Oxford: Blackwell.

Walker, S. (1991) 'How are you motivated?', *Probation Journal* **38** (4): 177–80.

Wasik, M. and von Hirsch, A. (1988) 'Non-custodial penalties and the principle of desert', *Criminal Law Review*, 555–71.

Watson, W. (1993) Letter to the *Guardian*, 24 September.

Weaver, C. and Benstead, J. (1992) 'Thinking for a change', *Probation Journal* **39**: 196–200.

Weston, B. (1993) Letter to the *Guardian*, 10 September.

Woolf, Lord Justice (1991) *Prison Disturbance April 1990: Report of an Inquiry* (Cm 1456), London: HMSO.

Wright, M. (1991) *Justice for Victims and Offenders*, Milton Keynes: Open University Press.

Zehr, H. (1990) *Changing Lenses: A New Focus for Crime and Justice*, Scottdale, Pennsylvania: Herald Press.

Index